BLOOD AND IRON

ALSO BY C. G. SWEETING

Hitler's Squadron: The Fuehrer's Personal Aircraft and Transport Unit, 1933–45
Hitler's Personal Pilot: The Life and Times of Hans Baur
Combat Flying Clothing: Army Air Forces Clothing through World War II
Combat Flying Equipment: U.S. Army Aviators' Personal Equipment, 1917–1945

BLOOD AND IRON

The German Conquest of Sevastopol

C. G. Sweeting
Foreword by Conrad Crane, Ph.D.

Potomac Books, Inc.
Washington, D.C.

Library of Congress Cataloging-in-Publication Data

Sweeting, C. G.
   Blood and iron : the German conquest of Sevastopol / C.G. Sweeting ; foreword by Dr. Conrad Crane. — 1st ed.
      p.   cm.
   Includes bibliographical references and index.
   ISBN 1-57488-796-3 (alk. paper)
   1. World War, 1939–1945 — Campaigns — Eastern Front.   2. Sevastopol' (Ukraine) — History — Siege, 1942.   I. Title.
   D764.S96   2004
   940.54'21771 — dc22   2004006289
   ISBN 1-57488-797-1 (paperback)

Printed in the United States of America on acid-free paper that meets the American National Standards Institute Z39-48 Standard.

Potomac Books, Inc.
22841 Quicksilver Drive
Dulles, Virginia 20166

Book design and composition by Susan Mark
Coghill Composition Company
Richmond, Virginia

First Edition

10   9   8   7   6   5   4   3   2   1

Theirs not to reason why,
Theirs but to do and die. . . .

. . .

Cannon to right of them,
Cannon to left of them . . .

. . .

Volley'd and thunder'd;
Storm'd at with shot and shell, . . .

. . .

Into the jaws of Death,
Into the mouth of hell,
Rode the six hundred.

ALFRED, LORD TENNYSON
"The Charge of the Light Brigade"
Crimean War, 1854–56

CONTENTS

"Me or You!" The war on the Eastern Front was characterized by some of the most savage and brutal combat ever experienced in modern warfare. *From* Die Wehrmacht, *No. 20, 24 Sept. 1941*

ILLUSTRATIONS

FOREWORD

I FIRST BECAME fascinated with World War II many years ago while still in elementary school. I devoured all the holdings of our local library, beginning with books dealing with the American campaigns which I had heard my parents and uncles describe. In the midst of this reading frenzy I stumbled upon an impressive looking tome entitled *Lost Victories* by Field-Marshal Erich von Manstein. As a result I became aware of a whole different war, the momentous death struggle between the Germans and the Russians on the Eastern Front. And I developed an admiration for the skills and candor of the German general whom B. H. Liddell Hart labeled "the Allies' most formidable military opponent."

C. G. Sweeting has provided a thorough description of von Manstein's career in the Epilogue, but some highlights are worth mentioning here. Von Manstein developed and championed the operational concepts that evolved into the campaign that overwhelmed France and amazed the world in 1940. He also contributed to that victory as commander of a corps. During the Russian campaign he advanced rapidly from corps to army to army group command. After the disaster at Stalingrad, he stabilized the German front and even produced a brilliant victory at Kharkov, inflicting great losses on Soviet forces despite being heavily outnumbered. His efforts enabled the German armies to retain enough initiative to mount one more major offensive at Kursk in 1943. Von Manstein's disagreements with Hitler over the conduct of that failed campaign contributed to his final falling out of favor. Though von Manstein had proved to be a master of mobile warfare, and fought tenaciously and successfully even when outnumbered, his continuing and growing friction with Hitler led to the end of his active service in 1944.

Von Manstein's conquest of the Crimea must rank high among his many significant accomplishments. Yet the campaign has drawn surprisingly little attention from historians. The coverage appears even sparser when compared to the many books dealing with the British actions around Sevastopol during the Crimean War of the 1850s. But von Manstein had no Tennyson to immortalize his exploits in epic verse, or Errol Flynn to glorify them on the movie screen.

However, the student of military history can learn much from this detailed description of von Manstein's campaign. Despite the popular image of *Blitzkrieg* emphasizing charging Panzers and screaming Stuka dive-bombers, the German army that carried out such operations was predominantly infantry. Most of its logistics still relied on horses. But the new German doctrine relied more on a fresh way of thinking than new technology, and von Manstein displayed intellectual creativity in abundance. His mental agility was particularly evident when the Russians made major landings behind him at Kerch while he was trying to invest Sevastopol. He was presented with a problem similar to that faced by Caesar against Vercingetorix in the siege of Alesia in Gaul. They both had to besiege an important enemy city while worrying about the possibility of being attacked themselves from the rear. Both came up with innovative approaches and achieved decisive victories. Relying primarily on traditional ground combat arms of infantry and artillery, with very effective air support, von Manstein orchestrated a finely coordinated series of actions that protected his own forces while eventually conquering the heavily defended city. He displayed adept maneuver and keen judgment throughout the campaign, maintaining the initiative and keeping his enemy off balance. He even found a way to work effectively with his Romanian allies, whose military record on the Eastern Front was lackluster at best, disastrous at worst.

Von Manstein was also able to overcome the obstacles presented by the complex Crimean terrain. The combination of rocky, hilly topography with modern fortifications and a major city was daunting. Many commentators have predicted that future adversaries will try to negate the technological advantages of American and other Western armies by drawing them into urban areas, forests, or mountains. Relevant insights may be gained from von Manstein's approach to those environments.

Just as Erich von Manstein was no ordinary general, and the German siege of Sevastopol no ordinary campaign, C. G. Sweeting is no ordinary author. He has been collecting reference books and manuals about what he terms "the things of war" for over fifty years, and owns many thousands of titles. He also collects artifacts, once even providing 3,000 German military items to the Imperial War Museum in London. As a result he possesses a rare feel for soldiers and their equipment. This is very evident in his extensive coverage of the "tools of war" on both sides in the Crimea.

He further honed his technological expertise as a curator at the National Air and Space Museum in Washington, D.C. His descriptions of air combat over Russia are exceptional and add rich detail to his descriptions of German operations. This close coordination between ground and air forces was another essential element of *Blitzkrieg*, and readers will find many such examples in the pages of this book.

Sweeting further enriches his descriptions with a rich and varied selection of maps and photographs. While stationed in Germany as a community relations specialist with the U.S. Air Force, he spent much of his time talking with the inhabitants about their wartime experiences and those of their families. A number of these acquaintances showed him personal snapshots and other original pictures which he has reproduced for this book. Many of the images on these pages have not been published before.

C. G. Sweeting has provided readers with far more than an illustrated narrative of the siege of Sevastopol. He builds up to that action with a thorough summary of the war in the East. Throughout World War II most of the German Army was engaged there, and the vast majority of its combat casualties were suffered at the hands of the Russians. He describes how leaders thought and acted, soldiers fought and died, and equipment worked and failed. He explains how a brilliant German general orchestrated a difficult campaign that flowed back and forth over the Crimean peninsula. He furnishes insights into the intellectual agility and tactical prowess that were so important for German success, but also gives glimpses of the determination and recuperative powers that would eventually give the Russians final victory. And he tells a rousing good story. Readers will be both educated and entertained by this book; perhaps they will be inspired to do further research into the lesser known campaigns of the War in the East and World War II in general.

Dr. Conrad Crane
U.S. Army Military History Institute
Carlisle Barracks, Pennsylvania

PREFACE

A FLOOD OF books on World War II has poured forth from the presses since the end of hostilities in 1945. Virtually every leader, campaign, invasion, battle, and weapon in the European Theater has been examined in detail, and even most minor events have been recorded in books and articles. Dozens of books have been written on the major battles including Stalingrad, Leningrad, Kursk, Normandy, the Bulge, and Berlin, to name just a few. It is therefore surprising that no detailed, objective account has been published in English dealing with the last major German victory: the battle for the Crimean Peninsula and the conquest of Sevastopol.

Considered the world's strongest fortress, Sevastopol was a vital port for the Soviet Black Sea fleet, and because of its terrain and the strength of its fortifications, well suited to resist a siege indefinitely. From the German standpoint, it was necessary to conquer the Crimea and capture Sevastopol to prevent their use as a Soviet air and sea base from which the Soviets could attack Axis forces from the rear. How this victory was achieved by the German and Romanian forces, under the leadership of General Erich von Manstein, is the subject of this book.

A brief account has been included of the events that transpired after the beginning of *Barbarossa*, the German invasion of the Soviet Union, that began on June 22, 1941. The vital role played by the German Air Force and the Romanian Army is also discussed. The tools of war are described, including the German secret weapons and the biggest gun of all time.

The Wehrmacht came very close to defeating the Red Army in 1941 and with the fall of Sevastopol in early July 1942, appeared to many to be omnipotent and well positioned to deal the Russians a final, knockout blow during the German summer offensive. But the seeds of Axis defeat had already been sown. This was partly because of the overextension of the German armed forces and the growing might of the Western Allies and the Soviets, but not least from the disastrous errors in judgment made by Adolf Hitler, who masterminded and micromanaged his war on the Eastern Front as well as the entire struggle throughout Europe and Africa.

I have drawn on a number of German, American, and Russian sources during the research and writing of this book, and many are listed in the endnotes. While working on this book with so many subject areas, I was fortunate to be able to call upon several very knowledgeable people for advice. I wish to thank everyone who has generously shared expertise on a variety of subjects. First, my special thanks to Lt. Gen. (Ret.) Guenther Rall. His experiences in the Crimea and throughout World War II are legendary. It was my privilege to give General Rall a tour through the Smithsonian's National Air and Space Museum (NASM) in Washington on two occasions, and I found his comments most informative, especially during his visits to the World War II aviation gallery.

Among others making important contributions were Donald S. Lopez, Deputy Director, NASM and Dr. Von Hardesty, Curator, Aeronautics Division, NASM, and authority on Russian aviation. Col. Walter J. Boyne, USAF (Ret.), pilot, historian, author, and former NASM director; Dr. John R. C. Schmitt, weapons and ammunition consultant; Dr. Denys Volan, historian, who as always provided encouragement and inspiration; and Andrew Mollo, British historian and expert on the Red Army.

Dr. Jack Atwater, Director, and the staff of the U.S. Army Ordnance Museum, were very helpful and kindly shared photographs and information from the museum archives. Klaus J. Knepscher, German aviation historian was, as usual, a good source of information concerning German military history and provided some rare German official photos. The late Dipl. Ing. Karl Ries, Luftwaffe historian and author, was always generous in sharing his extensive knowledge and outstanding collection of rare photos. Glenn Hyatt, Director, Fredericksburg Memorial Military Museum, and computer expert, greatly assisted in preparing many of the photos for this book. This was particularly important since a number of them were small, original snapshots, taken by German soldiers on the Eastern Front, and given to me over the years by veterans of Barbarossa.

Concerning photographs identified as a "German official photo": While serving with the U.S. Air Force, I made numerous flights to Berlin between 1956 and 1959. In addition to many German military books and manuals acquired in antiquarian bookshops, I obtained a number of original German government photos from World War II, still with the paper labels glued to the back. Some are of famous officers, aces, and men decorated with the Knight's Cross, while others are scenes of combat, mainly on the Eastern Front. The labels usually list the *Kriegsberichter* (war correspondent) who took the photo, the general location or battle, and a brief explanation concerning the person or event.

Another source of original glossy photos are those contained in three remarkable albums titled *Grossdeutschland im Weltgeschehen* (*Greater Germany in World Happenings*), covering the years 1940, 1941, and 1942. Prepared by the Nazi Ministry of Propaganda, the majority of the fascinating photos glued in the albums are from the war fronts, as well as from events inside the Third Reich. Most have never been published in the West. These photos form a unique historical record, and some are included in this book.

Other good sources of information and photos include the U.S. National Archives at College Park, Maryland, custodian of the Luftwaffe Photo Collection, and the archives of the National Air and Space Museum. Ms. Kris French, archivist of the Map Department of the National Geographic Society, was very helpful in locating and providing a detailed wartime map of the Crimea, which turned out to be surprisingly rare.

Last but certainly not least, my sincere thanks to my wife Joyce for her invaluable patience and assistance, and to my son Thomas, who has forgotten more about computers than I will ever know.

C. G. Sweeting
Clinton, Maryland
2004

INTRODUCTION

THE RED ARMY sentries manning the fortifications in the northeast quadrant on June 2, 1942, were jolted from their drowsiness by a tremendous explosion. The switchboard at Soviet headquarters inside the port city of Sevastopol lit up with calls reporting the blast. In the dark, quiet hours before dawn, the noise had echoed for miles and led some to believe that an ammunition dump had exploded. Others thought that a high-flying German warplane had dropped a large bomb on the massive masonry battlements.

Then, another huge blast hurled chunks of concrete and tangled steel into the air, followed by new explosions every few minutes. It was soon apparent to the Soviets that their defensive lines were under bombardment by giant German guns. At the first glimmer of dawn, German artillery of all calibers joined in, and soon Stuka dive-bombers screamed down to hurl their bombs, equipped with Jericho sirens, to add to the storm of steel lashing the strong points ringing the city on the north, east, and south. It was obvious to all that the long-awaited German offensive to capture Sevastopol had begun.

In a camouflaged command post on a hill behind German lines, Colonel General Erich von Manstein, commander of German and Romanian forces besieging the city, watched developments with keen interest. Through a large scissors telescope he observed the devastating effects of the super-heavy artillery on the selected targets. The huge two-ton shells from three 60cm (600mm—about 26-inch) *Karl* howitzers, burst with great force, shattering even the most sturdily constructed fortifications. They blasted craters in the earth 30 meters (98.42 feet) wide, flinging debris and mangled body parts hundreds of feet in the air.

"Dora" roared into action early on the morning of June 5. The 80cm (800mm, or 31.5-inch) railway gun was the biggest cannon of all time. Its enormous shells began exploding on their targets, causing unparalleled destruction. The very earth shook, and clouds of smoke and dust billowed high into the sky. Even deep inside the massive, reinforced concrete forts, the tremendous concussion of the high-explosive projectiles produced such great changes in air pressure that they ruptured the lungs of many hapless Russian soldiers. It took great courage for soldiers to continue to perform their duties during days and nights of such merciless bombardment. *Dora*, known earlier as *Schwerer Gustav*, was operated by a crew of 450 men, and required a small army of about 5,000 to lay the rail spur and assemble the gun.

Von Manstein sat patiently at his field desk, reading reports that arrived frequently by phone, radio, and messenger from his commanders and forward observers. Trainloads of ammunition and supplies were still arriving on the recently rebuilt rail line down the Crimean Peninsula. The Russian railroads had always been a different gauge than that used in Germany and other European countries, probably so designed in the mid-1800s when the invasion of Russia by Napoleon was still fresh in people's minds. Now German and Romanian infantry and combat engineer (Pionier) troops were in position along the front, which stretched in a great arc along the northern and eastern outskirts of the port city. German troops were supported by aircraft and self-propelled assault guns, armed and ready for the final offensive.

But first, the strong Soviet defenses had to be softened up for five days by one of the heaviest artillery bombardments since the siege of Verdun in World War I. As hours turned into days, von Manstein had plenty of time to sit back in his camp chair, sip ersatz coffee, and review the battle plans with his staff. During a lull in the shelling on the night of June 4, he pondered the significant events that had transpired in the year since the beginning of *Operation Barbarossa,* the German invasion of the Soviet Union.

Like most German officers, von Manstein was surprised and concerned when he was finally informed of Adolf Hitler's decision to invade the Soviet Union. In his postwar memoir, von Manstein stated that unlike the *Blitzkrieg* in the west against France in 1940, which

incorporated his brilliant strategy for an armored thrust through the Ardennes, he was not consulted on the advisability or method of conducting a campaign against the Soviet Union. At the time von Manstein, although an infantry officer, was commander of the LVI Panzer Corps, and the operation order for his Corps was not received until a late date—in May 1941.[1]

The German supreme command reviews plans for Operation Barbarossa, the invasion of the Soviet Union. Left to right, Gen. Field Marshal Wilhelm Keitel, chief of OKW; unknown officer; Gen. Field Marshal Walter von Brauchitsch, commander in chief, German Army; Adolf Hitler; Col. Gen. Franz Halder, chief of the army general staff. *German Official Photo*

Most Germans had long feared the menacing Bolshevik colossus in the east with its aggressive policy of expanding communist domination abroad. The National Socialists and others had battled the German Communist Party for years prior to Hitler's gaining power in January 1933. In theory, the idea of destroying the Soviet Union appealed to many German military and Party leaders who recognized communism as a significant threat to Germany and Europe. Hatred of communism continued to be a basic tenet of National Socialist propaganda until the Hitler-Stalin Nonaggression Pact was signed in August 1939. But the German generals remembered all too well the disastrous consequences of fighting on two fronts during World War I, and in 1941 Great Britain and her empire remained undefeated and growing in strength.

Members of the General Staff, in particular, viewed a war in the east with trepidation because European Russia was vast and was known to have poor, mainly unpaved roads and severe weather conditions. They recognized that logistics would therefore be extremely difficult. Most important, these experts on strategy and capabilities knew that the Soviet Union possessed a huge army and air force with almost unlimited manpower reserves.

A number of senior officers who opposed Hitler's audacious plan tried to dissuade him from attacking Russia, at least at this time. Some appealed to Field Marshal Walter von Brauchitsch, Commander in Chief of the Army (OKH), while others urged Field Marshal Wilhelm Keitel, Chief of Armed Forces High Command (OKW), to prevail on Hitler to cancel or delay the invasion, but to no avail. Foreign Minister Joachim von Ribbentrop continued to oppose Barbarossa, but even his opinion did not deter the Fuehrer in any way. Grand Admiral Erich Raeder, Commander in Chief of the Navy (OKM), and Colonel General Franz Halder, Chief of the General Staff, raised strong objections to Barbarossa and were against invading Russia at all.

Secrecy was of paramount importance, so the plans for Barbarossa were divulged only to those with a need to know. Reichs Press Chief Otto Dietrich, along with most of the Gauleiters and senior Party leaders, was not informed until hours before the attack.

Hitler told the skeptics that Germany must attack Russia before Stalin joined with Britain to attack Germany. He firmly believed that a powerful Blitzkrieg (Lightning War) campaign, with the element of surprise, could defeat the Red Army within three to four months and precipitate the collapse of the Soviet government. Hitler was confident that Stalin's bloody purge of the Army leadership corps in 1938 had weakened the armed forces. He also felt that the forced collectivization of the farms and peasants, and the deplorable conditions in the Soviet Union for over twenty years, had undermined the people's loyalty to the state. When Field Marshal Gerd von Rundstedt obtained an audience with the Fuehrer, in an effort to convince him to cancel or at least postpone the attack, he was told, "You have only to kick in the door, and the whole rotten structure will come crashing down."[2]

Also, Hitler did not believe the intelligence reports concerning the size, strength, and morale of the Red Army. He discounted even the information obtained from Luftwaffe overflights of Soviet territory. Russian forces had performed poorly in the winter war with Finland during 1939–40, and this surely influenced Hitler's low opinion of the Soviet military capability. For centuries, Germany had coveted the rich natural resources of the east and viewed European Russia as its logical area for expansion, for needed *Lebensraum*. The oil, food, and labor available in a conquered Russia would provide Germany with the means of successfully prosecuting the war and establishing a "New Order" in Europe under German hegemony.

Hitler's increasing medical problems, real and imaginary, and his obsession with his health, may also have prompted him to accelerate his ambitious agenda. Despite all the objections, the Fuehrer's will prevailed and the plans for Barbarossa proceeded on a priority basis, with the original starting date of May 15, 1941.

The British incursion in Greece that spring posed a threat to Germany's southern flank that required immediate action. Hitler was incensed by the anti-Axis coup in Yugoslavia and was determined to help Benito Mussolini, the Italian dictator, who had commenced an ill-fated invasion of Greece the previous October. On April 6, the Wehrmacht, with its Italian ally, launched a Blitzkrieg that quickly defeated the armies of Yugoslavia and Greece. Although another remarkable victory, the campaign in the Balkans delayed the beginning of Operation Barbarossa for several crucial weeks, with perhaps fatal consequences. Hitler reluctantly set June 22 as the new date for the attack on Russia. However, the troop movements and redeployments had inadvertently helped mask the preparations for the invasion of the Soviet Union. Even while war raged in the Balkans, thousands of German troops, with all the grim tools of war, moved quietly into camouflaged positions along the eastern frontier. They trav-

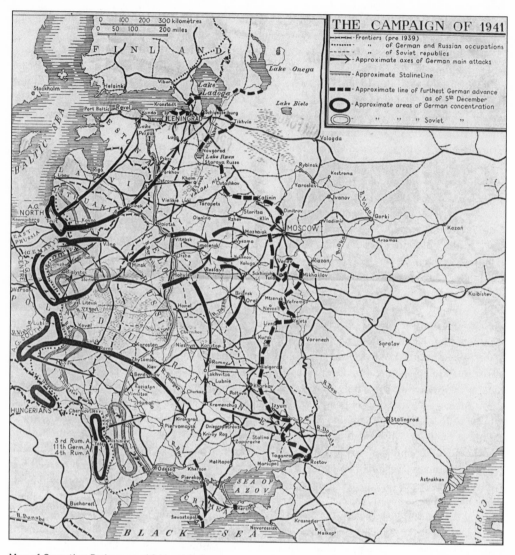

Map of Operation Barbarossa, 1941. *U.S. Army*

eled mainly at night, in complete radio silence, in what turned out to be a masterly example of deception.

Fuehrer Directive No. 21, dated December 18, 1940, outlined the plan for *Unternehmung* (Operation) *Barbarossa*. The main goal was to "destroy the 'Russian Army' by daring operations led by deeply penetrating armored spearheads." The enemy was to be prevented "from withdrawing into the depths of Russia." After defeating the Red Army, the Wehrmacht was to establish a line deep enough in European Russia to make air attack on Germany impossible, thereby "erecting a barrier against Asiatic Russia on the general line 'Volga-Archangel.'"[3]

By mid-June the Wehrmacht was almost fully deployed in three great army groups along the frontier of over nine hundred miles (1,145 kilometers). Army Groups North, Center, and South fielded 145 divisions, including 19 Panzer (armored) divisions, with 3,350 tanks. Army Group Center was the strongest, with more tank units. Initially two Finnish and fourteen Romanian infantry divisions participated, later joined by Italian, Hungarian, Slovakian, and Spanish contingents. Each army group was supported by a Luftwaffe air fleet, with a total of 2,230 aircraft.[4] Despite the recent combat operations in the Balkans, the Wehrmacht was at the peak of its power, well trained, adequately equipped, and with important combat experience at all levels of command. Morale was good and the troops had confidence in their commanders and themselves.

The actual invasion plan was quite simple. Fast-moving Panzer divisions were to carve up and encircle the Red Army formations in swift, deeply penetrating pincer movements. The slower-moving infantry and artillery, advancing mainly on foot, were to destroy or force the surrender of the encircled Russian units. The main objective was not the occupation of territory or large cities, but the destruction of the Soviet armed forces. Even the capture of Moscow was not Hitler's primary goal, and it should be noted that the Army High Command (OKH), did not agree with Hitler's evolving strategy as the campaign progressed.[5]

Von Manstein had no opportunity at the time to worry about the reasons or strategy for Barbarossa, but he later stated that he thought "Hitler's strategic aims were based primarily on political and economic considerations. These were (a) the capture of Leningrad, a city he regarded as the cradle of Bolshevism, which would allow him to join up with the Finns and dominate the Baltic and (b) possession of the raw material regions of the Ukraine, the armaments centers of the Donetz Basin, and later the Caucasus oil fields. Seizing these territories would cripple the Soviet war economy completely."[6]

Although Hitler stated in Fuehrer Directive No. 21 that the destruction of the Russian Army was the main goal of the campaign, and this was the contention of the OKH, von Manstein believed that Hitler wanted both to defeat the Red Army and to capture and exploit the economic objectives immediately. According to von Manstein, Germany simply did not possess adequate forces to accomplish Hitler's overall plan as he directed, and it was on this divergence of basic strategy that the German conduct of operations ultimately foundered.[7] None of this would be obvious during the first heady months of dramatic German victories.

Unlike the Wehrmacht, the Red Army on the eve of Barbarossa was in a state of transition. Many of its most competent and experienced commanders had been executed during Stalin's mindless purges of the 1930s. Although the Army was huge, most armaments were obsolescent. However, the Soviet armed forces were modernizing and incorporating lessons learned during its war with Finland. New and improved weapons, such as the formidable T-34 tank, were replacing old equipment. At the time of the German invasion the Red Army actually possessed a total of 203 divisions, plus 46 armored brigades, most deployed in western Russia. At least 158 infantry divisions faced the Russian-German frontier.[8] These forces fielded over 7,000 tanks, most obsolete.

The Soviet Air Force was much larger than the Luftwaffe, but most of its airplanes were obsolete and inferior to those of Germany. Its strength was estimated at 8,000 aircraft, with about 6,000 in western Russia and the rest in Asia. Like the Army, the Air Force was receiving improved equipment, and most of the new planes were for support of the ground forces.

Although spies had reported the German preparations, and even the British Government had warned of the German intention to invade, Stalin did not believe that Germany would attack. He believed an attack was unlikely since Germany was involved in the war in the west and in North Africa, and the Wehrmacht had just completed the campaign in the

Balkans to expel the British Expeditionary Force from Greece. Furthermore, both Russia and Germany had been complying with the terms of the Hitler-Stalin Non-aggression Pact. As a result, the troops of the Red Army were caught by surprise, with only a last-minute alert coming down the chain of command.

As the date for Barbarossa approached, Hitler's confidence and enthusiasm began to convince some top military leaders of the certainty of a speedy German victory. According to General Heinz Guderian, "The Fuehrer had succeeded in infecting his immediate military entourage with his own baseless optimism."[9] Preparations for Barbarossa now proceeded with new confidence at OKW and OKH on the premise that a Blitzkrieg could quickly defeat the Soviets and prevent them from attacking Germany when least expected. None of the German generals are known to have resigned to show their opposition to Barbarossa.

The German public knew nothing about this momentous undertaking. Even the soldiers in the field did not know the real reason for all the troop movements and preparations. One rumor circulated that German forces were to be allowed transit through Russia to attack the British in Iraq or Iran and to secure the oil resources for Germany.

Hitler, an insomniac even under normal conditions, was unable to sleep during the day and night before the beginning of Barbarossa. He stated on September 17, 1941 that " . . . I needed great spiritual strength to take the decision to attack Bolshevism."[10] On the morning of June 21, he paced slowly back and forth in his opulent office in the new Reichs Chancellery, wrestling with his fateful decision to launch the greatest invasion in history. At the noon situation conference he was informed that the Wehrmacht was in position and that all preparations for *Fall Barbarossa* were completed. But there was still time to cancel the order to attack and thus to avoid war with the Soviet Union. Even at this late date it is unlikely that many senior officers would have complained if Hitler had called off the invasion.

When Hitler returned to his study he paused to gaze at his favorite painting, the portrait of King Frederick the Great of Prussia by Anton Graf. The picture of the monarch he strived to emulate seemed to inspire him and to confirm his final decision to attack Communist Russia. He then went to his desk and began to write a letter to Mussolini explaining why he was launching Barbarossa.

As the final hours ticked away there was tension in the military headquarters in the *Bendlerstrasse*. The generals nervously eyed the clock as it neared 1:30 P.M., the final moment that the chain of events could be stopped and the attack canceled. When no word was received from the Fuehrer, they knew that Barbarossa would proceed as scheduled. Hitler, ignoring the great physical and spiritual costs that this new war would bring, launched one of the most brutal conflicts in history. With his unlimited power, he callously sealed the fate of millions of soldiers and civilians, and even that of his own country. The Third Reich was now definitely on the road to Armageddon.

CHAPTER I

STORM ACROSS THE STEPPE

At exactly 3:15 A.M. on Sunday, June 22, 1941, sleepy Russian sentries saw blinking white lights across the frontier to the west. Within seconds, roaring and whistling sounds announced the arrival of the first volley of shells from some 7,200 guns of all calibers, followed by crashing explosions as the artillery barrage began bursting in the Soviet defensive positions. In some parts of the long front, from the Baltic to the Black Sea, the barrage was light or even nonexistent, in other more vital areas it was devastating. The shelling continued until the local commanders determined that the opposition had been crushed. Then red flares appeared overhead and tanks, self-propelled guns, and infantry surged forward from their camouflaged positions to storm the Red Army frontier outposts. At first light warplanes of the Luftwaffe were roaring east to strafe and bomb airfields and important targets along the front.

Operation Barbarossa was underway!

During the first hectic days the German offensive seemed irresistible; in places the stunned Russian soldiers retreated in disarray or were captured while still in their billets. Others began fighting tenaciously in uncoordinated groups until overrun and decimated by the advancing tanks and troops of the German Army and Waffen-SS (Armed SS). Fast-moving Panzer divisions, with close air support, destroyed large Soviet Army formations in giant battles of encirclement. During the first weeks hundreds of thousands of Soviet troops were killed or taken prisoner, and thousands of tanks, guns, and vehicles were wrecked or captured. But the Wehrmacht still could not land a final knock-out blow on the Red Army.

Unternehmung Barbarossa was named by Hitler for the Holy Roman Emperor Friedrich Barbarossa (Red Beard), 1152–1190. The operational plan for the Barbarossa Blitzkrieg, prepared during the winter and spring of 1941, provided for the three great army groups to launch a series of main-effort penetrations by infantry, supported by artillery and assault guns, accom-

1

Junkers Ju 87D dive-bombers returning from a precision attack on targets during the summer of 1941. The Stuka, with a crew of two, was slow at 255 mph (410 km/h) and vulnerable because it lacked maneuverability, but it could carry up to 4,032 pounds (1,800 kg) of bombs. *Smithsonian Photo*

panied by secondary infantry frontal attacks. The breakthroughs were quickly exploited by enveloping attacks by *Panzer* (armored) forces. These tactics pinned many enemy troops in their frontier positions, cut off their escape to the rear, and forced them to fight on an inverted front. As the armor developed its exploitation, it became the outer ring of envelopment; the infantry moved up as rapidly as possible to form an inner ring and effected the destruction of the encircled hostile forces. The Germans dubbed these tactics *Keil und Kessel*, or wedge and trap; essentially it was a process of taking huge bites out of the enemy position by means of multiple penetrations followed by double envelopments.[1] During this period communications and air-ground cooperation with the Luftwaffe were excellent, greatly contributing to the remarkable series of victories.

The Wehrmacht was initially fully equipped with a complete range of armored vehicles. The well-trained and experienced crews used multipurpose half-tracks, armored personnel carriers, armored cars, and command and reconnaissance vehicles. Principal tanks in 1941 included the light PzKw IIJ weighing 9.5 tons, armed with a 2cm (20mm) gun, the PzKw IIIH of 21.6 tons with a 5cm (50mm) gun, and the PzKw IVF-1, a 22.3 ton tank with a 7.5cm (75mm) gun, and a few other older types that were used in the first months, including the Czech-built PzKw 38(t) light tank with a 3.7cm (37mm) gun. Assault guns on tank chassis, usually armed with a 7.5cm (75mm) gun, provided close support for the infantry. The high-velocity 8.8cm (88mm) Flak 18, 36, and 37 guns were widely used with telling effect in both the antiaircraft and antitank roles. Antitank guns of 37mm,

Armored vehicles of the 3d Panzer Division wait for orders by radio to form up for an attack during a *Kesselschlacht*, or battle of encirclement, at Minsk on June 26, 1941. In the foreground is a Sd.Kfz. 260/4 communications half-track; behind on the left and center are PzKw IIIJ tanks with 5cm KwK guns. Additional steel trackshoes were carried on the front for added armor protection. *From* Die Deutsche Panzerwaffe *(Berlin, 1942)*

42mm, 50mm, and 75mm were in use along with field and heavy artillery of various calibers. The main German problem was the amazingly small number of tanks available in June 1941; according to an account by General Wilhelm von Thoma, there were only 2,434, excluding the very light "sardine cans."

Contrary to popular belief, the Wehrmacht was not fully mechanized. There were only nineteen Panzer and ten motorized divisions in action during the first months of Barbarossa. Most of the German army, like its Soviet enemy, marched on foot accompanied by horse-drawn vehicles and artillery.

The Russo-German war was unprecedented not only in size and scope, but in unmitigated savagery. Never in history had a nation sustained such losses as the Soviet Union and still survived. The Russian soldier soon proved to be a formidable foe. While not as well trained or efficient as German troops, at least initially, Russians were tough and accustomed to privation. They evidenced strong patriotism for their motherland in the course of the conflict despite the hardships of combat and the repression that characterized the Soviet system.

Stalin's purges of the army officer corps in the late 1930s caused considerable difficulty during the first year of the war. Leadership in the Red Army suffered because of the loss of many of the most capable and experienced officers. Because of the general atmosphere of fear and repression, officers, noncommissioned officers, and men often hesitated to demonstrate initiative or make decisions until orders were received from higher authority or requests were approved. For example, on the first morning of the German invasion, some commanders reported that they were being attacked and asked, "What should we do?"[2] This attitude is understandable in such a totalitarian state, but it added to the general confusion and often fatal lack of prompt response to enemy action or changing circumstances. Units with both a commander and political commissar assigned had a form of dual control, which often led to additional confusion and difficulties. In practice, Soviet commanders and commissars cared little about the lives of the soldiers.

Discipline in the Red Army

Soldiers of the Red Army surrender to rapidly advancing German troops in summer 1941. Hundreds of thousands of Russians were taken prisoner in the great battles during the first months of the invasion. *From OKH*, Infanterie im Osten *(Graz, 1943)*

was brutal; retreat or failure was often punished by the political commissar attached to each unit or the firing squads of the NKVD, the dreaded security police organization. During the first chaotic weeks of war, thousands of Russian soldiers surrendered in the hope of finding freedom. The enormous number of prisoners of war in the initial phases of Barbarossa at times overwhelmed the German capability to guard and care for them. Many escaped into the forests and swamps where they eventually joined with civilians to fight German occupation forces.

Some German troops, especially in Ukraine, were welcomed as liberators with bread and salt. Hundreds of thousands of Ukrainians had been killed by the Soviet secret police before the war.[3] The German political administrators, *SS Einsatzgruppen* (Special Action Groups), and police forces, following along behind the army, quickly alienated the civilian populace with harsh repression, executions, and exploitation for the benefit of the German war effort. It was soon obvious that the Germans came not as liberators from Communist bondage but as conquerors. The atrocity at Babi Yar is an example of the terror that the civilian population continued to suffer during the war.[4] The SS Einsatzgruppen were under orders from Reichsfuehrer-SS Heinrich Himmler not only to stamp out resistance but also to liquidate Communists, especially political commissars, Jews, and others believed by Hitler to stand in the way of his planned "New Order" in Europe. On September 29 and 30, 1941, over 33,000 people, mostly Jews, were shot by the SS, with the aid of local fascist-minded and anti-Semitic extremists, and their bodies dumped in a ravine outside Kiev.[5] This was just one of many horrific episodes of this type in World War II that includes the Katyn massacre, where over 4,400 Polish officers and civilians were executed by the Soviet Secret Police in early 1940.[6]

The partisan warfare that developed behind German lines greatly hindered their war effort. Sabotage soon led to brutal confrontations as daring attacks were made on German supply lines, camps, hospitals, and headquarters. After seeing the dead, often mutilated bodies of their comrades, German retaliation was quick and cruel. This lead to an unending cycle of violence that added to the pathetic plight of innocent peasants and townspeople in rear areas. In areas recaptured by the Soviets, anyone believed to have cooperated with the Germans was either executed, imprisoned, or deported.

Although the Russian armed forces of 1941 were, man for man, division for division, grossly inferior in military effectiveness to their German foes, they made up for their deficiencies in mass, if not quality. This great army of foot soldiers was poorly fed and supported. They moved like locusts across the land, commandeering whatever they needed. Many of their units remained an "armed horde" throughout the war.[7] As the conflict progressed, the Germans learned the hard way that Soviet soldiers, unlike most of those encountered in the west, frequently fought to the death. Prisoners or wounded would sometimes attack their German captors by surprise, even with their bare hands, leading to bloody retribution. There was no shortage of heroism and barbarity on both sides among both soldiers and civilians caught up in this terrible struggle. The war may have begun mainly as a conflict of ideologies, but it soon developed into a war for survival.

The Red Army was armed with some of the best and worst weapons. Although there was no radar and up-to-date communications, and medical and other technical equipment was in short supply, the Soviets had more tanks and artillery than any other army in the world. However, most armored vehicles were obsolete; modern tanks were just entering service in limited numbers at that time.

The best Russian tanks in 1941 included the T-26 light tank variations, weighing about 9.4 tons, and armed with a 37mm or 45mm cannon; the excellent new T-34 medium tank of 26.3 tons, with a 76mm cannon; and the KV-I and KV-II heavy tanks. The KV-I, at 47 tons, was well armored and over twice as heavy as the German PzKw IV. It had a powerful 76mm gun like the T-34. The KV-II, discontinued in production shortly after the beginning of Barbarossa because of poor mobility, weighed an impressive 57 tons and was equipped with a huge turret, usually mounting a 152mm howitzer. These heavy tanks were practically impervious to the fire of German 37mm and 50mm antitank guns and usually had to be dealt with by 88mm cannon. The main problem for the Soviets at that time was not so much the tanks themselves, but how they were used.

Before considering the events that transpired during the first months of Barbarossa, it is useful to take a brief look at Romania, Germany's major ally in the campaign to conquer southern Russia, the Crimea, Sevastopol, and beyond.

The Kingdom of Romania was traditionally an agrarian country with only minor industrial capacity. Romania sided with the Western Allies in World War I and became a major battleground. France exerted considerable influence in the years between the wars, including supplying some arms and training for the Romanian Army.[8] After a series of political upheavals during the Great Depression, a Fascist government was elected in 1937 and the country soon came under increasing German influence, politically and economically. By 1939, the Fascist Iron Guard organization, which had been suppressed, reemerged, resulting in violence including the assassination of the Prime Minister. Out of the political turmoil came absolute allegiance to Nazi Germany.[9]

German Army gunners shout with glee and relief after scoring a direct hit at point-blank range with their 5cm Pak 38 antitank gun on a Soviet T-34 tank. *German Official Photo*

Kaboom! A Soviet heavy tank loaded with fuel and ammunition explodes in a giant fireball after a direct hit from a German 8.8cm Flak gun firing in the antitank mode. *From* Die Deutsche Panzerwaffe *(Berlin, 1942)*

In June 1940, the Soviet Union presented Romania with an ultimatum. They seized two Romanian provinces, Bessarabia and Northern Bukovina, claiming they were traditionally Russian territory. Other areas were lost as a result of German-Italian machinations, and on September 6, King Carol abdicated, naming his son, Mihai (Michael) regent. Young Mihai later was crowned king, but the real power was now firmly in the hands of Prime Minister Ion Antonescu, backed by the Iron Guard. Antonescu controlled the authoritarian government that allied itself with Germany and Italy by signing the Tripartite Pact on November 23. Twelve German Army divisions had entered Romania, supposedly to protect the country, and began training the Romanian military on a priority basis. The Germans found the Romanians not only inferior in organization and training, but poorly equipped.

The Romanian Army in 1941 was a walking arms museum. Even the army's basic weapon, the Mannlicher Model 93 6.5mm rifle, manufactured under license in Romania, was not standard issue throughout the army.[10] Obsolete weapons of several types and calibers, most of French, Czechoslovakian, Austrian, English, and Russian origin were in use even within a regiment. A good example from the hodgepodge of weapons was the French M1915 8mm Chauchat light machine gun, used by the U.S. Army in France in World War I, and proven to be probably the worst piece of automatic junk ever produced. Romania intended to replace it with the excellent 7.9mm Czech Z.B. 26 (Praga) light machine gun, from which the British caliber .303 Bren gun was developed, as funds became available. Even the steel helmets in use were of two types, a French and a Dutch model.

Romanian infantry fire a Czech-made 7.9mm ZBvz/53 (German MG 37[t]) heavy machine gun on a tripod from the cover of a cornfield while advancing through Bessarabia in July 1941. *German Official Photo*

The same situation existed with heavy equipment including the limited number of armored vehicles and field and heavy artillery. Some English Carden Lloyd light tanks, Czech LT 35 light tanks, and light French tanks were purchased before the war, but few trucks were in use by the army. Some civilian trucks were requisitioned in 1941, but the Romanian Army depended mainly on boots and horse-drawn transport. The Germans provided some captured French arms and equipment during the winter and spring of 1941, but the supply of ammunition and spare parts of so many types became a severe problem after the first few weeks of war against the Soviet Union. Germany was therefore compelled to provide weapons and equipment of their own manufacture, as well as training, to improve Romanian combat capability.

The Romanian Navy and Air Force were small and their equipment was mostly obsolete. The largest ships in the navy were four old destroyers and miscellaneous gunboats and patrol craft on the Danube River and along the coast. It was no match for the Soviet Black Sea fleet and played only a limited role in the war in the east.

Serious attention was given by the Germans to improving the capabilities of the Romanian Air Force. Germany supplied some bombers, including the Junkers Ju 88. One was delivered to the Allies in good condition by a defecting Romanian aircrew when they flew it to an island in the Mediterranean in 1943. It was flown to Wright Field, Ohio, for testing and evaluation and is now on display at the U.S. Air Force Museum. Messerschmitt Bf 109 fighters were also provided, and some were used in air defense of the vital Ploesti oil fields. Ploesti supplied one third of all German fuel oil requirements and was considered essential to the German war effort. German fighter units were also assigned to protect the oil fields and refineries when attacks were made by Soviet Air Force bombers and later by the U.S. Army Air Forces (USAAF). The Romanians had some good pilots. The top Romanian fighter ace, Prince Constantine Cantacuzene, is reported to have shot down sixty aircraft.[11]

In his postwar memoir, Field Marshal Erich von Manstein stated that Marshal Antonescu was a real patriot, a good soldier and a most loyal ally.[12] According to von Manstein, the Romanian Army had a number of weaknesses. The Romanian soldier, who was usually of peasant origin, was modest in his wants and usually a capable, brave fighter, but the possibility of training him as an individual fighting man who could think for himself in action, let alone as a noncommissioned officer or officer, was to a great extent limited by the low standard of general education in Romania. Experience and training were lacking; there was no NCO corps as we know it, and most of all, the Romanians lacked that close link between officers and men which tends to be taken for granted in the German Army. In the Romanian Army, flogging was still used as a punishment. Their management was entirely devoid of the "Prussian" tradition.[13] Lastly, von Manstein stated that Romanians had little appetite for pushing further into Russia after the reconquest of Bessarabia, their fundamental war aim.

In order to ensure good coordination between the German and Romanian armies, German liaison staffs, with considerable authority, were assigned to Romanian units down through division level, and sometimes even to regiments. Germans often directed operations and facilitated supply of Romanian troops in the field. The Germans felt this was necessary to prevent retreat or panic among Romanians in difficult combat situations. Similar arrangements were made with the armies of other German allies. The procedure worked with varying results until the debacle at Stalingrad when Romanian divisions on the German flanks collapsed during the great Soviet offensive in late November 1942.

In the summer of 1941, columns of black smoke from burning tanks and villages smudged the sky over the vast Eastern Front. After breaking through the Soviet frontier defenses, the Wehrmacht surged forward to clash with the massive formations of the Red Army. Clouds of dust billowed up as great armies marched across seemingly endless fields of grass, sunflowers, and maize. Over three million German and allied troops struggled in the heat with equal numbers of Russian soldiers, in

Tank versus tank. The commander of a German PzKw III tank surveys the battlefield while clouds of smoke from burning vehicles smudge the sky. The PzKw III was the principal German tank during the battles in 1941. *From OKH*, Allen Gewalten zum Trotz *(Berlin, 1942)*

countless battles and skirmishes. Thousands of tanks and vehicles roared, belched blue smoke, and maneuvered through forests and plains in the deadly game of armored combat and mechanized destruction. Hitler had launched his fateful crusade to destroy Communism and seize an eastern empire, and the massive Soviet Army was determined to defeat the invader on this, the greatest battlefield in modern history.

During the first weeks Army Group North (*Heeresgruppe Nord*), commanded by Field Marshal Wilhelm *Ritter* von Leeb, fought through difficult terrain in the Baltic states, seized by the Soviets in 1940, where the Germans were welcomed by the indigenous population. At that time, General of Infantry Erich von Manstein, commanding the German LVI Panzer Corps, made a brilliantly executed advance in the direction of Leningrad, the main objective.

Army Group Center (*Herresgruppe Mitte*), led by Field Marshal Fedor von Bock, was the strongest German formation with the most armored vehicles. It broke through Soviet defenses and advanced spectacularly in the general direction of Moscow. Eventually even the fortifications of the so-called "Stalin Line," behind the old 1939 Russian frontier, were breached. The powerful armored pincers closed a big *Kessel* (pocket) at Minsk by mid-July, enfolding 323,000 prisoners, 3,000 tanks and 1,800 guns, which were either captured or destroyed. The swift-moving jaws then opened in another thrust as the Panzer and motorized units crossed the Dnieper River, with the help of engineers, to bag an additional 100,000 prisoners, 2,000 tanks and 1,900 guns. Other great successes were achieved in August with the capture of 310,000 prisoners and the capture or destruction of 3,200 tanks and 3,200 guns in the battle for Smolensk. Yet another victorious battle was waged south of the Divina River, but as at Smolensk, many Russians managed to escape and fought on, while German losses in men and machines began to mount.[14]

Army Group South (*Heeresgruppe Sued*), with which we are mainly concerned in this account, was commanded by Field Marshal Gerd von Rundstedt. It fielded three armies, the Eleventh, Seventeenth, and Sixth, the latter with most of the armor. The total strength of Army Group South included five Panzer divisions, three motorized infantry divisions, twenty-six infantry divisions, six mountain and light infantry divisions, and three security divisions. Von Rundstedt's command also included Romanian, Hungarian, Slovakian, and Italian units, but the taciturn field marshal managed to get the best out of this multinational force. This was in spite of the fact that there was animosity and distrust between some of the foreign contingents, notably the Romanian and Hungarian armies. These two formations always had to be separated by German or other forces.

On the far right flank or southern wing was the German Eleventh Army, technically part of Army Group South, but attacking out of Romania. Colonel General Eugen *Ritter* von Schobert commanded this army, with the Romanian Third and Fourth Armies on its left and right flanks during the initial phases of the offensive. The Eleventh Army had 7 German divisions, while the Romanians fielded 14 infantry divisions, 4 cavalry brigades, and a tank brigade.[15]

On the afternoon of June 21, a short message for the commander was received in Army Group South headquarters. It was marked not only *Geheime Kommandosache* (Secret Document) but *Streng Geheim* (Top Secret). When Field Marshal von Rundstedt read the decoded message he noted the special code word *"Dortmund,"* which signaled that *Fall Barbarossa* would begin as scheduled at 3:15 the next morning. He called his staff together and had the final instructions for the offensive transmitted to subordinate unit commanders. Later, a special *Tagesbefehl* (Order of the Day) from the Fuehrer was disseminated and read during the night to all the troops by their immediate commanding officers. It said in part: "Soldiers of the East-

ern Front," followed by a short explanation to the effect that Russia
was a threat that must be eliminated and that they were going to
save the whole of European civi-
lization and culture. "German soldiers! You are about to join battle,
a hard and crucial battle, the destiny of Europe, the future of the
German Reich, the existence of our
nation, now lie in your hands
alone. May the Almighty help us
all in this struggle."[16]

Army Group South faced the
largest Russian forces, which were
evidently deployed to cover the
Ukraine, called the "breadbasket of
Russia," which also was the location of many important industries.
Since the Soviet forces could withdraw to the east behind successive
river lines, the best method of preventing such a withdrawal was a
strong attack with armor on the
left, driving in a southeasterly direction to cut off the Russians before they could reach the Dnieper,
and to push them against the Black
Sea on the south. Von Rundstedt
concentrated his greatest strength
in the section between Lublin and
the Carpathians. His main effort

Soviet infantry firing an 8.2cm M1941 mortar during a counterattack.
The wheels have been removed during firing. The Red Army used more
mortars than any other army in World War II. *Sovfoto*

was made by the Sixth Army, followed by the First Panzer Group. The latter exploited in the
direction of the Dnieper River bend once the infantry broke through the defenses. The Seventeenth Army protected the First Panzer Group's right flank against an attack from the large enemy forces cut off in the south. The Carpathian sector was held by Hungarian forces; the
German Eleventh Army, supported by the Romanians, launched frontal attacks across the
Prut to hold the Russians in the south. The Romanians were, of course, most anxious to lib-
erate their province of Bessarabia from the Soviets. The Pripet Marshes, which separated
the zones of action of Army Groups Center and South, provided some protection for von
Rundstedt's left flank.

The advance of von Rundstedt's Army Group South to the Dnieper River bend was an
operation that proceeded concurrently with the successful drive to Smolensk by von Bock's
Army Group Center. Von Rundstedt's forces achieved the same surprise on June 22, as did
the other German armies in breaking through the Russians' thin border positions. By noon the
Panzer divisions of Colonel General Ewald von Kleist's First Panzer Group had moved forward to the attack, eventually encountering counterattacks by strong Soviet armored forces.

The formidable Soviet T-34 medium tank with sloping front armor plate, and armed with a 7.62cm gun, came as a considerable shock to the Germans when first encountered in July 1941. It weighed 26 tons, had 13–45mm armor, and a speed of 34 mph (55 km/h). With its firepower, speed, armor, and wide-track mobility, the T-34 provided the greatest challenge to the German Panzer forces during the first two years of war. Near the end of 1943, an improved model was introduced, the T-34/85 with an 8.5cm gun. *From Hans Albertz*, Die wichtigsten Panzerkampfwagen unserer Gegner *(Munich-Berlin, 1943)*

Nevertheless, the German Panzer divisions continued to gain ground; since they soon threatened the rear of the Russians around Prezemysl, who had held the Seventeenth Army to small gains up to the 27th, those Russian forces began to withdraw, pursued by the Seventeenth Army.

In the following days Lwow fell but von Rundstedt had made modest gains in comparison with those of von Bock; having broken up the numerous Russian armored counterattacks, it was hoped he would now have greater freedom of action as he continued his drive to the east. The Sixth Army was supporting the Panzer spearheads, and in the south the Eleventh Army and the Romanian divisions were ready to launch their attack into the Ukraine.

During the next two weeks von Rundstedt continued his offensive with the main effort on his left. The First Panzer Group was still the spearhead, with the Sixth Army following behind to protect von Kleist's flanks. Further south the Seventeenth Army advanced on a broad front as the enemy executed a general withdrawal under cover of armored rear-guard action. Rain created road conditions that slowed down operations, but the First Panzer Group, moving forward in a wedge formation, continued to make steady progress.

On July 11 one Panzer division reached the outer defenses of the city of Kiev, but that day heavy Russian counterattacks were launched with a furious tank battle fought around Berdichev causing heavy losses to both sides. By July 16 von Kleist concentrated his armor south of Kiev to continue the attack to the southeast along with the Seventeenth Army.

As a result of the first three weeks of fighting, the southern group of armies had pushed forward along its entire front, but it

The German PzKw IVF-2, introduced early in 1942, featured the long-barrelled, high-velocity KwK 40 7.5cm gun with muzzle brake, that replaced the short-barreled 7.5cm gun. The PzKw IVG, shown here, was similar except for the double-baffle muzzle brake. It was a fair match for the Soviet T-34. *From U.S. Army Ordnance Department*, Catalogue of Enemy Ordnance Materiel *(Washington, 1943)*

had not yet succeeded in executing any spectacular encircling maneuvers or in destroying any major parts of Soviet Marshal Semen Budenny's armies. The Russians had lost heavily in their counterattacks against the more experienced German forces, but in general they had succeeded in withdrawing into the Ukraine and the area north and west of Kiev. They had also gained some time for the evacuation of the large industrial area in the Dnieper River bend. The Germans were aware of the heavy rail movements in the rear areas, but the Luftwaffe was busy providing air cover for the German armies, and the significance of the evacuation of the Ukrainian industries to the east was not appreciated until much later in the war. In a systematic "scorched-earth" program, the Soviets were now demolishing anything of importance they could not take along.

Hitler, often at odds with his generals, had changed his orders and sent Colonel General Heinz Guderian with his powerful Second Panzer Group south to come up behind Kiev and ensure the completion of the destruction of the Russian forces in front of the Seventeenth and Eleventh Armies. Soviet counterattacks and new formations delayed the Germans; nevertheless, all available German forces converged on the town of Uman to trap the Russians before they could withdraw behind the Dnieper River. On August 1, one of the divisions of von Kleist's First Panzer Group reached the Bug River and other corps from the First Panzer Group and the Seventeenth Army were closing in on Uman.

In the meantime, the Eleventh Army forced a crossing of the Dnieper River on July 17, and by the end of the month it had reached the Bug southwest of Uman. Within this ring of German divisions, elements of over twenty Russian divisions were trapped between Uman and the Bug. Hundreds of Soviet tanks and vehicles were burning from shelling by artillery and attacks by aircraft. Within days the 150,000 Russians in the Uman pocket were forced to surrender, including the commanders of the Soviet Twelfth and Sixth Armies, which included elements of sixteen infantry and six armored divisions. The victory at Uman was the first major battle for the troops of the Italian Expeditionary Force that had recently entered action in Russia. Italian dictator Benito Mussolini was making a visit to Hitler at that time at *Wolfsschanze*, the Fuehrer's new, secret headquarters located near Rastenburg in East Prussia. They decided to visit the site of the battle, and Hitler and Mussolini arrived promptly in the Fuehrer's special transport aircraft, Focke-Wulf Fw 200 Condor, *Immelmann III*, piloted by Hitler's personal pilot, *SS-Oberfuehrer* Hans Baur. After meeting with Field Marshal von Rundstedt, and reviewing some of the German and Italian troops, they flew away well satisfied with the results of the battle.[17]

The Soviets were still counterattacking from Kiev, and by now the Germans were not only tired but critically short of fuel, ammunition, and rations. However, during the next two weeks, with reinforcements from the Seventeenth Army and the

Barbarossa was a war of movement until the snow and bitter cold of the Russian winter froze virtually everything in its tracks. Here a German Army supply wagon, loaded with ammunition, gallops past a burning Soviet T-26S light tank. The turret and 4.5cm gun are aiming to the rear. *From 5th Infantry Division, Mit uns im Osten (Stuttgart, 1942)*

First Panzer Group, von Rundstedt cleared out the Dnieper bend and began regrouping for the next operation. In the south, the Eleventh Army moved up to the coast of the Black Sea, and the Romanians tried unsuccessfully to take the port city of Odessa, held by four Russian divisions. In heavy fighting, the Sixth Army and the First Panzer Group managed to cross the Dnieper on August 30 and the Eleventh Army forced a crossing of the Dnieper east of Kherson.

During this time the Russians had continued a determined resistance around the important city of Kiev. The Germans had now reached the Dnieper River from the Black Sea to north of Kiev. Unfortunately for the Germans, Hitler and the High Command could not decide on the next major effort. The Red Army had suffered great losses but remained undefeated. Army Group Center was still in the vicinity of Smolensk, and von Bock, with his entire Army Group Center, and Guderian with his Second Panzer Group, wanted to drive straight on to Moscow, thereby paralyzing Russia's resistance by striking at her heart. Field Marshal Walter von Brauchitsch, Army Commander in Chief, agreed, and hoped to fight the decisive battle in front of Moscow. The indecision continued until August 21, wasting good campaigning weather, when Hitler finally announced his orders. The Soviet armies in front of Moscow, and the capital itself, would not be the final objective. Instead, the Caucasus, with its vast and valuable oil fields that sustained the Red Army, would be the final goal. The Russian armies around Kiev would be the immediate objective of the next series of operations.

In early September, five German armies were converging on the Russian salient between the Desna and Dnieper Rivers. German forces included 6 Panzer, 5 motorized, and 35 infantry divisions, while the Russians were estimated to have five armies of about 35 divisions under Marshal Budenny's Southwest Front. The Germans attacked immediately with all available forces and strong air support. The German plan called for the First Panzer Group to strike to the northwest and the Second Panzer Group to the south for a junction on the Sula River and then jointly attack the enemy in the Desna-Dnieper area from the rear. The Sixth Army would hold the enemy in the vicinity of Kiev by continuing its frontal attacks. After a series of maneuvers and battles von Kleist and Guderian linked up at Sencha. The resulting pocket behind Kiev was the largest in military history. Five Soviet armies, amounting to over 665,000 men, were trapped with all their equipment. By September 18, chaos and demoralization seemed to overtake the Russians in the pocket; only a few organized attempts to break out were noted. On September 19, the Germans reported:

> The German war flag was raised over the citadel of Kiev at 1200. The enemy commanders apparently have fled the fortress by plane. The troops have thrown away their rifles. Wild chaos. All bridges are down. Three of our divisions have penetrated into the city, one from the north, two from the south.[18]

The Germans claimed to have captured 665,000 prisoners, 886 tanks, and 3,718 guns in the liquidation of the Kiev pocket. The five Soviet armies of the southwest front were practically destroyed, and for the time being Marshal Budenny was without an effective fighting force. Despite their tremendous losses in this great battle of encirclement, the Russians had kept the Germans occupied for a month and provided time for strengthening defenses deeper in the interior and for completing the evacuation of vital industrial personnel and equipment. Colonel General Franz Halder, Chief of the German Army General Staff, stated in his war diary that although a great victory, concentrating on Kiev and objectives in the southeast instead of Moscow was the greatest blunder in the eastern campaign.

Fortunately for the Germans, the enemy had been comparatively inactive in other sectors of the long front while so much German strength was committed in the Kiev area. Even around Smolensk, the Russians had assumed a more passive role while bringing up reinforcements and strengthening the defenses in front of Moscow. When Hitler finally launched the long-delayed advance on Moscow on October 2, the Russians were again caught by surprise.

In another battle of encirclement around Vyasma and Bryansk, the Soviets were defeated and another 600,000 troops were captured and started the long march to prisoner of war camps in the rear. But the German troops were exhausted and at the end of their supply lines. The offensive stalled in front of Moscow in the face of desperate resistance and the difficulties of winter warfare. Hitler refused to retreat to better defensive positions for the winter and the Wehrmacht suffered its first big defeat. Floundering in the deep snow, the Germans were thrown back with severe losses of both men and materiel as they endured the coldest winter in 150 years.

Seemingly endless columns of Russian prisoners of war plodded off into hastily constructed camps during the first months of Barbarossa. The Germans claimed to have captured an incredible 3,006,867 POWs by December 1, 1941, while the Russians admitted to losing 2,122,000 killed, wounded, and missing in action. The plight of POWs on both sides was horrific. The huge number of POWs overwhelmed the German ability to guard and care for them, and many thousand eventually perished from starvation, neglect, and maltreatment. German losses from all causes were 743,112 by December 1, even before the onset of winter, and those well-trained and experienced veterans could never be replaced. *German Official Photo*

The Germans listed their total casualties up to the end of September as approximately 551,000.[19] This included 116,900 killed, 409,000 wounded, and 24,500 missing. Although far greater damage had been inflicted on the Russians, the cost was proportionately much more for the Germans, who lacked Russia's manpower reserves. Also important was the loss of so many trained and experienced combat soldiers. But these losses in men and equipment were minor compared with the casualties to be suffered by the Wehrmacht during the coming winter before Moscow. Supply lines were now greatly extended, and with the autumn rains, the Russian tanks and trucks, followed by the Germans, turned the dirt roads into rivers of mud. By November, the ground froze and maneuver and transportation became easier until the heavy snows began. After so much marching and combat, the troops were tired and equipment needed repair. It was now obvious to almost everyone that this was not going to be a short campaign. The same situation confronted the Luftwaffe, which had been in action continually since the beginning of Barbarossa.

Nevertheless, on the southern front during the latter half of September, the German Sixth Army completed the mopping-up of the Kiev pocket and by the twenty-ninth had started moving eastward to take up its position on the north flank of von Rundstedt's Army Group South. While Guderian and his Panzers were now able to move north, von Kleist and his armored columns attacked to the southeast toward the Germans' Dniepropetrovsk bridgehead. By the end of the month he had reached this vital bridgehead and was preparing to advance to the south against a strong Soviet force that had been built up on the Eleventh Army's east flank. Just north of the Black Sea, by the third week of September, the LIV Infantry Corps was making probing attacks at the Perekop Isthmus, the narrow neck of land that separates the Crimean peninsula from the Russian mainland.

On September 12, while the great battles were raging around Kiev, an event occurred near the Perekop Isthmus that had a profound effect on the future conquest of the Crimea and the capture of the fortress city of Sevastopol. Colonel General Eugen *Ritter* von Schobert, the respected commander of the Eleventh Army, met a soldier's death in action. While flying that morning with his pilot in a Fieseler Fi 156 *Storch* reconnaissance plane, they either encountered engine failure or were hit by ground fire and were forced to make an emergency landing. Unfortunately for them, they landed on a Russian minefield and both were killed instantly. When this information reached Hitler at his supreme headquarters at Wolfsschanze in East Prussia, he conferred briefly with Field Marshal Wilhelm Keitel, Chief, OKW, the High Command of the Armed Forces, and Lieutenant General Alfred Jodl, Chief of the Operations Staff of OKW, concerning a replacement. Keitel phoned Field Marshal Walter von Brauchitsch, Army Commander in Chief, who made a recommendation, but Hitler's mind was already made up. The man chosen by the Fuehrer for this important post would soon earn an even greater reputation as a brilliant military leader and strategist: *General der Infanterie* (General of Infantry) Erich von Manstein.[20]

CHAPTER II

LUFTWAFFE:

The "Air Weapon" in Action

I spotted the Pe-2 aircraft at long range, chased him, and he saw me. He was damned fast, and he dived. I couldn't close on him in my Me 109. Finally in a left turn I pulled what I thought was the right amount of lead. I knew I was really "reaching" because he was somewhere near the limit of my bullets' trajectory. I fired. I immediately saw the explosions at his wing root peppering him in a fiery shower. His wing came off and he spun in. With his high speed he was at the limit of his aircraft's structural strength. The slight extra impact of my bullets caused his wing to shear, and he spun to the ground in seconds.[1]

THIS VICTORY in air-to-air combat over southern Russia occurred during just one of hundreds of sorties flown in World War II by Luftwaffe Major Guenther Rall, on the eastern, southern, and western fronts. Rall achieved an amazing 275 victories to become the third-highest-scoring ace of Germany and the world. He was awarded the Knight's Cross with Oak Leaves and Swords for his heroism and remarkable accomplishments. Rall survived the war to become a lieutenant general in the postwar German Air Force.

His story is just one of thousands involving individuals and incidents that make up the complex history of the *Luftwaffe*, the Air Force of the Third Reich. There are probably more myths and greater misinformation about the Luftwaffe than any other branch of the German armed forces, with the possible exception of the Waffen-SS. It is necessary to emphasize the important role played by the Luftwaffe in the remarkable successes achieved by the Wehrmacht during the first months of Barbarossa, as well as the achievements of the Air Force in preventing a German debacle during the Soviet counteroffensive in the frigid winter of 1941–42. Emphasis will, of course, be placed on the Fourth Air Fleet supporting Army Group South, including the German Eleventh Army and the Romanian Army.

The fact that Germany had the most powerful air force in the world at the beginning of the war in September 1939 is a remarkable story in itself.[2] The air forces of the Imperial German Army and Navy were disbanded after World War I in compliance with the Armistice agreement and the Treaty of Versailles. The 100,000-man army of the Weimar Republic in the 1920s was not permitted to possess tanks, heavy artillery, chemical weapons, and aircraft, but still found a way to train some pilots in the Soviet Union. After Adolf Hitler was appointed Reichs Chancellor on January 30, 1933, he quickly turned Germany into a totalitarian state under National Socialism and launched his ambitious program to make Germany the dominant nation in Europe.

Hitler believed that to regain German power and influence the nation had to rearm. He correctly perceived that a powerful air force would become the most important weapon in his emerging propaganda campaign. To accomplish this he charged his loyal supporter and World War I ace Hermann Goering with the task of creating an air weapon, the Luftwaffe, with which he could not only intimidate neighbor nations but defeat them if they stood in the way of regaining lost territory and establishing German hegemony over Europe.

Goering, now Air Minister, appointed Lufthansa Airline director Erhard Milch as his deputy and State Secretary in the Reichs Air Ministry. They began a secret but rapid expansion of the aviation industry and aeronautical research. By March 1935, the new German Air Force had been organized and was announced to the world as a powerful force. At this time it was mainly a paper force, but between 1933 and 1939 the Luftwaffe, established as an independent branch of the armed forces, expanded into the most formidable air force in the world. However, the rapid development of the Luftwaffe during the 1930s was not without mistakes. Financial limitations during the Great Depression as well as political and propaganda considerations prevented Hitler and his regime from acquiring all of the new armaments that they desired. A fateful decision was made to defer the development and production of a long-range, heavy bomber in favor of more fast, twin-engine medium bombers and single-engine dive-bombers for precision bombing in support of the Army. This made sense at the time, when German ambitions focused on nearby neighbors Poland, France, and Czechoslovakia, as possible enemies in a future international confrontation. The concept of strategic bombing was recognized by the leaders of the Luftwaffe, but the new concept of *Blitzkrieg* (Lightning War) called for aircraft and tactics capable of efficient air-ground combat support of the Army.[3] Blitzkrieg tactics emphasized bombers, not fighters.

The new aircraft were impressive, but had certain design limitations. Some improvements were made as a result of combat experience gained by future German leaders aiding General Francisco Franco during the Spanish Civil War (1936–1939). However, the so-called "fast bombers" such as the Heinkel He 111 and Dornier Do 17, which at the time of introduction were as fast if not faster than the biplane fighters of France, Italy, and Great Britain, were designed with only light defensive armament. This originally consisted of only two or three 7.9mm (rifle caliber) MG 15 hand-held flexible machine guns. The standard dive bomber, the Junkers Ju 87, was sturdy and efficient for the job, but it was slow and lacked maneuverability. It was called the *Stuka*, short for *Sturzkampfflugzeug*, and was a favorite of General Ernst Udet, from 1936 chief of the Technical Office of the Air Ministry, and the man responsible for aircraft design, production, and inspection. Udet also favored fighters, and two standard types were produced in quantity. The Messerschmitt Bf 109, also referred to as the Me 109, was a fast, short-range, single-engine design that was very maneuverable. The Messerschmitt Bf 110 twin-engine fighter, intended as a long-range escort, eventually proved that it lacked the maneuverability so essential in air-to-air fighter combat. However, it served well during the war as a night-fighter and on the Russian Front as a fighter-bomber.[4]

The Luftwaffe emerged in the late 1930s as a tactical air force primarily designed for close air support of the German ground forces. Ground attack was especially important for the new Panzer (armored) divisions, which would form the spearhead of any army offensive. During the German invasion of Poland in September 1939, which launched World War II, the Luftwaffe operated with deadly efficiency, destroying the Polish Air Force on the ground and in the air during the first days of the war. The short distances involved posed no problem for German Bf 109 fighters, and the bombers with their rather limited bomb loads could fly multiple missions each day to attack key targets such as fortifications, bridges, depots, artillery, troop concentrations, and headquarters. Forward air controllers were employed at the front to coordinate rapid and effective air strikes. The emphasis was on offensive warfare so until mid-World War II, bombers, not fighters, received priority in personnel and aircraft production.

The Luftwaffe performed efficiently against limited resistance in the occupation of Denmark and the conquest of Norway, a major seaborne invasion supported by German airpower.

An even more impressive Blitzkrieg began on May 10, 1940, with the German invasion of France and the Low Countries.[5] The French Army was actually larger and had more and heavier tanks than the German Army, but the French high command was mired in the defensive strategy of World War I. Ensconced behind its vaunted Maginot Line of fortifications, the French Army, supported by the British Expeditionary Force (BEF), planned for another war of attrition. They soon learned that wars are not won by defense alone. The seemingly invincible German air-ground team quickly defeated France and drove the BEF off the continent. When the British refused Hitler's peace offer, he ordered preparations for an invasion of England.

As the smoke cleared across defeated France, Goering stood on a cliff at Calais and looked confidently across the choppy, gray waters of the English Channel. His Luftwaffe had failed to prevent the evacuation of most of the BEF from Dunkirk, but he now expected it to defeat the Royal Air Force (RAF) and pave the way for a seaborne invasion of southern England. A successful invasion across the Channel could only be made after the establishment of German air supremacy over southern England. But now, for the first time, the limitations of Luftwaffe capabilities became apparent. When the Luftwaffe confronted the RAF, they found it to be an efficient, modern, highly motivated force with a radar-guided Fighter Command equipped with a new generation of high-performance fighter planes.[6] The British intended to defend their nation to the bitter end.

The "Battle of Britain" began in the summer of 1940 with German attacks on Channel shipping and RAF airfields along the southern coast. The Germans soon realized that their bombers required fighter protection to survive against the heavily armed RAF Hurricane and Spitfire fighters, guided by radar and ground control.[7] For example,

Reichsmarschall Hermann Goering (center), Commander in Chief of the Luftwaffe in addition to his many other duties, discusses the air campaign with Hitler and Field Marshal Wilhelm Keitel, the Fuehrer's main military advisor. *German Official Photo*

Lt. Gen. Adolf Galland, famed fighter ace with 103 victories, served as General (actually chief) of Fighter Forces from December 1941 until dismissed in late 1944 when he clashed with Goering and Hitler over the use of fighters. Awarded the coveted Diamonds, Oakleaves and Swords to the Knight's Cross, he was injured in 1945 flying the Me 262 jet fighter in combat but survived to become a successful aeronautical consultant. This photo was given to the author in 1983 during Galland's second visit to the Smithsonian's National Air and Space Museum. It is inscribed "*Hals und Beinbruch*" (Break your neck and legs), the German fighter pilot's good luck slogan. *Author's Collection*

the gunner lying in the rear of the lower gondola on the He 111, armed with only one 7.9mm MG 15, referred to this gun position as the "Starbebett" (deathbed). The Bf 110 was no match for the nimble British fighter planes and along with the Ju 87 Stukas had to be withdrawn from combat over England. The Bf 109 fighter was more or less an even match for the RAF fighters but lacked the range to escort the bombers all the way to inland targets. Their limited flying time did not allow them to challenge the RAF in dogfights while protecting the bombers over England. And, of course, there were no long-range heavy bombers available to the Luftwaffe and only a limited number of Focke-Wulf Fw 200 Condors for use as commerce raiders in cooperation with the U-boats in the Atlantic. Nevertheless, by early September the RAF was nearing the end of its ability to continue the battle when providence seemed to intervene.

Hitler and Goering, angry over an RAF raid on Berlin, switched the focus of attacks from RAF airfields and factories to the city of London. The resulting destruction and loss of life did not break British morale and will to resist, and because of mounting German losses, daylight raids were discontinued in favor of night attacks. This dramatic duel in the sky showed that there was no shortage of heroism on both sides. However, with the RAF Fighter Command undefeated, and inclement weather arriving, Hitler decided to abandon his plans for invasion of England and turned instead to preparations for the conquest of a greater and richer prize: the Soviet Union.

The Luftwaffe regained its prestige during April and May 1941 when the landing of British troops in Greece exposed Germany's southern flank to attack. Hitler decided to join his Italian ally in invading Greece and defeating Yugoslavia in the process. Another successful Blitzkrieg, made possible by strong Luftwaffe air support, culminated in the first aerial invasion in history, the German conquest of the Mediterranean island of Crete.[8] Now the Luftwaffe was defending western Europe against attack by the RAF, fighting in the deserts of North Africa, and aiding the U-boat war at sea. At the conclusion of the Balkan campaign, Hitler declared: "For the German Wehrmacht, nothing is impossible."[9] It is obvious that Hitler believed his own propaganda.

The campaign in the Balkans interfered with Hitler's plans and forced a delay in the beginning of the German invasion of the Soviet Union, code name *Barbarossa*. It also allowed little time for the Luftwaffe and army units involved to rest, refit, and regroup for their most ambitious challenge. Originally scheduled for May 15, the new date with destiny was set for June 22, 1941. Plans for the air war against the Nazi's traditional Communist enemy involved employing the bulk of the Luftwaffe combat forces for the initial surprise attack. To help mask the secret German preparations for the invasion, the Luftwaffe high command deployed their air units at the last minute to bases in East Prussia and along the frontier, from the Baltic to Romania.

Just before dawn on June 22, aircraft of the Luftwaffe crossed the Soviet frontier at high altitudes, so as not to alert Russian defenses, then dropped to attack altitude to pulverize airfields and facilities. As with the Americans at Pearl Harbor, less than six months later, the Soviet aircraft were lined up in neat rows on their airfields, facilitating the Luftwaffe's grim task. Soon great pillars of black smoke rose into the sky as Russian aircraft exploded and burned, along with fuel storage and ammunition dumps. Those few aircraft that managed to get permission to scramble and take off soon fell to the guns of veteran German fighter pilots. Most Soviet aircraft at that time were obsolete and were being replaced by more advanced planes. For example, the old I-16 *"Rata"* fighter, although maneuverable, was powered by an M-25 radial engine of 715 hp, which gave a top speed of only 282 mph (458

This squadron was fortunate to have a special bus for their headquarters, which was linked to group headquarters by telephone and radio. *From* Dr.-Ing. *Lt. Wolf Ruemmler*, Ein Fliegerkorps im Einsatz Ost *(Munich, 1943)*

km/h) at altitude. It was armed with four 7.62mm machine guns.[10] By contrast, the German Messerschmitt Bf 109F had a DB 601E-1 engine of 1,350 hp and a top speed of 388 mph (625 km/h) at 21,325 feet (5,000 meters). The Bf 109F was armed with one 20mm MG 151 cannon and two 7.9mm MG 17 machine guns.[11]

With the Soviet Air Force decimated, the Luftwaffe then turned, as in previous campaigns, to close air support of the advancing German ground forces. Stuka dive-bombers were soon screaming down to attack fortifications, tank columns, troop concentrations, and points of resistance, with devastating efficiency. The amazing success of the Wehrmacht at the beginning of Barbarossa tended to confirm Hitler's belief in an early victory. Although some Luftwaffe leaders opposed Barbarossa, including Reichsmarshall Goering, Field Marshal Albert Kesselring optimistically approved of the invasion. He wrote in his postwar memoir that "Hitler's contention that Russia would seize the first favorable moment to attack us seemed to me indisputably right."[12]

At the beginning of Barbarossa the Luftwaffe deployed three air fleets with 2,200 aircraft, or 65 percent of their frontline strength, organized to support the three major army groups, North, Center, and South. The Soviet Air Force had an estimated 8,000 aircraft, with somewhere around 6,000 spread across European Russia, Poland, and the Baltic states.[13] The stunning success of the Luftwaffe in the first days led most German leaders and the Luftwaffe high command to believe that after Germany broke the back of the Soviet Air Force, the Russians would not recover.

Even more than the Luftwaffe, the Soviet Air Force was mainly capable of ground support of the Red Army. Soviet airmen and ground personnel were not trained to the standards of efficiency of the German and other Western air forces.

The rapid advance of the German ground forces called for the highest degree of mobility on the part of the close support forces, and the ground organization of the Luftwaffe in the field proved itself generally capable of maintaining the serviceability and operational efficiency of units under very difficult conditions. The Blitzkrieg bogged down in the late fall for a number of reasons, one of them the declining combat readiness of the flying units. The wear and tear on airplanes, crews, and support personnel caused by the continuing combat and moves to new locations in the vast theater of war was taking its toll. Unlike previous campaigns, there was no time to rest and refit, and few reserves to press into combat.

The extent to which reconnaissance was carried out after the beginning of the campaign was one of the most striking features of the German Air Force activities during the first months of Barbarossa. This extended into the Russian rear areas as well as covering the fighting zones, and there is little doubt that the German High Command must have constantly been able to form a clear picture not only of Russian movements and of troop and tank concentrations, but also of the general situation on an extensive front, where the fighting was often fast-moving and very confused. Through reconnaissance the huge size of the Red Army now became frighteningly apparent.

The experienced German veterans of Poland, France, and the Balkans found the Russians far easier prey than the British pilots of the RAF. In the first weeks, Soviet aircraft of all types were shot down in droves, and totals on the Eastern Front rose more rapidly than at any other time in the history of aerial warfare. In the words of Johannes "Macky" Steinhoff, who ended the war with 176 victories, "It was like shooting ducks."[14] The typical Russian fighter pilot, a product of a system that sought to extinguish individuality, was unable to meet his German foe on equal terms. The superiority of the German fighter pilot was not only technical, but psychological. Even after the Russians later redressed their technical disadvantage, the Germans retained their psychological edge. All the qualities of individual intelligence, independence, and enterprise which fitted German fighter pilots temperamentally for the highly individualized art of aerial combat were encouraged and developed in their training.[15]

Freie Jagd, a fighter sweep without ground control, was the preferred type of mission on the Eastern Front, most often flown by *Schwaerme* against Soviet bombers and attack aircraft. An example of this type of air-to-air combat was related by (then) *Hauptmann* (Captain) Guenther Rall. He was on a fighter sweep over southern Russia in his Bf 109, flying with a wingman in a *Rotte,* as part of *Schwarm* (two Rotte formations). Eventually he spotted a Russian fighter flying below and across his path and dove on him:[16]

> I knew I had him. We were hurtling along together, with me on his tail. He could not escape; both fighters were at the same speed and at deck level. He finally made a shallow left turn, which gave me my opportunity. I squeezed the trigger. Blam! I hit him with the first few (cannon and machine gun) shots and he went in immediately, kicking up a tremendous shower of sand. Nothing remained of him but a bunch of scattered debris.

German aviators dreaded forced landing and capture by the Soviets. Some flyers, particularly high-scoring fighter pilots known to the enemy, are known to have committed suicide rather than be captured and tortured by the Russians. It is said that Soviet Lieutenant Vladimir D. Lavrinekov (thirty victories), shot down a Bf 109, which crash-landed in a field. The German pilot ran to a nearby ditch to hide. Lavrinekov landed his plane beside the Bf 109, ran over to the ditch, choked the German to death, then took off again.[17] Brutality characterized the entire war on the Eastern Front.

The dedicated technicians and ground support staff had an increasingly difficult job keeping their squadron aircraft flying as the war in the east ground on. There was often little if any shelter at the airfields behind the rapidly moving front. The summer heat, dust, rain, and mud and finally the winter snow, wind, and cold made life miserable for Luftwaffe ground personnel and flak crews, just as it did for Army troops. Many men required to work outside wore their gas masks with filters removed to protect their faces from freezing in the bitter winter wind and snow. Thousands of soldiers and airmen died from the cold or were incapacitated by frostbite.

As the front expanded deep into the Russian hinterland, the shortage of parts, fuel, and equipment became more serious. The constant flying and fighting, with little opportunity to rest, put an increasing strain on pilots, crewmen, and ground crews alike. As winter came on, servicing and repairing damaged aircraft in the open slowed aircraft turnaround. All sorts of improvisations were employed to maintain the combat capability of the units. When gasoline heaters to warm up the engines were not available, or failed to work in the intense cold, crews copied the crude but effective Russian method of building bonfires under the engines and keeping them going all night to prevent freezing up. This was dangerous, but an airplane with a frozen engine was useless anyway.

For German personnel across the far-flung battlefront, sleeping in an abandoned farmhouse or any building in winter, instead of in a tent, was a real luxury. Many houses had been destroyed in the fighting or burned by the retreating Russians as part of their scorched-earth program. In many areas there was little wood for fires. But whether indoors or out, avoiding vermin was virtually impossible. Fleas and lice plagued soldiers everywhere, exacerbated by the difficulties of bathing and sanitation.

By the end of July 1941, the great distances and poor transportation system contributed to a logistical nightmare for both the German Army and Air Force. The shortages of fuel, parts, spare engines, ammunition, rations, and other necessities were becoming

A Messerschmitt Bf 110 waits for the next mission while a member of the ground crew watches for enemy aircraft next to a 7.9mm MG 15 on a makeshift anti-aircraft mount. Aircrews and support personnel usually lived in tents on improvised airfields behind the front. Because of the lack of roads, units were frequently supplied by air with Junkers Ju 52/3m transports. *National Archives, Luftwaffe Collection*

acute and required continued improvisation. In emergencies, the sturdy Junkers Ju 52/3m transports, and even Heinkel He 111 bombers, were used to rush essential supplies to the front on short notice. To further complicate the situation, the autumn rains affected not only the dirt roads but caused airplanes to bog down in the mud so they could not take off or land safely. An additional hazard emerged at airfields and supply lines in rear areas. Security had to be provided by Luftwaffe personnel against attack by partisans. By midsummer, attacks by fighters and bombers of the Soviet Air Force also became a reality. By late fall, all of these factors contributed to reducing aircraft operational ready rates, thereby having a negative impact on the whole force structure.

However, in the first weeks of the invasion, German air superiority, and in many areas complete air supremacy, allowed the Ju 87 Stuka dive-bombers, Bf 110 *Zerstoerer* fighter-bombers, and medium bombers, to operate almost with impunity. With the Soviet Air Force swept from the skies, the main threat was from antiaircraft fire, but this did not deter the Luftwaffe from providing excellent close air support and interdiction for the Army. The constant strafing and bombing, in conjunction with artillery fire and attacks by Panzer and motorized infantry divisions, helped to restrict and confuse Red Army movements and counterattacks. Devastating close air support lowered morale and even caused panic at times among green Russian troops, thus hastening the surrender of soldiers trapped in the great German battles of encirclement.

Luftwaffe antiaircraft units also took part in ground combat. Flak artillery, especially the high-velocity 88mm guns with their flat trajectory, were employed with telling effect against enemy tanks and defensive positions. The call "Flak vor!" was often heard when guns were urgently needed in the front lines during Soviet attacks with heavy tanks.

Only in the area of strategic bombing was the Luftwaffe noticeably lacking in initiative. Without a fleet of long-range, four-engine heavy bombers, it was impossible to strike distant targets such as the growing concentration of arms factories in the Urals and other remote areas of the Soviet Union. But with the constant demand by the army for close air support, the Luftwaffe often lacked the strength even to attack strategic targets within range of twin-engine bombers. (The Heinkel He 177 strategic bomber never became fully operational.)

In late July, with the seizure of airfields near Smolensk, the Luftwaffe was at last within bombing range of Moscow. Moscow was not just the political capital and the seat of government and the center of the Communist Party, it was also the military, economic, transportation, and communications center of the Soviet Union. Hitler wanted Moscow "razed to the ground" and demanded that it be bombed as soon as possible. Even though the experience of bombing London indicated otherwise, Hitler believed that attacks would undermine Russian morale and disrupt the war effort. Raids were then ordered by *Reichsmarschall* Goering, Luftwaffe commander in chief, and reluctantly approved by Field Marshal Albert Kesselring, commander of Luftflotte 2. A composite force was hastily organized, comprising several *Kampfgeschwader* (Bomber Wings); KG 53 and KG 55 with He 111s, and KG 3 and KG 54 with Ju 88s. In addition, these units were supplemented by bombers from KG 28 with its two pathfinder *Gruppen, Kampfgruppe 100* and *III/KG 26*.[18]

The mission briefing was especially long and detailed for the crews of the bomber units, including those of *1. Staffel, II. Gruppe* (1st Squadron, 2d Group), *KG 53*, equipped with Heinkel He 111H bombers. This was not because the crews were inexperienced, for until recently they had been flying missions from a base in northern France against London and targets elsewhere in the British Isles. However, this was a special mission, the first bombing raid on Moscow.

By the evening of July 21, 1941, ground crews had completed servicing the aircraft and loading a full cargo of bombs. The commander of the 1st Squadron and his flight crew boarded the lead plane and when the signal was finally given, he eased forward on the throttles, taxied out, and went bumping down the airstrip to lift off into the gathering dusk on this historic mission. Forming up with other squadron aircraft, the C.O. joined the three groups of KG 53, and those of other wings, in a loose formation that included a total of 127 bombers. The distance to Moscow was either 280 miles (450

A Luftwaffe major, probably the bomber-group commander (second from right, facing camera), arrives with his crew at an airfield in an Austrian Stoewer—Greif car. The group is part of KG 54, the *Totenkopf—Geschwader* (Deathshead Wing), equipped at that time with Heinkel He IIIH bombers. *Author's Collection*

km) or 380 miles (611 km), depending on whether the unit was flying from advanced bases around Orsha, Minsk, Vitebsk, or Chatalovska. Take-off times were coordinated to form up in one long bomber stream.

The formation climbed steadily, and as night fell they maintained their positions by watching the running lights of other squadron aircraft. In the moonlight the white borders of the large, black *Balkenkreuz* (cross) insignia on the wings and fuselages were clearly visible. Interception

by Russian fighters flying at night was not expected, and because of the distance, no fighter escort was provided. The gunners couldn't help feeling a bit nervous, and once airborne, fired a short burst from their machine guns to make sure they were functioning properly. Everyone kept an alert eye on the sky, but so far the mission was uneventful with just the steady, reassuring hum of the two 1,350 hp Jumo engines droning in their ears.

As the formation flew on it gradually turned northeast so it could reach Moscow from the north. On approaching the suburbs, searchlights suddenly flashed on and some pathfinder aircraft at the head of the formation were illuminated in the blinding white light. Some *Gruppen* managed to fly undetected almost to the city center,

A ground crew prepares to load an SD 1700 bomb (left), about 3,750 pounds (1,703 kg), into the bomb bay of a Heinkel He 111H bomber. Note the *Kopfring* (head ring) to prevent excessive penetration. The bomb at right appears to be an SD 500 of 1,179 pounds (535 kg). *Smithsonian Photo*

but then the entire city came alive as seemingly countless powerful searchlights, and light and heavy antiaircraft guns, opened up with a massive barrage, with red tracers climbing high into the night sky. Antiaircraft shells burst with bright flashes, but the sounds were drowned out by the roar of the engines. The German planes arrived over downtown Moscow at 10:00 P.M. and after flying in the dark, the bomber crews were dazzled as they were pinned like giant moths in the crisscrossing beams of over 300 searchlights. This made the recognition of objectives more difficult; crews who had bombed London during the "Blitz" stated that the air defenses of Moscow were almost as strong. Fortunately for the Germans, the inexperienced Russian AAA gunners had a lot to learn about hitting aircraft, especially at night.

Flying through the flak over the Soviet capital, the Luftwaffe bombardiers squinted into their *Lotfe* bombsights as they tried to get their assigned targets into the crosshairs. Lead planes dropped brilliant magnesium flares that seemed to hang in the sky above the blacked-out metropolis below. During this raid 104 tons of high explosive and 46,000 incendiary bombs were dropped without achieving any concentration.[19] The Kremlin was situated on a hill above the

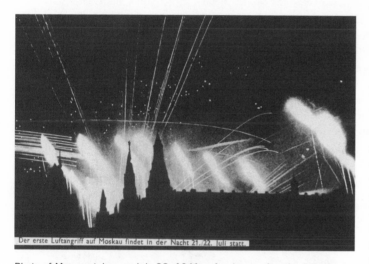

Der erste Luftangriff auf Moskau findet in der Nacht 21./22. Juli statt.

Photo of Moscow taken on July 22, 1941, a few hours after the first air attack on the Soviet capital. *German Official Photo*

Moskva (Moscow) River, which gleamed eerily in the moonlight. It was the target of He 111s of II/KG 55, and they were sure that they hit it with hundreds of *Electronbrandbomben* (incendiary bombs). Demolition bombs also hit the Kremlin, a huge fortress, extensively camouflaged with nets, imitation houses painted on walls, and fake windows painted on an enormous roll of canvas with fireproof paint.[20] During an evaluation of the raid the next day, a former German air attaché to Moscow suggested that the Kremlin roof was covered with so many layers of seventeenth-century tiles that the incendiary bombs failed to penetrate or set the buildings on fire. As the German formation left the Moscow area and turned west, the crews managed to relax somewhat and pass around thermoses of hot, ersatz coffee and bars of chocolate.[21]

Moscow was raided again the following night by 115 bombers, and on the third night by a hundred. Other pressing requirements reduced the number of aircraft on subsequent raids to fifty, then thirty and even fifteen. A total of seventy-six raids were made on Moscow, continuing spasmodically through the remainder of 1941, with few tangible results. An estimated fifty-nine raids were carried out by as few as three to ten bombers and were little more than harassing attacks or reconnaissance missions.[22] Although the raids caused only minor damage, the initial attacks did have considerable psychological impact. They made good propaganda for the Germans, and Stalin is reported to have begun considering evacuation of the leadership from the endangered capital. The German military defeat before Moscow during the winter of 1941–42, made such drastic measures unnecessary.

The pilot (right) and copilot-bombardier, in the cockpit of this Junkers Ju 88, are wearing standard Wehrmacht M35 steel helmets over their flying helmets as protection against enemy flak. A 7.9mm MG 15, on a flexible mount firing forward, is at the upper left. *National Archives, Luftwaffe Collection*

Luftwaffe general Wolfram *Freiherr* von Richthofen, cousin of the famous World War I air ace and commander of *Fliegerkorps VIII,* ordered a firebomb attack on Leningrad in August that caused huge fires in the city's center. Nevertheless, for the most part, the demands and tempo of ground operations kept the Luftwaffe sufficiently occupied to preclude significant aerial attempts at city busting, with the notable exceptions of Sevastopol and Stalingrad. These cities, however, were destroyed as part of ground battles and not as strategic objectives.

The Germans used dive-bombing to good effect in France, the Balkans, and on the Eastern Front. Dive-bombing was actually pioneered by the U.S. Navy in the 1920s as an antiship weapon and, as mentioned earlier, General Ernst Udet pushed development of the Junkers Ju 87 Stuka for use by the Luftwaffe in precision bombing. Udet had learned about this technique while visiting the United States, and dive-bombing worked well with the Blitzkrieg concept as long as the Luftwaffe enjoyed air superiority. The Stuka was also used for "tank-busting" when armed with two 37mm flak guns mounted under the wings.

The most famous dive-bomber pilot of all was *Oberst* (Colonel) Hans-Ulrich Rudel, who became the most highly decorated soldier in the Third Reich. He was the only recipient of the Knight's Cross of the Iron Cross with Golden Oak Leaves, Swords, and Diamonds, presented to

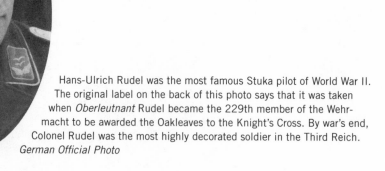

Hans-Ulrich Rudel was the most famous Stuka pilot of World War II. The original label on the back of this photo says that it was taken when *Oberleutnant* Rudel became the 229th member of the Wehrmacht to be awarded the Oakleaves to the Knight's Cross. By war's end, Colonel Rudel was the most highly decorated soldier in the Third Reich. *German Official Photo*

him personally by Hitler. Rudel flew an amazing 2,530 combat missions, mainly against the Soviets, and was credited with having personally destroyed 532 tanks, 150 gun emplacements, and 800 combat vehicles. He also damaged or destroyed bridges, rail lines, depots, three large warships, and seventy smaller craft. The following is a short account of perhaps his most famous exploit, the sinking of the 23,600-ton Russian battleship *Marat* during the siege of Leningrad in September 1941. The *Marat* and other warships were holding up the further advance of the Army and moving up and down the coast intervening in battles with their formidable naval guns. Rudel and his squadron commander, *Hauptmann* Steen, were sent out to bomb the *Marat* on September 16, even though the special 2,000 pound (907-kg) bombs had not arrived at his unit. With clouds as cover, Rudel managed to locate and dive-bomb the *Marat* with 1,000 pound (450-kg) bombs, causing major damage, but it did not sink. On September 21, the big armor-piercing 2,000 pounders arrived, and the next day Rudel, Steen, and the squadron took off to attack the *Marat*, which had been located in Kronstadt Harbor.[23]

> In the brilliant blue sky we are chased by Rata fighters at 2,750 meters [about 9,000 feet], and then encounter heavy flak. At an angle ahead of me I can already make out the *Marat* berthed in the harbor. The guns boom, the shells scream up at us, bursting in flashes of livid colors and forming small fleecy clouds around us. Steen dives, I follow suit; we are close beside each other. Our diving angle must be between seventy and eighty degrees. I have already picked up the *Marat* in my sights and we race down towards her, slowly she grows to a gigantic size. All their A.A. guns are now directed at us. We retract our diving brakes and go all out to get down more quickly. I increase my diving angle with all the strength I have got—it must surely be ninety degrees—sit tight as if I were sitting on a powder keg. My Ju 87 keeps perfectly steady as I scream down, I see sailors running across the deck. I press the bomb release switch on my stick at not more than 275 meters [900 feet] and pull with all my strength. I see nothing, my sight

is blurred in a momentary blackout, a new experience for me. My head has not yet cleared when I hear my rear gunner Scharnovski's voice: "She is blowing up sir!" Now I look out; we are skimming the water at three meters [10 feet] and I bank around a little. Yonder lies the *Marat* below a cloud of smoke rising to 365 meters [1,200 feet]; apparently the magazine has exploded. We head for home at low level because of heavy flak and Ratas.

After landing, Rudel and all the crews were paraded in front of the squadron tent where Hauptmann Steen told them that the wing commander had already phoned to congratulate the squadron on its achievement. In an ensuing operation Rudel sank a cruiser and participated in other attacks in the Leningrad area until transferred with his unit to the front before Moscow. Captain Steen was killed in a dive-bombing attack on the Russian cruiser *Kirov* in late September. Rudel was awarded the *Deutschekreuz in Gold* (German Cross in Gold) in December, and at the beginning of January 1942, General von Richthofen arrived at his base in a Fieseler Fi 156 Storch and, in the name of the Fuehrer, presented Rudel with the *Ritterkreuz*, the Knight's Cross of the Iron Cross. The citation, in a red leather folder, especially mentioned his successful destruction of ships and bridges. Rudel later served in the Crimea and in most major battles until being seriously wounded in February 1945.[24]

While great battles raged on the northern and central fronts, the Eleventh Army, part of Army Group South, and its Romanian ally, had crossed the Prut River and were pursuing So-

A dive-bomber is serviced prior to another mission against Soviet targets. The Ukrainian Russian Orthodox Church in the background indicates this photo was taken in the Ukraine. The "K" on the fixed landing gear of the Ju 87D may indicate that it is assigned to the 2. *Staffel* of Gruppe I of its *Geschwader*. On tanks and vehicles a white "K" indicated that they were part of the First Panzer Army commanded by (then) Col. Gen. Ewald von Kleist. *National Archives, Luftwaffe Collection*

viet troops as they cleared the Russians from Bessarabia. Army Group South was supported by the Fourth Air Fleet under command of Colonel General Alexander Loehr, former commander of the Austrian Air Force before the *Anschluss* (union) of Austria and Germany in 1938.

The mission of the Fourth Air Fleet in support of Army Group South's operations was as follows:[25]

1. Attack the Soviet air forces, achieve air superiority, and thereby prevent any counter-air action against German Army units.
2. Render direct and indirect support to the army group, concentrating on the left flank as the Sixth Army and First Panzer Group advanced to the Dnieper River at Kiev to prevent the withdrawal of strong Russian forces across the river.
3. Attack and eliminate the Soviet Black Sea Fleet and its bases.
4. Interdict Russian merchant shipping on the Black Sea and the Sea of Asov.

The IV Air Corps, commanded by *General der Flieger* (General of Aviation) Kurt Pflugbeil, a part of the Fourth Air Fleet, was linked with the operations of the Romanian Air Force and cooperated in protecting the vital Ploesti oil fields and facilities from Russian attack. They supported operations of the Eleventh Army and the Romanian Third and Fourth Armies, and attacked the Soviet naval bases around the Black Sea.

The V Air Corps, under *General der Flieger* Robert *Ritter* von Greim, was assigned the task of operating against Soviet air forces on the northern wing and securing air superiority within the first few days of the campaign.

The staff of the Luftwaffe Mission in Romania under *Generalleutnant* (Lieutenant General) Wilhelm Speidel was directly responsible for the air defense of the Ploesti area as well as bridges and other vital targets in Romania. Elements of *Jagdgeschwader 52* (JG-52), including the 8th Squadron, with Captain Guenther Rall, were sent to Romania before the beginning of Barbarossa and on June 23 attacked Soviet bombers, which were flying without fighter escort and attempting to bomb the oilfields. Flying from a grass airstrip with primitive facilities. Rall and his pilots downed between forty-five and fifty Russian bombers in the ensuing five days, and brought Soviet airstrikes against the oilfields to an abrupt end.[26]

As in the areas of Army Groups North and Center, the Russians were completely surprised by the Luftwaffe's attack in support of Army Group South. By employing all units to the utmost—Luftwaffe bomber squadrons flying from three to four missions daily and fighter units carrying out six to seven missions a day—Russians were dealt a decisive blow. For example, from June 22 to 25, units of the V Air Corps alone attacked 77 Russian airfields in 1,600 sorties, destroying 774 Soviet planes on the ground and 136 in the air. By the third day of warfare air operations could be shifted mainly to direct and indirect support of the German ground forces. For the period June 22 to 30, the Fourth Air Fleet reported 201 Soviet tanks, 27 bunkers, and 2 armored fortifications destroyed.[27]

Subsequent battles included strong attacks in support of Army units breaking through the Stalin Line of fortifications and in mobile operations. Army commanders agreed that the Luftwaffe should claim much of the credit for the success of major battles because its close fighter cover of German tank spearheads prevented effective Soviet counter-air measures and eliminated all threats to the German flanks. The destruction of bridges and rail junctions, and the interdiction of rail and road traffic by bombers, prevented the advance of Russian reinforcements in many crucial operations and caused the Soviets heavy losses. Hundreds of Soviet tanks, trucks, and convoys of troops were destroyed when caught on narrow roads in open country. One unexpected problem was the inability of German bombers to carry the heaviest bombs on takeoff because of the poor condition of runways and airstrips during the advance. In a special operation, IV Air Corps bombers repeatedly mined the ports of Nikolayev, Odessa, and Sevastopol on the Black Sea, with good results.

Army commanders, however, continually demanded close air support. Every Army unit wanted fighters overhead and bombs dropped ahead of its front. Over such a great area with so many battles and skirmishes in the often trackless terrain, the Luftwaffe eventually had to reject numerous requests, applications, and demands for air support, sometimes even in urgent situations. This situation was exacerbated when attrition gradually reduced the combat readiness of the Luftwaffe, and it was only natural that

A ground crew with a special lift loads an SC 250 high-explosive general-purpose bomb, weighing 548 pounds (248 kg), under a Messerschmitt Bf I09E fighter-bomber. The Luftwaffe provided outstanding close air support to the German ground forces during the first months of Barbarossa. *From Dr. Heinz Orlovius*, Fliegen und Siegen *(Munich, ca. 1942)*

some friction and discord developed between Army and Luftwaffe commanders. At times, Army Group South and the Fourth Air Fleet had to decide which ground units and operations were to be supported and by what air units. Nevertheless, in some serious situations, such as during the Soviet counterattack across the Dnieper River south of Kiev, the V Air Corps, on its own initiative, immediately attacked with every unit available and annihilated the Soviet tank and cavalry forces that had broken through.

The Luftwaffe organization best trained and equipped for close air support was the VIII Air Corps, commanded by General Wolfram *Freiherr* von Richthofen. This large, versatile, and highly effective unit was employed on the Eastern Front from the beginning, after performing well in the German campaign in the Balkans and Crete. In Russia, it was often used as a "fire brigade" in critical battles and emergencies along the front. It also participated in the conquest of the Crimea and the fortress city of Sevastopol. The VIII Air Corps was equipped with a variety of aircraft, including the Junkers Ju 87 Stuka and the older Henschel Hs 123 dive-bomber and attack aircraft, the Ju 88 bomber, which could also serve as a dive-bomber, and the Messerschmitt Bf 109, often used as a fighter-bomber. In May 1942, the VIII received the Henschel Hs 129 ground-attack aircraft, and the Hs 129B-1 became operational in the Crimea.

In the skies over southern Russia, fighter pilots of the IV Air Corps continued to shoot down dozens of Russian aircraft but, of course, not every aerial duel was successful. *Oberstleutnant* (Lieutenant Colonel) Dietrich "Dieter" Hrabak, *Kommaodore* (Wing Commander) of JG-52, was credited with 125 victories, all but 18 on the Eastern Front. He recounted an attack by members of his unit on an IL-2 *Stormovik* ground attack plane, which was famous as the most durable Russian airplane of the war. According to Hrabak, who had fought against almost every type of Soviet plane, he had considerable respect for this plane because he never saw any aircraft that could absorb battle damage and still fly as did the armored IL-2.[28]

I was flying with one of my formations and a Schwarm of four Me 109s set upon a solitary IL-2. One by one the fighters emptied their guns into the Russian machine at point-blank range. The IL-2 continued to fly on, unfazed by the storm of bullets and shells. I was astonished. "What's going on down there?" I asked on the radio. Back came the answer: *"Herr Oberst, you cannot bite a porcupine in the ass."*

Even before the final German victory at Kiev, new battles were developing to the southeast, north of the Crimea and the Sea of Azov. The Fourth Air Fleet continued to support the ground forces as strongly as possible. In the huge area of southern Russia, interdiction of Soviet rail and road traffic became even more important, as did attacks on Russian Navy bases and shipping on the Black Sea. Thus, attacks on Soviet movements of reinforcements and supplies had a significant effect on future operations.

A Soviet IL–2 Stormovik, shot down by a German Bf IO9F. This heavily armed and armored ground attack plane symbolized the emphasis of Soviet air power on simple design, rugged construction, and tactical deployment. *National Archives, Luftwaffe Collection*

Successful use of air power at points of main strategic significance was the decisive factor in the summer campaigns of 1941. It was stated that the Fourth Air Fleet had skillfully conducted its operations and that its practice of assigning missions daily had proven to be correct, although the number of demands made it "far from easy" to select the most essential tasks.[29]

The IV Air Corps was ordered to support the Eleventh Army and Romanian units battling north of the Sea of Azov where enemy resistance and strong counterattacks had compelled them to go over to the defensive. Romanian forces attacking Odessa also required air support. Then a new front opened for the Eleventh Army and the IV Air Corps: breaking through the strong Soviet defenses in the Perekop Isthmus and invading the Crimean peninsula.

A formal Luftwaffe funeral with an honor guard of flying officers from the squadron of the deceased. Because of the rather elaborate ceremony, this may have occurred early in the campaign in the east when the unit was still flying from a permanent air base in East Prussia. *Author's Collection*

CHAPTER III

BREAKTHROUGH AT PEREKOP ISTHMUS

*G*ENERAL DER INFANTERIE Erich von Manstein, commander of the LVI Panzer Corps, was sitting in his tent on the rainy evening of September 12, 1941, playing bridge with two of his staff officers while waiting for the evening situation reports to arrive at his headquarters. The field telephone rang with a call for von Manstein from *Generaloberst* Ernst Busch, commander of the Sixteenth Army. General Busch, an old friend, read him an order that had just arrived by teletype from OKH, the Army High Command: "General of Infantry von Manstein will leave forthwith for Army Group South to assume command of Eleventh Army."[1]

Von Manstein was, of course, proud and delighted to be selected to command an entire army, but he regretted leaving the fine officers and brave soldiers of his armored corps. There was no time allowed for home leave or even a transition of command, he had to say goodbye to his staff officers that night and bid farewell to his division commanders by telephone. Von Manstein departed the next morning for Sixteenth Army headquarters, where he officially turned over command of the corps to Colonel General Busch. He could take only three members of his staff with him, his young aide-de-camp, *Leutnant* "Pepo" Specht, and his faithful personal aides and drivers, Sergeant Fritz Nagel and Sergeant Hans Schumann.

Eleventh Army headquarters was located at that time at Nikolayev, the Soviet naval base and shipyard at the mouth of the Bug River. Von Manstein and his three aides arrived on September 17 in a Junkers Ju 52/3m transport, one day after the funeral and burial of Colonel General Eugen *Ritter* von Schobert. They were met at the plane by a couple of staff officers who welcomed them warmly and escorted them to headquarters in a staff car and two *Kuebel-wagen* with armed guards.[2] Eleventh Army headquarters was housed in a former Soviet Navy office building. For von Manstein, a new and challenging chapter in his life was beginning. For the German war effort, and the Soviet enemy, his assignment was an event that would have great impact on the campaign in the Crimea and southern Russia.

Death and destruction characterized the war on the Eastern Front. The German Sturmgeschuetz III, SdKfz 142 assault gun, was highly regarded by the infantry to which they were assigned. They provided a mobile armored vehicle with a 7.5cm KwK L/24 cannon that was able to advance with the foot soldiers and destroy strong points where supporting artillery was not available or capable of doing the job. Based on the PzKw III tank, with a crew of four and a weight of 19.5 tons, the Stg III entered service in 1940. *From Eugen Beinhauer*, Artillerie im Osten *(Berlin, 1944)*

While Lieutenant Specht and the sergeants arranged his quarters, von Manstein met the other members of his staff and joined them for lunch in the officer's mess. That afternoon, von Manstein received a thorough briefing on the status and composition of the Eleventh Army and the current military situation on their front. He also discovered that the Third Romanian Army would be under his command, and this meant a new requirement for political and diplomatic cooperation. The Eleventh Army, although subordinate to Army Group South commanded by Field Marshal Gerd von Rundstedt, was one of the few armies that was able to operate independently in a segregated theater of war and was rather free from interference from Hitler and the Supreme Command. Romanian Marshal Ion Antonescu, at this time, retained operational control only of the Fourth Romanian Army, which was involved in the siege of the Black Sea port of Odessa.

Since the beginning of Barbarossa, the Eleventh Army and the Romanians had fought

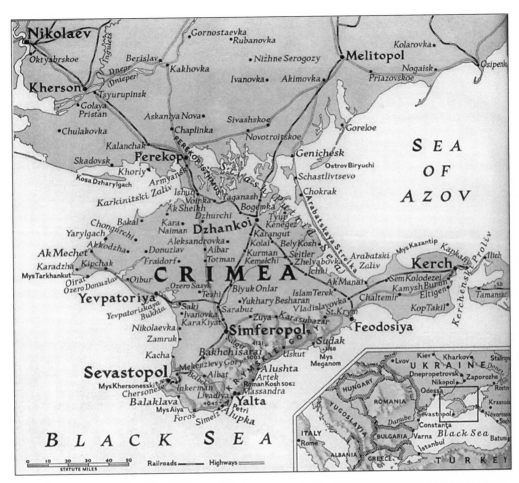

Map of the Crimean Peninsula. ©*National Geographic Society* (National Geographic, *April 1945*)

their way across southern Russia. Von Manstein now learned that the Eleventh Army had been assigned two missions by the Supreme Command that would require advancing in two divergent directions. The army was to push on to the east along the north shore of the Sea of Azov to capture Rostov, as well as to break through the Isthmus of Perekop and capture the Crimean peninsula. The highest priority was the Crimea since it was considered the gateway to the Caucasus and the oilfields that would not only solve all of Germany's fuel problems but deny vital oil to the Soviet war machine. Soviet forces in the Crimea also threatened the German southern flank, and the Russians could originate bombing attacks on the Romanian oilfields from there.

The main strength of the Eleventh Army was the XXX Infantry Corps and the IL Mountain Corps, now pursuing a retreating enemy toward the east. The LIV Infantry Corps was moving south toward the Perekop Isthmus. It was known that the Soviets had already fortified a line from Melitopol to Nikopol and were bringing up reinforcements. The Third Romanian Army, west of the Dnieper River, was not enthusiastic about advancing further into the interior of Russia now that they had secured their main war aim, the reoccupation of Bessarabia.

Upon taking command on the seventeenth, von Manstein soon determined that the task assigned to the Eleventh Army was unrealistic. He conveyed this opinion to Field Marshal von Rundstedt, who agreed. The forces available to von Manstein, which did not include armored units, were simply not strong enough to accomplish both missions in that vast area. Von Manstein decided to concentrate on the conquest of the Crimea. He ordered the LIV Corps to attack the Perekop Isthmus to open the approach to the Crimea, into which part of the enemy forces had retreated. Romanian troops and a German infantry division were ordered to take the place of the LIV Corps on the march to the east.

Von Manstein studied maps, aerial photographs, and reconnaissance reports on the Perekop Isthmus. Initial probing attacks confirmed that breaking through the narrow isthmus would be difficult indeed because of the strong Soviet defenses. The isthmus was the only entrance to the Crimean peninsula from the Russian mainland. The major all-weather highway leading into the Crimea ran through the village of Perekop and the neck of land that was only five miles (8 kilometers) wide. It consisted of a flat, arid, treeless plain that did not provide any cover.

A company commander from the LIV Infantry Corps surveys the front through a scissors telescope in preparation for the assault on the Soviet defenses at the Perekop Isthmus, gateway to the Crimea. *From Eleventh Army*, Bessarabien, Ukraine-Krim *(Berlin, 1943)*

The Soviets had transformed the entire area into a fortified system just over 9.3 miles (15 kilometers) deep. The defenses included bunkers, some concrete pillboxes, trenches, minefields, and barbed wire entanglements. Tank obstacles were especially formidable since they incorporated the "Tatars' Ditch," an extensive earthwork that was at least 15 feet (5 meters) deep and up to 50 feet (15.2 meters) deep in most of its length. Called the *"Tatarengraben"* by the Germans, this ditch, almost a ravine, had been dug straight across the isthmus in the fifteenth century as a defense against invasion by the "Rus" (Russians).[3] Not only did the Soviets have strong natural and prepared defensive positions, they occupied the fortified zone with three infantry divisions supported by approximately 125 tanks and 150 artillery pieces. Some of the tanks were dug in for use as pillboxes. There were also a number of antiaircraft guns, and ammunition and supplies for their personnel were stored in underground bunkers. Air support was provided by Soviet aircraft flying from bases in the Crimea.

It was obviously impossible to bypass the defenses because the Black Sea was on the west and the shallow Sivash salt marsh lay to the east. Von Manstein wanted no delay and ordered the LIV Corps to attack on September 24, with their three infantry divisions and all the artillery, combat engineers, and antiaircraft guns that could be mustered. Strong air support was then arranged, including dive-bombers, for a special effort coordinated through the IV Air Corps. Although the LIV Corps had no tanks, each infantry division had assault gun units with *Sturmgeschuetz III, SdKfz 142*, armed with a 7.5cm short-barreled KwK L/24 gun. By early 1942, new *SdKfz 142/1* assault guns were introduced with a high-velocity, long-barreled 7.5cm gun. The lack of tanks in the Perekop fighting was not such a great problem for the Germans;

the terrain was not suitable for armored warfare because of minefields, the Tatars' Ditch, and lack of room to maneuver. Passes through the Tatars' Ditch would have to be made by knocking down the sides by shelling, bombing, or blasting by engineers.

The situation at the Perekop Isthmus would have been a good opportunity for the use of paratroops or airborne troops to land south of the isthmus and attack from the rear. Coupled with a frontal assault from the north, it is likely that the Soviet defense would have collapsed. Unfortunately for the Germans, the *Fallschirmjaeger*, the Luftwaffe paratroops, were still recovering from the heavy losses sustained during the aerial invasion of the island of Crete in the Mediterranean the previous May. There was also no longer a large fleet of Junkers Ju 52/3m transports available for such an undertaking. An amphibious landing operation was out of the question because of the strength of the Soviet Black Sea fleet and the lack of Axis warships and appropriate transport vessels. The assault on the Perekop Isthmus would have to be made as a straightforward frontal attack.

The German offensive began before dawn on September 24 with a maximum artillery barrage. At first light, Ju 87 Stuka dive-bombers screamed down to hurl their loads of high explosive on the Soviet positions. The 45th and 73d Infantry Divisions stormed forward in bright sunshine across the barren salt steppe against a determined enemy that fought fiercely for every single strong-point and trench. The intense combat continued day and night with the desperate troops of the Red Army counterattacking even as they were forced back. The soldiers on both sides knew the critical importance of this battle and fought on through the smoke, dust, and noise. Hunger and thirst plagued the attackers and defenders. In the constant hail of lead it was also difficult to evacuate the wounded.

The concentrated and accurate German artillery bombardment and sustained air attacks helped turn the tide, and the soldiers in sweat-stained field gray managed to cross the Tatars' Ditch, with the help of engineers, on September 26. After three more days of intensive fighting, including savage hand-to-hand combat, the Germans broke through the enemy's defensive zone and, after capturing the strongly defended locality of Armyansk, finally emerged into more open country.

The Russians fell back to strong field fortifications between

German infantry wearing only assault packs and armed with Kar. 98k rifles, grenades, and MG 34 light machine guns, climb out of a Russian antitank ditch to storm a bunker at Perekop. *From* Bessarabien, Ukraine-Krim, *op. cit.*

the Ishun Lakes and took up new defensive positions, forming a bottleneck. Three fresh Soviet infantry divisions were brought up from the south, making a total of six divisions facing the weary troops of the German LIV Corps. German losses had been heavy, but the Soviets suffered thousands killed and left behind 11,000 prisoners, 112 tanks, and 135 artillery pieces in German hands.[4] Von Manstein knew that reinforcements were necessary for the final offensive and intended to bring up the IL Mountain Corps and the crack troops of the 1st SS Panzer Division *Leibstandarte-SS Adolf Hitler*. The armored forces would participate in the final assault, breaking through into the Crimea and then overrunning the Russians trying to escape to the south. However, this plan was thwarted by enemy action to the north, and the invasion of the Crimea was stalled.

On September 26, the Soviets on the mainland launched an offensive against the German eastern front between the Sea of Azov and the Dnieper River with two new armies, the Ninth, under Gen. Y. T. Cherevichenko, and the Eighteenth, commanded by Lt. Gen. Smirnov. Their

main intention was to prevent the German advance into the Crimea. The blow fell with initial success on the Romanians in the Nogay Steppe, holding the northeastern flank of the Eleventh Army. The Romanians gave way and a dangerous threat developed as it became obvious that the Soviets intended to cut off the Eleventh Army and force it back against the sea. Fortunately for the Germans, they were able to slow the attacks, allowing the IL Mountain Corps to turn back from its march to the Crimea and help counter the Soviet drive. After the successful battle of encirclement around Kiev, Col. Gen. Ewald von Kleist's powerful First Panzer Army, as it had now been designated, was free to come to the rescue. Von Kleist's armored forces

A Panzer division deploys during a battle on the vast steppe along the Dnieper River, north of the Crimea. A PzKw II, *Ausfuerung* C, SdKfz 121, with a 2cm KwK gun, pauses in the foreground. In Russia, this light tank was used mainly for reconnaissance with tank regiments. Beyond are dozens of PzKw III and PzKw IV tanks, and smoke from burning Russian armored vehicles. *German Official Photo*

led a drive down the Dnieper, striking the Soviet northern flank and rear, while elements of the Eleventh Army simultaneously resumed the attack. Their efforts were aided by air support from the IV Air Corps.

By early October, the Soviet threat was eliminated and the battle turned into another German victory. The main forces of both Soviet armies were encircled north of the Sea of Azov with between 65,000 and 100,000 prisoners taken, along with 125 tanks and 500 artillery pieces reported captured.[5]

The advance eastward towards Rostov was now assigned to von Kleist's First Panzer Army, along with the Leibstandarte-SS Division and the IL Mountain Corps. This allowed the bulk of the Eleventh Army to concentrate solely on the invasion of the Crimea.

With the successful conclusion of the battle north of the Sea of Azov, the *Oberkommando des Heeres* (OKH) ordered a redeployment of the Eleventh Army forces and a resumption of the attack on the Ishun Lakes bottle-neck now blocking the way to the Crimean peninsula. The two remaining Eleventh Army Corps, the XXX with the 22d, 72d, and 170th Infantry Divisions and the LIV Corps with the 46th, 73d, and 50th Infantry Divisions, faced the IX Soviet Corps. Additional German reinforcements were on the way but would not arrive until after the battle had been decided. They included the 42d Infantry Corps, which would be referred to as Command Group 42, commanding the 24th and 132d Infantry Divisions. The Third Romanian Army was assigned responsibility for the defense of the coast along the Black Sea and the Sea of Azov. Von Manstein reached an agreement with Marshal Antonescu that the Romanian Mountain Corps, with one mountain and one cavalry brigade, would follow the Germans into the Crimea to help exploit the promised breakthrough.

Von Manstein now concentrated his forces for the offensive against the Ishun Lakes defensive zone just south of Perekop. The road was repaired, ammunition and supplies were brought up, and the artillery was redeployed. This operation again involved an attack against a well-prepared system of field fortifications that was rapidly being reinforced by the Soviets. The terrain was the same type of barren salt steppes that did not permit any covered approach, and any possibility of an encirclement on either flank was impossible because of the lakes, sea, and marsh. German troops, towed artillery, and assault guns were brought forward under cover of darkness be-

The Wehrmacht enjoyed the advantage of superior communications. A company command post receives instructions from battalion headquarters using the *Tornister Funkgeraet b1* (Pack Radio Type b1), a transmitter/receiver with a separate case for battery and accessories. This radio, also used by the artillery, had a voice range of 10 miles and a C.W. range of 25 miles (16 and 40 km). Note BMW heavy motorcycle and sidecar, which has seen plenty of use. *From* Mit uns im Osten, *op. cit.*

German infantry inspect a captured Soviet T-35B 45-ton heavy tank, knocked out during the breakthrough at Perekop. This obsolete tank was armed with one 7.62cm gun, two 4.5cm guns, and six 7.62mm machine guns. *Author's Collection*

cause of Soviet air attacks. The Russians knew that holding the Germans at Ishun was critical, and their troops were ordered to hold at all costs. The (then) six divisions of the German Eleventh Army were now confronted by eight Soviet rifle divisions and four cavalry divisions, which, of course, could also fight on foot. The Soviets had evacuated Odessa with the help of the Black Sea Fleet and by the middle of October had transported the troops by sea to the Crimea. The evacuation was not without losses caused by attacks by German bombers of the IV Air Corps. It was now or never, and the Germans went over to the attack.

The Soviets at this time controlled the air over the Crimea and were continuously bombing and strafing the German troops exposed in the narrow, bleak section of land at Ishun. Even horses and vehicles in the rear had to be protected by trenches or foxholes. It was a great relief when Colonel Werner Moelders, then commander of fighter forces, was brought in and directed fighter operations that soon cleared the Russian aircraft from the sky, but only during the day. At night the Russians continued to attack the Germans from the air. German squadrons continued fighter sweeps over the battlefield, and on October 20 the 77th Fighter Wing under command of Major Gotthardt Handrick scored its 800th aerial victory.[6] Now German bomber units of the IV Air Corps increasingly attacked enemy airfields in the Crimea, in order to strike the enemy at his bases and thus decrease his effectiveness. Concurrently, dive-bombers struck the strong ground positions on the isthmus.[7] German dive-bombers and level-bomber units hammered incessantly at the enemy. Field positions, concentrations of artillery, bunkers, pockets of resistance, troop concentrations, and assembly areas lay under the daily hail of bombs

A hail of shells from this German Army 2cm Flak 30, mounted on a SdKfz 10/4 half-track, lashes an enemy field fortification during the German assault. *From* Die Wehrmacht, *No. 21, 8 Oct. 1941*

from the IV Air Corps, whose strength on November 1 consisted of six bomber, three dive-bomber, and four fighter groups.[8]

When the German assault at Ishun began early on October 26, it found the Soviets grimly prepared for the worst. An example of this type of close combat is included in a study by the U.S. Army based on personal experiences of Germans who actually took part:[9]

At 0800 the massed guns of the artillery opened fire. As the hail of shells struck the Soviet positions it obliterated some of the enemy observation posts. Patches of dried-out steppe grass burned freely and reddish clouds of dust and smoke enveloped the area depriving the Russians of visibility in some places. Meanwhile, the first German assault wave moved forward. When NCOs with 27mm flare pistols fired a signal flare to indicate they were entering the Russian defensive positions, the artillery fire was shifted. The assault detachments opened gaps in the center and the difficult task of ferreting out the enemy force dug in began. The assault forces fanned out from the initial points of penetration and moved forward firing well-aimed bullets at anything that moved. Whenever Russians from a nearby foxhole or bunker returned the fire, they were silenced by a well-placed hand grenade. The main fortified positions were neutralized by teams carrying portable flame-throwers. Whenever a particularly fanatic Russian force could not be flushed out by the assault troops, they fired a signal flare to pinpoint the target for the German artillery pieces and mortars. Dive-bombers, flying in waves, made low-level attacks against tanks, dug-in tanks, and antitank guns, while the infantry continued to storm Russian machine gun nests and strong points. This bloody fighting continued for days.

Von Manstein, who was constantly on the road to issue orders and provide advice, noted that German losses were mounting and the troops were nearing exhaustion. According to von Manstein, after continuous vicious fighting, "the fate of the battle was balanced, so to speak, on the keen edge of the blade. This hour must prove that the will of the attacker, by giving his utmost, is stronger than the will of the defender to resist."[10] Soldiers of the LIV Corps' 22d, 46th, and 73d Infantry Divisions continued their frontal assault along the three narrow strips of land into which the isthmus was divided by the lakes lying within it.

In a last supreme effort the Germans overcame the Russian's frantic resistance and after one more brutal day of savage combat the Germans' attack was crowned with success. On October 28, in a final burst of bitter fighting, the defense collapsed, and the Russians began a rapid retreat to the south, into the heart of the Crimean Peninsula. The Germans then had to gather their forces and begin a pursuit.

(Then) Lt. Gen. Erich von Manstein (left front) prepares to shake hands and congratulate a master sergeant of an infantry unit after the successful breakthrough of the Ishun Lakes defensive zone, opening the way to the Crimean Peninsula. *From* Bessarabien, Ukraine-Krim, *op. cit.*

Breaking through such strong and hard-fought defenses was indeed an arduous and

Two infantrymen, a private (left), and a technical sergeant, both newly decorated with the Iron Cross Second Class, pause and ponder their new orders to pursue the Red Amy into the Crimea. Both are armed with the 9mm MP 38 submachine gun, and both carry M24 stick grenades in their belts. The NCO also has a pair of 7x30 binoculars and a dispatch case. *From* Bessarabien, Ukraine-Krim, *op. cit.*

costly undertaking, but there was no time for celebration or even a rest for the weary troops. Von Manstein was impressed with the fighting quality and spirit of the soldiers of his command and the efficiency and professionalism of his staff.

Now came the real challenge — the conquest of the Crimea.

CHAPTER IV

CRIMEAN COMBAT

AFTER TEN DAYS of exceptionally hard fighting, the German breakthrough down the isthmus through Perekop and Ishun had been achieved, opening the way to the Crimean Peninsula. With the collapse of Soviet resistance on October 28, 1941, Russian troops began hurriedly streaming south, splitting into two main groups.[1] The German victors were tired and badly needed to rest and regroup, but this was no time for delay. General von Manstein ordered the troops of his Eleventh Army to begin the pursuit immediately, by employing every motor vehicle available, as well as forced marches.

The XXX Corps with two infantry divisions was sent south in the direction of Simferopol, an important commercial town and the key-point of the only good road network in the southern Crimea. The LIV Corps with two infantry divisions, including the newly assigned 132d Infantry Division, and a recently organized motor brigade, was ordered to pursue the Russians in the direction of the port city of Sevastopol on the southwest coast. The newly arrived Command Group 42, with three divisions, was assigned the mission of pursuing major Soviet forces fleeing southeast in the direction of Feodosiya and the Kerch Peninsula.

Most of the northern and central parts of the Crimean Peninsula consist of flat, grassy steppes or plains with no natural features on which the Russians could establish defensive positions or even rearguard actions. However, the Simferopol region is a rich, green agricultural area. Beyond Simferopol, to the south, the rugged Yaila Mountains, called the *Jailagebirge* by the Germans, formed a stark contrast to the steppes that characterized most of the Crimean terrain.

Despite the fact that von Manstein had no Panzer or motorized infantry divisions that could have quickly caught, encircled, and wiped out the major Soviet units at this most vulnerable time, the Germans made remarkable progress in pursuing their disorganized enemy. In addition, fighters and bombers of the IV Air Corps harried the retreating Russians with strafing and bombing runs on the columns of troops, horse-drawn vehicles and trucks, caus-

Even horses often had to have help traversing the Russian roads, usually unpaved and either dusty, sandy, snowy, or muddy, and sometimes impassable. These infantrymen, carrying only combat packs, struggle to move a supply wagon through the soft dirt of a road churned up during the advance. This was an easy task compared to the problems of blown bridges over rivers and hidden land mines.
From Mit uns im Osten, *op. cit.*

ing numerous casualties. Air attacks helped prevent the Soviets from establishing organized resistance to delay the rapidly pursuing troops of the German Eleventh Army.[2]

The motorized *Panzerjaeger* (antitank) unit of the XXX Corps raced south to the city of Simferopol, followed by some heavily armed infantry riding mainly in Soviet trucks captured at Perekop. They took the city by storm after a short firefight. This cut the paved highway from Simferopol to Sevastopol, hindering the escape of Russian units heading for the fortress city. During the chase, the Russian soldiers lost almost all weapons except small arms. As the bulk of the German XXX Corps' two divisions arrived, they pushed through the mountains to the southern coast with a strong contingent, firmly cutting Soviet forces in two. In a battle with a Soviet group that had fled into the mountains east of the Simferopol—Alushta highway, the Germans trapped and annihilated the Soviets almost to the last man.

German Command Group 42 and Romanian forces arrived in record time at the isthmus of Parpatsch, leading to the Kerch Peninsula, at the eastern end of the Crimea. They immediately clashed with troops of the Red Army trying to establish a front and overran the Russians with little difficulty. The Germans promptly seized the port city of Feodosiya and with the capture of the harbor prevented the embarkation of sizable enemy forces. On November 15, German forces captured the town of Kerch on the far eastern end of the peninsula and soon rounded up the last Russian prisoners of war. Only small numbers of Soviet troops were able to escape across the narrow Straits of Kerch to the Kuban, and all heavy weapons, tanks, and vehicles were left behind.

The view toward the port city of Kerch shortly after its capture by the Germans in mid-November 1941. At left, two disarmed Russian soldiers help a wounded comrade on the way to a prisoner of war collection point. *From* Mit uns im Osten, *op. cit.*

The wild chase was now over and the entire Crimean Peninsula was in German hands except the fortified port city of Sevastopol. The six divisions of the Eleventh Army had wiped out two enemy armies totaling twelve rifle and four cavalry divisions. During the battles for Perekop Isthmus and Ishun, and during their retreat, the Soviet armies of around 200,000 men suffered many casualties and lost over 100,000 as prisoners. The Germans also captured or destroyed 700 guns and 160 tanks.[3] During the rout, Russian forces used detachments of cavalry as rearguard to delay the German and Romanian pursuers. Romanian cavalry clashed with Russian cavalry in small battles that resembled those of the nineteenth century. Romanian cavalry, with sabers drawn, also hunted down Russian stragglers in open terrain far off the roads.

The German LIV Infantry Corps and Romanian units were now astride the highway which led to Sevastopol and were advancing toward the port city on the southwest coast. Aerial reconnaissance disclosed that the Soviets, with command of the sea, were bringing in reinforcements and supplies and intended to make a firm stand in the city and vicinity. Unfortunately for the Germans, time was on the side of the Red Army. The only armored and motorized unit that the German Army controlled at this time in the south was the *Leibstandarte-SS "Adolf Hitler,"* and it was far away, north of the Sea of Azov, advancing on Rostov with von Kleist's First Panzer Army. By the time the Eleventh Army was able to deploy strong infantry forces around Sevastopol, it was too late for a surprise attack.

The city of Sevastopol was ringed on the north, east, and south with permanent and field fortifications built into the rough terrain. The Black Sea was on the west. Some of the masonry forts dated back to the Crimean War of 1854–1856. That war had been precipitated when Turkey declared war on Russia, but France and Great Britain were soon drawn into the conflict. In January 1854, the Allies had landed troops in the Crimea, intent on capturing the Russian naval base at Sevastopol. A series of costly battles ensued, including the famous Battle of Balaklava featuring the British Light Brigade, the "six hundred." Despite cholera and logistical difficulties, Sevastopol finally fell to the Allies the following year, after a most difficult siege. The Crimean War ended in February 1856, after great losses to both sides, a high proportion having died from disease and deprivation. Now General von Manstein and the German Eleventh Army, with their Romanian ally, were intent on capturing the city without delay.

Meanwhile, von Manstein moved the administrative branches of Eleventh Army headquarters into Simferopol, a small city of 89,700. His tactical headquarters was established in Sarabuz, a sizable village north of town. At Sarabuz, von Manstein's headquarters was set up in a new school building. Soon the communication center was operating, a mess had been established, and the staff functions were operating smoothly to cope with the inevitable *Papierkrieg* (paper war). Von Manstein's *Bursche* (orderly and driver), Sergeant Fritz Nagel, moved the general's meager personal belongings into a room in a small farmhouse located in an orchard on a nearby collective farm. The army's chief of staff also had a room in the farmhouse. Von Manstein's furniture consisted of a folding cot, a table and chair, a stool for the washbowl to stand on, and a few clothes hooks. More comfortable furniture could have been acquired in Simferopol, but he did not believe that staff officers, or even the commander, should live in comfort while the troops were camping in *Zelte und Schuetzenloecher* (tents and foxholes). As for the headquarters building, heating was a problem in winter, so two small brick stoves, like the Russian type, were built in the rooms in the school building. This was necessary because the heating system had been wrecked by the Soviets before their hurried departure. Everyone was tired after the work and stress of the previous weeks; on the day after von Manstein's arrival, Sergeant Nagel managed to barter with a peasant for some potatoes, pork, and a wurst, and had the cook prepare for the general a *Bauern Schmaus* or "peasant feast," one of von Manstein's favorite meals.

There was no time for relaxation. For the assault on Sevastopol, von Manstein brought up all available troops of the Eleventh Army. Command Group 42, with the 46th Infantry Division, had to be left on the Kerch Peninsula to the east, and a Romanian cavalry brigade was assigned the job of securing the remaining eastern coast. A Romanian mountain brigade was ordered to combat partisans in the Yaila Mountains to make sure that the most important highways and lines of supply and communication were held open.

The advantage at Sevastopol lay with the defenders. The Soviet forces in Sevastopol had reorganized and were constantly being reinforced by sea. The original garrison and the remnants of the units that had retreated into the fortified zone, along with newly arrived troops, now totaled nine divisions. The main Soviet force in Sevastopol was the Separate Maritime Army, commanded since October 5 by General I. Y. Petrov. The defenders had artillery and even some aircraft flying from camouflaged airstrips. Thousands of soldiers and civilians were seen building new field fortifications, and with winter closing in, time was of the essence. The Luftwaffe, because of the winter weather conditions and its reduced strength, was no longer able to cut off Soviet supply by sea.

In addition to forts, field works, and antitank ditches, defensive positions were built into the caves, rocks, and stony hillsides. The total extent of the Soviet defense line around the land side of Sevastopol was 21.7 miles (35 kilometers). The

Marshal Ion Antonescu (center, facing troops), CinC of Romanian forces, visits his troops on the south coast of the Crimea. Most Romanian soldiers wore the odd Dutch-style steel helmet adopted just before the war. *German Official Photo*

terrain was generally quite rough, hilly and broken, but to the north it was comparatively open, in contrast to the eastern sector with almost impenetrable thickets. To the south a range of rocky mountains presented a difficult obstacle, and German forces on the coast could have been attacked by the Russian Black Sea Fleet.

After studying all the factors, including the weather, von Manstein decided to launch the attack against the northern front with its more favorable terrain, which included the deep Belbek Valley. The area between this and the Severnaya Bight, which opened to the sea, was heavily fortified. However, the German assault artillery could be deployed more easily here, and it would be easier to supply ammunition and fuel during the assault. Hills and valleys ran all the way to the city proper, on the south side of the Severnaya Bight, or bay.

Von Manstein directed that the attack from the north would be made by the LIV Corps with four infantry divisions, supported by the greater part of the heavy artillery and strong air attacks. The plan was to have an additional infantry division in reserve for the attack, but the crisis that developed at Rostov required Army Group South to order the transfer of this division out of the Crimea; it was now moving north towards Perekop. A holding attack along the southern portion of the eastern front was to be conducted by the XXX Corps with two infantry divisions. The original date for the assault on Sevastopol was set for November 27. This was the earliest date that the army could be ready for the attack because many of the troops in the Kerch Peninsula had to march the entire distance on foot. It was also taking considerable time to bring up the artillery and ammunition over the hills and rough terrain.

In December, the German railroad engineers and skilled workers of the *OT*, the Todt Construction Organization, managed to complete the repair and changing of the rail gauge on the railroad leading south into the Crimea all the way to Simferopol and on to Sevastopol. This permitted the swift movement of troops, ammunition, and supplies to the battlefront.[4] However, heavy snow on the mainland to the north immobilized four of the only five train engines then available south of the Dnieper and further delayed the arrival of essential supplies and artillery ammunition. There were also ice jams on the Dnieper River, while to the south in the Crimea heavy rains soon turned unpaved roads into quagmires. Winter was definitely the Soviets' ally.

As a result of the onset of winter weather, the attack on Sevastopol was postponed until mid-December. This benefited the Soviets, who continued to reinforce and strengthen their fortifications.

Snow in the mountains and freezing rain and wind made life miserable for the soldiers in the field with little shelter. The thousands of German troops that had completed their march from the Kerch Peninsula and elsewhere dug in around the Soviet defensive perimeter. Artillery was moved into position with great difficulty and ammunition was stockpiled by soldiers living in trenches, hastily constructed bunkers, and tents. The Russians, of course, frequently harassed the Germans with artillery fire and local probing attacks. Even though Yalta on the south coast was called the "Russian Riviera," by December the Crimea was seized in winter's icy grip. Soldiers who a few weeks before had been sweating in their field gray woolen uniforms were now delighted when they received warm blankets, overcoats, and other items of winter clothing. Eventually the troops, artillery, ammunition, and assault guns were in position. Von Manstein's staff had established a command post for him behind the defensive perimeter from which he could personally direct the coming battle. The German campaign so far had been costly and tiring, but dramatically successful, and morale in the Eleventh Army was high.

The attack on Sevastopol was preceded by an intense and sustained artillery barrage. The boom of artillery and the thump of explosions echoed through the hills, and soon Stuka dive-bombers of the Fourth Air Fleet screamed down, lobbing their bombs, equipped with Jericho Whistles, onto the Soviet defenses. The Russians returned the artillery fire in a deadly duel of destruction.

Hitler addressed the Reichstag in Berlin on December 11, 1941, to announce his declaration of war against the United States. Although Reichs Press Chief Otto Dietrich (second from right) and the Reichstag members approved this momentous decision and declared their loyalty to the Fuehrer, no amount of propaganda could alter the grim reality of war with America. *German Official Photo*

The actual attack began early on December 17. Now, in the smoke, dust, and noise, German combat engineers worked their way forward over the rocky ground under a smoke screen from *Nebelwerfer* (wheeled rocket launchers, which also fired high-explosive projectiles). Explosive charges and flamethrowers were directed against firing ports and other vital parts of fortifications, while small arms fire attempted to suppress Russian defensive fire. Deep penetration was made into the enemy outer defense lines, which were mainly field fortifications and small fortified positions forming a deep defensive area.[5] Artillery and assault guns moved up under cover of smoke and darkness and fired point-blank at the larger forts, many of which were located between the Belbek Valley and Severnaya Bay. The XXX Corps simultaneously attacked the heights along the southern sector of the perimeter.

By late December, the soldiers of the LIV Corps had fought through the deep antitank ditch and were approaching Fort Stalin. This was an important objective because the imposing fort overlooked the Severnaya Bay. With their artillery there, the Germans could have controlled this important body of water leading to the sea. Unfortunately for von Manstein and his troops, the 73d Infantry Division, that had been previously withdrawn for the attack on Rostov, was not available for the final assault. The German offensive ground to a halt at this point in front of the strong Soviet fortifications, with heavy casualties from gunfire from warships of the Soviet Black Sea Fleet, which included a battleship. Then came another serious shock that changed the entire situation, not only at Sevastopol, but in the entire Crimea.

An urgent message was received by von Manstein from Command Group 42, far to the east on the Kerch Peninsula. The Soviets had made landings in force at the town of Kerch and then at Feodosiya, under cover of the guns of the Black Sea Fleet. German forces on the Kerch Peninsula desperately needed reinforcements, and only von Manstein could provide them. Speedy action was essential to prevent a debacle, but von Manstein ordered one last attempt to break through on the northern sector, hoping to cause the collapse of the Sevastopol defenses. This would have released many of the Eleventh Army troops engaged in the siege, who would then be able to deal effectively with the Russian landings to the east. The German divisions had suffered heavy casualties and were tired. The attack on Sev-

In the Crimea, the situation was desperate in late December as German troops fought to thwart the Soviet landings on the Kerch Peninsula and break through Red Army defenses at Sevastopol. This army lieutenant continued to command his unit despite his wound. *From OKW*, Allen Gewalten zum Trotz *(Berlin, 1942)*

astopol stalled and had to be discontinued on December 30. The German troops then withdrew behind the Belbek River and took up defensive positions. The two divisions of the XXX Corps attacking along the southern part of the perimeter, and soon some of the units on the northern sector, were pulled out of the line and shifted to the eastern part of the Crimea. Again, the transfer of troops and equipment had to be accomplished without delay.

The halt in the attack on Sevastopol was a difficult decision not only for von Manstein, but for the troops who had made such sacrifices. But there was no alternative, and at least the gains made along the northern and southern sectors placed the Germans in a more favorable position for renewing their offensive against Sevastopol at a later date. In the meantime, von Manstein returned to his tactical headquarters at Sarabuz to confront the new crisis in the eastern Crimea.

Reports received by von Manstein indicated that the Soviet landings in the east were not intended just to relieve the German pressure on Sevastopol. The invasion developed into a full-scale offensive, ordered by Stalin himself, and was intended to recapture the entire Crimea. On January 28, 1942, all Soviet units operating in the Crimea were formed into the Crimean Front under General D. T. Kozlov.[6] In a short time, two powerful Soviet armies were ashore on the Kerch Peninsula, and were attempting, in conjunction with the Red Army units at Sevastopol, to attack and completely destroy the German forces in the Crimea. Suddenly, the attackers became the defenders—the fate of the entire Eleventh Army hung in the balance!

Personnel in von Manstein's headquarters worked around the clock. Moving thousands of men, weapons, ammunition, and supplies required excellent staff work and logistical planning on very short notice. Many of the troops had to march east in the bitter winter cold. Although this taxed the stamina and resolve of the men of von Manstein's command, by this time, his troops had complete confidence in their commander. To delay the Russians, Luftwaffe air strikes were called in to hit assembly areas in the Kerch Peninsula and aid the German and Romanian soldiers of Command Group 42, who now found themselves in a desperate situation as they prepared to defend against numerically superior Soviet forces.

Heavy fighting intensified on the Kerch Peninsula. Command Group 42 and the 46th Infantry Division, believing offense was the best defense, attacked the Russians who had made additional landings on the northern coast of the Kerch. However, Red Army forces ashore at Feodosiya, on the south coast, with the help of naval gun support, soon forced a withdrawal of the 46th Division from the Kerch Peninsula. Much of the 46th Division's artillery was lost because icy roads prevented it from being moved. The Straits of Kerch froze, allowing the Soviets to transport even more units to the peninsula. Even more discouraging, the counterattack made by the newly arrived Romanian Mountain Brigade failed, and the Romanians hastily retreated before the Soviet tanks as far back as the town of Staraya-Krym.

At this point the Soviets could have advanced, cutting the Dzhankoi-Simferopol railroad, thereby preventing any reinforcement and resupply of German forces. Apparently, due to confusion or indecision, the Soviets advanced hesitantly, allowing the Germans and Romanians time to build up a thin defensive line between the Sea of Azov, in the vicinity of Staraya-Krym, and the Black Sea. The German defenders consisted mainly of the depleted 46th Infantry Division and a regiment of the 73d Infantry Division that had been marching towards Rostov but had been stopped at Perekop, before they could leave the Crimea. These troops, with full equipment, arrived quickly by train. Von Manstein even sent soldiers from the staff of Eleventh Army headquarters to serve with the Romanians and help bolster their sagging morale. Spirited fighting held the Soviets at bay for the fourteen days it took for the XXX Corps, with its two infantry divisions, to arrive at the narrow neck of the Kerch Peninsula. They immediately attacked with some success at the port of Feodosiya. New danger arose suddenly when the Soviets made yet another landing, supported by warships, at the port of Yevpatoriya (Eupatoria) on the far western coast of the Crimea, north of Sevastopol.

The surprise landing at Yevpatoriya coincided with an uprising in the city, initiated mainly by partisans who had infiltrated the town. Hastily assembled German combat units had to be rushed to this new point of crisis and soon succeeded in annihilating the enemy landing force, along with 1,200 armed partisans, in bloody street fighting.[7] Urban warfare was something new for many of the German soldiers, including troops from rear echelon units. However, they had the advantage of a few assault guns with 75mm cannon and the small Pak 35/36 37mm antitank guns, which were used to good effect blasting nests of partisans firing automatic weapons or sniping from buildings. While the fighting in Yevpatoriya was going on, the Soviet

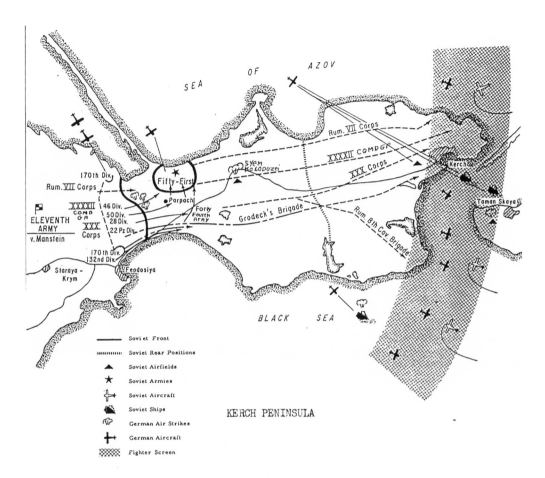

Map of the Kerch Peninsula battle zone. *U.S. Air Force*

forces in Sevastopol attacked in an attempt to break the German encirclement. The four German divisions remaining in the Sevastopol siege ring succeeded in throwing back the attacks and maintaining most positions.

By January 15, 1942, the Germans were strong enough in the eastern Crimea to attack Russian forces at Feodosiya. This effort was aided by strong Luftwaffe air strikes that started many fires in the town. During a fierce three-day battle, the Soviets were defeated and the city and harbor recaptured. The Germans had destroyed a numerically superior enemy fighting with the advantage of a built-up area. About 10,600 Russian prisoners were taken, along with 132 artillery pieces, 54 antitank guns, 85 tanks, 332 machine guns, and 81 mortars. An additional 6,700 dead Russians lay about the streets and on the surrounding battlefield.[8] Captured equipment that was still functional was pressed into service by the Germans.

The Germans and Romanians were not only tired but had suffered heavy losses. With the equivalent of only three and one-third depleted infantry divisions and the Romanian Mountain Brigade, they were unable to completely defeat the enemy on the Kerch Peninsula. The Soviets still had eight divisions and two brigades, but the Germans were able to retake the Parpatsch neck, thereby sealing off the Kerch Peninsula from the rest of the Crimea. Winter

The spoils of war. German soldiers pose in front of a captured Soviet heavy tank with captured chickens. There will be a welcome change in the evening meal for their unit from the usual monotonous army rations. The tank, a 47.5 ton KV-I, had a 7.62cm gun as its main armament. *German Soldier's Snapshot*

weather now hampered movement on both sides. The ground was frozen solid in this unusually cold winter, and foxholes and trenches had to be hacked or blasted out to aid in the defense. Shelter on the barren steppe was virtually nonexistent and many soldiers, in the open for weeks, suffered from frostbite or pneumonia. The Wehrmacht found itself ill prepared to cope with winter warfare in a climate as severe as Russia's. When it became apparent in the fall of 1941 that the war was going to drag on, a nationwide program was launched in Germany to collect furs and other winter clothing to aid the soldiers freezing on the Eastern Front.

Von Manstein now realized that the situation was at a critical point. The Soviets, with numerically superior forces, began the first of three attacks in an attempt to break through the Parpatsch neck and rout the Germans in the Crimea. Each of these major attacks was aided by assaults on the German divisions and Romanian Mountain Brigade surrounding Sevastopol. The Germans had the advantage in artillery but the Soviets in Sevastopol now consisted of seven rifle divisions, three brigades of marines, and a dismounted cavalry division. (The Russian horses were eaten during the siege.)

The first Soviet attack on the Parpatsch front began on February 27 with an artillery barrage. The German defenders were reinforced by a Romanian infantry division that arrived just in the nick of time. The Germans still had no tanks except for a few captured Russian tanks pressed into service with large German *Balkenkreuz* insignia painted on the sides of the turrets. The Soviets attacked with seven infantry divisions, two brigades, and several tank battalions in the first wave, with an additional six to seven divisions, two tank brigades, and one cavalry division waiting to exploit the expected breakthrough.

The Soviets advanced slowly over open ground against stubborn German resistance. Both sides knew the stakes were high. The Soviets managed to overrun the Romanian division on the northern flank, and the decision hung in the balance. The last German reserves were then thrown into the battle and, despite rain, strong Luftwaffe air support enabled the German-Romanian forces to hold and finally stem the enemy breakthrough on March 3.

Both sides were exhausted, and as a result a tense stalemate settled over the battlefield. The wounded who had not frozen to death were evacuated, and both sides regrouped for the next battle. The Soviet advance through the Romanian positions had created a wide salient that posed a danger to the entire defensive line. The Russians launched the second offensive on March 18, using eight rifle divisions and two tank brigades in continuous human-wave attacks. Again, the Germans and Romanians, fighting desperately, managed to repulse the "Ivans" with heavy losses.

The German units were weary and badly depleted, and they appeared to be at the end of their ability to resist the Soviet attacks. At this time, welcome reinforcements arrived in the form of a newly organized Panzer division, the 22d, commanded by *Generalmajor* Wilhelm von Apell, hurriedly sent by OKH. The Panzer division was ordered to make a surprise attack against the Russian salient in the German northern front and cut off the Soviet units. However, the green division did not as yet have the necessary training and combat experience to defeat such a well-equipped and determined enemy. The attack failed, but it came as a shock to the Soviets and gained valuable time for the Germans and Romanians to rest and prepare for the next enemy attack.

The situation for the Germans was serious if not critical, even though they now had armor available to counter a Soviet breakthrough. Preparations went on day and night, bringing up ammunition and strengthening their defensive positions.

On the morning of April 9, the thump of artillery and the whine of shells heralded the beginning of a new, and final, Soviet offensive. The Russians threw everything into this massive attack against the German positions around the Parpatsch neck, where the Kerch Peninsula connects to the rest of the Crimea. Artillery shells rained down, exploding in the German lines where troops cowered in foxholes and trenches. The barrage continued for an hour, with explosions occasionally hurling mangled body parts into the air. Then, out of the dust and smoke came the Russian tanks, grunting and rattling, belching clouds of blue exhaust and firing as they rolled forward. German antitank guns and artillery fired back and one by one the tanks were hit, sometimes bursting into flames, subjecting their hapless crews to a fiery death.

Wave after wave of Russian infantry followed the tanks, soldiers trotting grimly forward dressed in their brown, quilted "*telogreika*" M1941 winter uniforms, carrying M1891/30 Mosin-Nagant rifles with fixed, angular bayonets, or PPSh41 submachine guns. The sound of the fast-firing German MP 40 submachine guns and MG 34 light machine guns could easily be distinguished from the slower-firing Russian DP1928 light machine guns and the water-cooled PM1910 Maxim heavy machine guns, dragged forward on a mount with two small wheels.

Bodies piled up in front of the German positions but still the Russians bravely came on. German rifle and machine gun barrels glowed hot, and hand grenades and mortar shells arched through the haze, exploding in the Russian ranks as they stumbled forward. There was little natural cover on the grassy steppe, and the murderous mayhem continued with Russians here and there reaching German positions and assaulting their enemy in bloody, hand-to-hand combat. Bayonets, rifle butts, pistols, and trench knives took their toll on both sides as men wildly shouted, cursed, and died in fierce encounters, grappling and struggling in the dust and blood, over the bodies of their dead and dying comrades.

Finally, the Soviet tide ebbed, the German lines held, and the Russian survivors retreated as German fire kicked up dust around their heels. A grim silence descended over the battlefield, littered with hundreds of dead and dying men. Soon, flocks of crows, vultures, and other birds began circling this scene of ghastly carnage, landing to peck at dead eyes staring blankly at the sky. Burial parties, usually composed of prisoners, entered *Niemandsland* (no man's land), dragged stiff enemy corpses into shell holes, and unceremoniously covered them up. German dead were identified and buried under the supervision of the *Graeberoffizier* (Graves Registration Officer). For the living, war had become a struggle for survival.

When the smoke cleared after the three days of intensive battle, Soviet offensive power in the Crimea had been exhausted. Von Manstein, who had been promoted to *Generaloberst* (Colonel General) effective New Year's Day, 1942, could now begin preparations for a counteroffensive to again clear the enemy from the eastern Crimea. A short period of quiet now prevailed on the front around Parpatsch, as well as the Sevastopol perimeter, as both sides regrouped for the final showdown.

Each German army had at least one rest area behind the front where soldiers could recuperate from the stress and strain of combat. Upon arrival of a unit, the men first entered a delousing tent or building where they would remove their soiled clothing and rid themselves of any vermin. Their clothing would be washed and sterilized before reissue. A hot, soapy shower, followed by a good, hot meal, would do wonders for morale. The weary troops would then be allowed to enjoy a sound sleep, followed by another hot meal. There was always a facility for writing home through the *Feldpost*, the military postal system. Soldiers enjoyed the small pleasures such as sitting in a chair at a table after living for weeks or months in the field under primitive conditions.

Rest camps often had available a *Feldbuecherei*, a military field library, sometimes in a bus or van, where soldiers could obtain military newspapers and fiction or nonfiction books. Small softcover editions of books called *"Tornisterhefte"* (pack books or editions) were distributed by the Army and would fit

"On the hunt for '*Kleine Partisanen!*'" In German soldier slang, the vermin that inevitably infested their clothing in Russia were compared to the Soviet partisans who attacked German troops behind the lines. *From* Bessarabien, Ukraine–Krim, *op. cit.*

conveniently in the pocket or pack. Propaganda and motivational materials were also available in the form of paperback booklets. An example is a restricted booklet by the OKW, the Armed Forces High Command, dated 1940/41, titled *Frankreich—der ewige Reichsfeind* (*France—the eternal enemy of the Reich*). There was also an edition on the Soviet Union. Another booklet produced by the *Heerespersonalamt*, the Army Personnel Office, dealt with the reasons for the war from the German perspective. Titled *Wofuer Kaempfen Wir?* (*Why We Fight*), it was an illustrated paperback of 144 pages. Divisions and higher headquarters had assigned to them a *National-sozialistischer Fuehrungsoffizier* (National Socialist Guidance Officer), responsible for motivation and political indoctrination. As a political watchdog, his position was independent. There were also army chaplains available for religious services.

Rest camps usually had a *Kantine* or *Kameradschaftsheim* of some sort where soldiers could relax, buy a beer, and obtain small personal articles such as toothpaste and cigarettes. Last but not least, medics were available to treat minor medical problems such as blisters, rashes, and digestive disorders. Serious ailments were treated at a *Feldlazarett* (field hospital).

In towns in Germany and throughout occupied Europe, a *Soldatenheim* (Service Club) was established to provide food, quarters, movies, entertainment, and a place to relax for soldiers on leave, pass, or in transit. Some of these, like the one in Simferopol, were quite elaborate and comfortable and were a welcome haven in a foreign land where soldiers could stay out of trouble.

The really fortunate soldiers were those relaxing in a rest camp or at a service club when a traveling entertainment group arrived to perform for the troops. The German equivalent of the American United Service Organization (USO) was the *Wehrmachtbuehne*. Several of these traveling shows entertained troops behind the various fronts during the war. These shows featured attractive, talented young women singers and dancers, as well as comedians, and often gave short dramatic performances. The musical presentations were, of course, a welcome opportunity for the troops to forget the war for a short time and see professional entertainment. The shows raised morale wherever they were performed and were much appreciated.

Food is of vital importance, not only for the health and efficiency of the soldier, but also for maintaining good morale. German fliers were authorized special Luftwaffe rations (*Verpflegungsgegenstaende fuer Flieger*), but for the ordinary soldier the fare was usually unimaginative but adequate. The table shows a day's rations for one soldier in a division in June 1941:[9]

Bread	750 Grams
Cold food for the evening meal	120 Grams
Drink	25 Grams
Peas	180 Grams
Sugar	140 Grams
Salt	15 Grams
Meat	200 Grams
Cigars	2 each
Cigarettes	2 each

Note: 450 grams equal 1 pound, 225 grams equal ½ pound, etc.

Total rations for a division for a day totaled twelve tons, and included bread, meat, peas, wurst, butter or margarine, salt, sugar, and coffee.

Amounts and types of items were often substituted, depending on the season, location, and difficulties of transportation. For example, potatoes were frequently provided because they stored well during winter. On the march and at the front, hot food was prepared in the unit's field kitchen, usually mobile, and often referred to as the *Gulaschkanone*. The usual fare was goulash, *Schmoren* (stew), or a hearty soup, with ersatz coffee and *Kommissbrot* (G.I. bread). Several German veterans have remarked to this author that the bread baked by the *Feldbaekerei* (field bakery), was consistently good and tasty. Meat provided by the *Schlaechtereizug* (butchery platoon), or *Schlaechtereiabteilung* (butchery battalion or detachment), was subject to a health inspection by army specialists assigned to the *Fleischbeschau*. Water supplies were also inspected or boiled when practical.

The German Army in the field, like armies down through the ages, lived at least partly off the land, purchasing or requisitioning livestock, poultry, flour, vegetables, and other foods wherever they went. During harvest season this did not present major problems, especially in agricultural areas. However, in winter this practice frequently created severe difficulties and hardship, often alienating the civilian population. In fact, it was Emperor Napoleon Bonaparte of France (1769–1821), who sponsored the development of preserved foods that could be carried in the field, enabling large armies to campaign even in areas where no local food was available.

Resting after a hard battle, the soldiers in this photo have laid aside their MG 34 machine guns and rifles and are sharing slices of *Kommissbrot* (army bread), to eat with their mess kits of *Schmoren* (stew). *From Mit uns im Osten, op. cit.*

In combat or whenever the field kitchen was not available, soldiers carried one day's rations in their *Brotbeutel* (fabric pouch hung from the waist belt). One day's rations were carried in the unit field kitchen, two day's rations in the unit supply transport, and one day's rations in the divisional supply columns.

There was also an emergency ration called an *eiserne Portion* (iron ration) carried by each man, but this could be eaten only when authorized by his commander or other authority. It consisted of a small *Zwieback* (a twice-baked wheat biscuit) and a small can of *Dauerfleisch* (preserved meat). Preserved bread in a cardboard carton, called *Dauerbrot*, was also an item of issue. The usual evening meal at the front or in combat areas might consist of rye bread, margarine, and smoked sausage. At times on the Eastern Front boiled potatoes were the only food available, and the supply situation got worse as the war dragged on.

Supplies and reinforcements were just two of the problems confronting von Manstein and his staff. They had to quickly develop a plan for defeating the Soviets in the Crimea even though the German Eleventh Army was outnumbered by the Russians by about three to one. The Soviet forces, now under a command called the "Crimea Front," had 7 rifle divisions, 3 brigades, and 1 dismounted cavalry division in the "Coastal Army" at Sevastopol. The Soviet Fifty-first and Forty-fourth Armies on the Kerch front had over 17 rifle divisions, 3 rifle brigades, 2 cavalry divisions and 4 tank brigades, a powerful force with a total of 26 major units.

General von Manstein was joined by Marshal Ion Antonescu of Romania for a quick tour of the troops in the Crimea. Antonescu promised two more Romanian divisions for the coming offensive. OKH could provide no additional reinforcements other than the 22d Panzer Division, already at the Parpatsch front, and the recently arrived 28th Jaeger Division (A Jaeger division was a light division, similar in organization and mode of employment to the mountain division, except that some of the components had more motorization, permitting better employment in flat terrain).[10]

The German forces at von Manstein's disposal included the LIV Infantry Corps at Sevastopol, with three infantry divisions, and a new Romanian division that replaced the German 40th Infantry Division sent to the Kerch. The only German division on the southern perimeter at Sevastopol was the 72d Infantry Division. The Romanian Mountain Corps had to defend the entire south coast of the Crimea against surprise attacks from the sea and any remaining partisan groups in the mountains. German forces on the Kerch front included only five infantry divisions and the 22d Panzer Division. These were augmented by the newly arrived Romanian 7th Corps, with two divisions, one having been moved from the west coast, and a cavalry brigade. von Manstein commented that the usefulness of the Romanian forces in an offensive role was limited and the numerical disparity between the Soviet and German forces had now increased still further.[11] Decisive action first had to be taken on the Kerch front.

According to von Manstein's plan, the first objective was to deceive the Soviets

German soldiers in combat with Soviet troops and partisans in the rough Jaila-Gebirge, the mountains along the south coast of the Crimea near Sevastopol. The man on the left watches through binoculars while the soldier on the right remains ready with his rifle and M24 stick hand grenades, in his belt and lying on the rock. *From* Allen Gewalten zum Trotz, *op. cit.*

into believing that the main German attack would be on the bulge, attacked previously, and unsuccessfully, by the 22d Panzer Division. For this the Romanians, with two divisions and a cavalry brigade, would be used. German Command Group 42, with two divisions, would simultaneously conduct a holding attack in the center of the line.

The main assault would be made by the XXX Corps in the south with three infantry divisions and the 22d Panzer Division. This attack was intended not only to break through the Soviet front, but to make a deep penetration and destroy the bulk of the enemy forces. The infantry divisions, along with combat engineers, had to break through the strongly fortified Parpatsch position, with its deep antitank ditch, and seize territory to the east, in order to allow the advance of the tanks of the Panzer division. The XXX Corps, with the Panzers leading the way, was to swing to the north to trap the main Soviet forces in the bulge by striking them in the flank and rear and then forcing them against the northern coast where they would be encircled and destroyed. A special storm battalion, using only small assault boats, would land in the rear of the enemy to support the attack by the XXX Corps. The entire operation would be supported by artillery and the full weight of the VIII Air Corps. This was a complex and risky plan that required careful coordination, but action had to be taken immediately because *Fall Blau* (Operation Blue), the German summer offensive of 1942, was scheduled to begin on June 28.[12]

The Soviets had to be cleared from the Crimea without delay because the main forces of the Wehrmacht would be fighting on the mainland, far to the east, and would be very vulnerable to an attack from the Crimea in their rear. As the time for the attack approached, von Manstein and his staff moved to a command post close behind the Kerch front where he intended to direct the coming battle personally. He was then constantly on the move, visiting divisional staffs and front-line troops, but in constant radio contact. The cover name for the German offensive was *Trappenjagd* (Bustard Hunt), named after a large bird hunted on the steppes of the Crimea.

Operation Bustard Hunt began before dawn on May 8 with a heavy artillery barrage. At first light, the scream of Stuka dive-bombers of the VIII Air Corps could be heard over the sound of the exploding German shells and the Russian counter-battery fire. The shrieking of the Jericho Whistles attached to the fins on German bombs sounded like banshees from hell, adding to the demoralizing psychological effect on the Russian soldiers. The German infantry and combat engineers stormed forward through clouds of smoke and dust, following assault guns as they advanced. The Germans broke through the Soviet defenses; much credit must be given to the precision bombing of the squadrons of dive-bombers, which took a heavy toll of Russian defenders.

German infantry, accompanied by an assault gun, move forward in the Crimea in early 1942 to engage in another of the countless battles with the tenacious soldiers of the Red Army. This is one of the new Sturmgeschuetz IIIF assault guns with the high-velocity 7.5cm StuK 40 L/43 cannon. *From* Artillerie im Osten, *op. cit.*

The tanks of the 22d

Panzer Division then advanced, but like the assault guns, they were stopped at the antitank ditch. By the next day the combat engineers had prepared passes through the ditch allowing the tanks to exploit the breakthrough. After the tanks were through the fortified area, they swung to the north and were then involved in a counterattack by Soviet tank units. The German armor was again aided by the Luftwaffe and managed to thwart the Russian tank attacks on the open steppe. The weather then posed a new problem when heavy rain began to fall, resulting in the German tanks bogging down in the mud for almost 24 hours. Speed and sur-

A German 8.8cm Flak 36 arrives in the battered port city of Kerch, pulled by its crew in a Sd.Kfz. 7 half-track prime mover. *German Official Photo*

prise were essential to the success of the German offensive, and fortunately for the Germans, a motorized brigade, specially organized for this purpose, had advanced rapidly to the east before the rain and succeeded in preventing the Russians from building up a defense line further to the rear. The situation was confusing, and the Soviets, it seemed, had not as yet realized the German intentions and continued to hold their main reserve forces behind their northern flank.

The operation was now going according to plan, and on May 11 the tanks of the 22d Panzer Division reached the north coast. Eight Soviet divisions suddenly found themselves trapped in the pocket. Red Army troops below the pocket began a retreat, which turned into a rout, and in the pursuit and fighting entire Russian units were annihilated when caught in the open. On May 16, German troops of the 170th Infantry Division captured the town of Kerch, on the straits of the same name, and swiftly overcame resistance by disorganized Russian soldiers trying to cross the straits to the Kuban and safety. The beach was jammed with Russian vehicles, and the final annihilation of the troops along the coast was accomplished by artillery fire, in order to spare German infantry further losses.

By May 18, the battle of the Kerch Peninsula was over. Small groups of Russians, compelled to resist by a few fanatical commissars, continued to hold out in underground caves for weeks until finally forced to surrender. Both Soviet armies were destroyed and only a few thousand troops, without their heavy weapons or vehicles, had been able to escape over the Kerch Straits. Von Manstein even received a personal call from the Fuehrer congratulating him on this impressive victory. As the smoke cleared over the battlefields, von Manstein drove in an armed convoy to the town of Kerch with von Richthofen. All the roads were littered with Russian vehicles, tanks, and guns, and they passed long columns of prisoners plodding toward captivity in POW camps.

In his report to higher headquarters, von Manstein reported that they had captured about 170,000 prisoners, 1,133 pieces of artillery, and 258 tanks.[13] He stated that "By deceiving and surprising the enemy, we had succeeded in achieving an overpowering success by a frontal penetration and encircling operation. The victory was not one of superior numbers, but must be attributed to the initiative of the leaders in all grades and in the superior combat ability of the troops."[14]

German victory in the Crimea was by no means inevitable. The Red Army outnumbered the Wehrmacht, and the Germans came close to defeat on more than one occasion. German triumph over the odds at Kerch once again reinforced Hitler's belief in the ultimate superiority of German forces.

But now the Eleventh Army faced the most difficult challenge of all—the conquest of Sevastopol.

CHAPTER V

THE SIEGE OF SEVASTOPOL

The big, four-engine Condor circled the Simferopol Airport once, then skimmed in for a graceful landing. A staff car arrived shortly thereafter carrying Colonel General Erich von Manstein, Commander of the Eleventh Army, and an aide, Lieutenant Alexander Stahlberg. Stahlberg was carrying a large briefcase containing von Manstein's secret plans for destroying the Soviet forces in the eastern Crimea and the conquest of Sevastopol, the world's strongest fortress.

Von Manstein had been summoned to *Wolfsschanze*, Hitler's secret headquarters in East Prussia, for an audience with the Fuehrer, at which time he would explain his plans and present his requirements for the two-part campaign. Von Manstein had briefly explained his plans to Field Marshal Fedor von Bock, now commander of Army Group South, but approval must be received from Hitler as soon as possible — hence this quick visit to supreme headquarters in mid-April, 1942.

Hitler had advised that he would send his own transport for von Manstein, flown by his personal pilot, and because of the urgency of the situation, the general would be returned to the Crimea without delay. While the Condor was being refueled, von Manstein was introduced to the pilot, *SS-Oberfuehrer* (Senior Colonel) Hans Baur, who discussed the flight plan and then showed von Manstein and Stahlberg through the inside of the impressive aircraft. The plane was fully armed and had been modified for use as a transport from the maritime reconnaissance-bomber version manufactured by the Focke-Wulf Flugzeugbau A.G. of Bremen. The plane was not assigned to the Luftwaffe but was part of Hitler's personal transport squadron, the *Fliegerstaffel des Fuehrers* or *F.d.F.* Most of the pilots in the F.d.F. were former Lufthansa captains, now with commissions in the SS or Waffen-SS. However, the gun turrets were manned by experienced Luftwaffe sergeants trained on the 7.9mm MG 15 and 13mm MG 131 guns.

Focke-Wulf Fw 200C-4/Ul, registration CE+IB, had two passenger compartments, the forward cabin being reserved for Hitler's personal use. Baur invited von Manstein and Stahlberg to ride in this cabin and, with the refueling completed, entered the cockpit and prepared for takeoff. Von Manstein eyed Hitler's large, special armchair, located on the right side of the cabin, but chose to sit in one of the other comfortable seats. The thronelike chair had been specially made for Hitler, and was called the *Fuehrersessel*, or "Leader's armchair." It had 8mm armor built in, and a parachute was fitted into the seat of the chair, with the harness behind the cushion in the chair back. An escape hatch was built into the floor in front of the chair. In case Hitler had to bail out, he would don his parachute, pull a red lever on the wall; the hatch would fall away, and he would roll out and down, deploying the chute manually after clearing the plane. In any case, it never had to be used.[1]

During the flight a steward served meals and drinks from a small galley behind the rear cabin, on fine china and silverware that bore the NSDAP eagle insignia. Once airborne, Stahlberg went to the cockpit and Baur cheerfully explained the intricacies of flying the Condor, which Stahlberg found very interesting. The weather was good and they touched down at the airfield at Rastenburg in early afternoon.

Von Manstein and Stahlberg were met at the plane and taken by staff car to *Wolfsschanze*, where they passed through the check point at the reargate and entered the *Sperrkreis* (restricted area).[2] Driving through the compound, von Manstein observed that the camouflage provided by the dense Goerlitz Forest made the buildings, huts, and bunkers virtually invisible from the air. Every effort had been made to retain the foliage, and trees and vines had been planted in soil placed on the roofs of the bunkers. Roads and large structures were obscured by green and gray camouflage netting. Antiaircraft guns were placed in a few open areas, but no air attacks were ever made on Wolfsschanze.

Wolfsschanze was a self-contained complex complete with water storage reservoirs with pumps because water towers would be too conspicuous. Other facilities included an electrical power generating station, communications center, and a railroad spur. Most support and headquarters offices and barracks were located in the larger *Sperrkreis II*, inside the main compound. Hitler and his personal staff and aides numbering only twenty-one, including *Reichsleiter* (Reichs Leader) Martin Bormann, lived and worked in the smaller and more secure *Sperrkreis I*.

Von Manstein and Stahlberg were driven to Sperrkreis I where they were subjected to a more thorough security check that included examination of the *Soldbuch* of each visitor (the Soldbuch was a booklet carried by every German soldier that served as identification and included his photo and information on his rank, pay status, assignments, and authorized decorations). The driver delivered them directly to a massive concrete building called the *Fuehrerbunker*. The guards at the entrance snapped to attention and presented arms when von Manstein stepped from the vehicle. The general and his aide were escorted to the situation room where the daily military conferences were held at noon and midnight. Von Manstein was greeted cordially by Field Marshal Wilhelm Keitel, Hitler's main advisor, and Chief of the Armed Forces High Command (OKW), and Lieutenant General Alfred Jodl, Chief of the Armed Forces Operations Staff, OKW. Von Manstein and Stahlberg laid out the maps and documents on the long conference table and in a few minutes an orderly shouted "*Achtung!*" to announce the arrival of the Fuehrer.

This was the first time that von Manstein had seen Hitler since he had presented his views to him on the conduct of the offensive against France in February 1940. Von Manstein noted that Hitler seemed extremely well informed on every detail of the battles in the Crimea and listened carefully to the plans and proposals presented to him. Von Manstein was rather surprised and pleased that Hitler agreed with the Eleventh Army's view on the way to prosecute both the Kerch offensive and the eventual assault on Sevastopol. Hitler did not in any way interfere with von Manstein's plans, nor did he begin one of his rambling dissertations as he often did later in the war.[3]

Von Manstein then presented his request for reinforcements and advised that the use of additional heavy artillery, and the VIII Air Corps, would be necessary for the conquest of the fortress of Sevastopol. Hitler agreed and said that he had already ordered the transfer of *60cm "Karl" Moersers* to the Sevastopol front. He mentioned that he had already seen the work of the giant Karl Moersers used against the fortresses at Brest-Litowsk in June 1941, and knew they would be useful in the siege of Sevastopol. Hitler also promised that a new, super-heavy railway gun would be provided. This was a huge 80cm monster called *"Dora"* that Hitler stated was the biggest and most powerful gun ever built.

With this, Hitler shook hands with von Manstein, wished him well, and left the room. Keitel, Jodl, and a couple of staff officers remained to tie up the final details. After that, von Manstein and Stahlberg were returned to the airfield and boarded Hitler's Condor. Hans Baur, who had been resting in his office, returned them to Simferopol in a non-stop flight.

Back in the Crimea, von Manstein directed the final battles that destroyed the Red Army on the Kerch Peninsula and released most of his troops for use in the siege of Sevastopol. Only Command Group 42, with one division, and the Romanian units, remained on the Kerch Peninsula to defend it and the southern coast. Unfortunately for von Manstein, the 22d Panzer Division had to be withdrawn for the summer offensive on the mainland. However, as mentioned previously, the hilly, rocky terrain around Sevastopol did not lend itself to mobile tank operations anyway.

By mid-May, troops were being moved rapidly from the Kerch Peninsula to the Sevastopol front and assault guns, with their fuel and ammunition, and were taking up positions in the northern sector in preparation for the assault. Trainloads of ammunition and large numbers of heavy artillery pieces of all types were reaching the Eleventh Army in the Sevastopol

Col. Gen. Erich von Manstein, Eleventh Army commander (facing camera, second from right), consults with staff officers in a forward command post in the Kerch Peninsula. The officer to Manstein's left is believed to be Lt. Gen. Hans Sinnhuber, commander of the 28th *Jaeger* (light) Division. *German Official Photo*

area along with their experienced gunners. In some areas, roads had to be built in order to position the guns, ammunition, and supplies for the coming offensive.

Airfields in the Crimea were also improved to accommodate Luftwaffe aircraft, crews, support personnel, fuel, equipment, and supplies of bombs. Antiaircraft guns of the Luftwaffe were sent to Sevastopol. The 88mm Flak guns, with their high velocity and flat trajectory, were important additions to the arsenal for use against Soviet fortifications and other fixed positions.

Despite efforts by the Luftwaffe during the preceding months, the Soviet Black Sea Fleet had managed to transport supplies and ammunition, along with thousands of troops, to bring their combat units at Sevastopol up to full strength. By May, however, shipping losses increased to the point where supplies could be brought into Sevastopol harbor only in small, fast boats and submarines.

The latest German intelligence reports available to the Eleventh Army, including air reconnaissance, indicated that the Soviet Coastal Army, as it was referred to at that time, was very strong and well organized. It was commanded by General of the Army Ivan Petrov, and consisted of the 2d, 25th, 95th, 172d, 345th, 386th, and 388th Rifle Divisions, the 40th (dismounted) Cavalry Division, and the 7th, 8th, and 79th Marine Brigades.[4]

The official Soviet history of World War II states that the Sevastopol defense forces of the Independent Coastal Army, later called the First or Independent Maritime Army, included the 25th Chapayev Division, commanded by General T. K. Kolomiyets; the 95th Division under Colonel A. G. Kapitokhin; Colonel P. F. Gorpishchenko's 8th Marine Brigade; and Colonel Y. I. Zhidilov's combined unit of the 7th Marine Brigade. It also says that among the defenders cited for bravery were machine gunner Nina Onilova, sniper Lyudmila Pavlichenko, and scout Maria Baida. The total forces numbered more than 106,000 soldiers with 600 field guns and mortars. Only 38 tanks were said to be operational, most of them obsolete, and 53 aircraft were available.[5] These were no doubt mainly small Po-2 (U-2) biplanes used for training, scouting, and even light bombing, flying from small airstrips or roads. The Soviet history says that most aircraft, including a few fighters, were withdrawn and flown out to the east during the course of the battle.

As stated previously, the most daunting feature of the Soviet defensive system was the hilly, rocky terrain. Von Manstein determined that the northern sector was the least difficult and most accessible. Along the central sector of the perimeter was a dense forest of scrub and thickets growing among the rocks. In the south, rugged mountains formed a major obstacle to a German assault. Soviet permanent and field fortifications, which had been strengthened during the previous months, were arranged in depth. They were built in three main defensive rings that took advantage of the rough terrain, and there was also a long and very formidable antitank ditch. The defensive zone featured 19 modern forts and 3,600 pillboxes. Some artillery was installed in concrete fortifications and others were built into the rocks. A few heavy naval guns in calibers from 15.2cm to 30cm were in steel turrets, similar to those on warships, and now built into the fortifications including Forts Maxim Gorki I and II.

The German forces assembled for the offensive included the LIV Corps in the northern sector, the focal point of the attack, comprising the 22d, 24th, 50th, and 132d Infantry Divisions, commanded by Generals Ludwig Wolff,

Some German troops arrived by rail and air as replacements for casualties. These infantrymen, fresh from the Fatherland, with polished boots, clean uniforms, and full field equipment, were welcome additions to the depleted ranks of German units. *German Official Photo*

Baron Hans von Tettau, Arthur Schmidt, and Gerhard Lindemann, respectively. Each of these experienced officers had been awarded the Knight's Cross of the Iron Cross during the war, and Wolff and Lindemann later won the Oakleaves to the Knight's Cross.[6] A reinforced Infantry regiment, the 213th, was included in the assault force along with some other minor units including the 300th Panzer Abteilung equipped with the miniature unmanned, wire-controlled tanks containing high explosive, called *Goliath, SdKfz* 302.[7]

The XXX Corps was to attack in the south with the 72d and 170th Infantry Divisions and the 28th Light (Jaeger) Division, commanded by Generals Alfred Mueller-Gebhard, Erwin Sander, and Hans Sinnhuber, respectively, all three Knight's Cross winners.

The Romanian Mountain Corps in the center of the perimeter was responsible for pinning down the enemy on its own front. The Corps included the 18th Romanian Division on the left wing of the German LIV Corps and the 1st Romanian Mountain Division to the south where it was intended to support the XXX Corps northern wing.

The Germans had two important advantages in the coming battle for Sevastopol. First, they enjoyed air superiority and the capability for intensive bombing. The second factor in favor of the Germans was their great superiority in artillery, especially heavy artillery. The air units available for the battle included the Luftwaffe's powerful VIII Air Corps, sent into the Crimea by early June to participate in the German assault. Commanded by Colonel General (later Field Marshal) Wolfram Baron von Richthofen, it specialized in close air support. The famous bomber commander, Lieutenant Colonel Werner Baumbach, was dispatched to the Crimea in late May by General Hans Jeschonnek, the Luftwaffe Chief of Staff, to coordinate attacks by medium bomber units with von Richthofen. According to Baumbach, about 400 of von Richthofen's Stuka dive-bombers and fighters were assembled on airfields in the vicinity of Sevastopol with fuel, ordnance, and support personnel.[8]

Air raids had actually been continuing for months, carried out by planes of the IV Air Corps. From time to time heavy attacks were made on the city, harbor facilities, and shipping bringing in reinforcements and supplies for the Soviet defenders. Aerial photography greatly assisted the Luftwaffe and German Army artillery commanders in identifying key targets inside the defensive perimeter.

General von Manstein placed great confidence in the heavy artillery and his commanders, to defeat the strong Soviet fortifications and pave the way for the infantry. With 208 batteries, including the super—guns, the Germans were prepared to conduct a devastating bombardment of the Russian defenses. This assemblage of heavy artillery was probably the greatest concentration of firepower for a single battle in World War II up to that time. The Eleventh Army was also well equipped with self-propelled assault guns, most armed with 7.5cm cannon, so useful in attacks on defended positions. Because of requirements for the summer offensive elsewhere, no tanks were available for the battle. Preparation for the final assault on Sevastopol was a logistical challenge from the beginning, but now the guns were in position, ammunition had been brought up, and preparations were virtually complete.

Herbert Jaeger, the German artillery historian, stated that the following types of artillery were employed during the siege of Sevastopol:[9]

5cm & 8cm Granatwerfer (50mm and 80mm mortars)
7.5cm leichtes Infantriegeschuetz (75mm infantry support gun)
8.8cm Flak (the famous "88"), operated by Luftwaffe personnel
10cm Kanone 18 (100mm divisional field gun Type 18)
10.5cm leichte Feldhaubitze (105mm divisional light howitzer)

15cm schweres Infantriegeschuetz (150mm heavy infantry gun)

15cm schwere Feidhaubitze (deutsch) (150mm German heavy howitzer)

15cm schwere Feldhaubitze (tschechisch) (150mm heavy howitzer of Skoda, Czechoslovakian manufacture)

15cm Kanone 18 (150mm heavy field gun)

19.4 Kanone (franzoesisch) (194mm gun of French manufacture)

21cm Moerser 18 (210mm mortar, Type 18, considered by U.S. Army to be a howitzer if over 210mm)

24cm Haubitze (240mm howitzer)

28cm Kanone/Haubitze (280mm gun-howitzer)

30.5cm Moerser(t)(305mm howitzer of Czech manufacture)

35.5 Moerser M.1 (355mm howitzer M.1)

42cm Moerser (tschechisch) (420mm howitzer of Czech manufacture)

42cm Gamma-Moerser (420mm Gamma-howitzer)

60cm Moerser "Karl" (600mm "Karl" howitzer, on self-propelled carriage)

80cm Kanone (E) "Dora" (800mm "Dora" railway gun)

28cm Raketenwerfer (280mm rocket projector)

32cm Raketenwerfer (320mm rocket projector)

Von Manstein received a top secret teletype from Hitler emphasizing that it was imperative that Sevastopol be captured as soon as possible because Operation Blau, the German summer offensive of 1942, was scheduled to begin on June 28. The VIII Air Corps and other Luftwaffe elements would be required for action in support of the summer offensive.

In late May, Von Manstein had a close call when a small Italian motor torpedo boat in which he was riding on an inspection trip along the south coast was strafed by two Russian fighter planes. He was unhurt, but his longtime aide and driver, Sergeant Fritz Nagel, was killed. Von Manstein, greatly saddened, presided personally at a military funeral for his loyal and devoted comrade.[10]

At this time officers and men from von Manstein's staff, supervised by his chief of staff, Colonel Theodor Busse, established a forward command post in a small Tatar dwelling on a hill by the small village of Yukhary Karales. The general moved in early in June and found that he could observe much of the battlefield through a large observer's telescope. This included the Belbek Valley and northern sector, the Sapun Heights positions, and even the Severnaya Bight. This was one of the few times during World War II that a commander could actually view the battlefield with his own eyes.

By June 1 all was in readiness and von Manstein gave the order to launch the offensive on June 2, beginning with the preliminary artillery barrage before dawn, followed by heavy air attacks. It was now or never for the Eleventh Army, and *Operation Stoerfang* (Sturgeon Haul) was under way!

The boom of heavy artillery again echoed through the hills, and shells of all sizes began falling in and on the Soviet defensive positions. Artillery was under the direction of "*Harko*," the *306. Hoeheres Artillerie Kommandeur.* The two experienced chiefs of artillery were Lieutenant General Johannes Zuckertort, Chief of Artillery for the LIV Corps, and General of Artillery Robert Martinek, Chief of Artillery of the XXX Corps. The intense and sustained bombardment continued day and night for five days, making *Stoerfang* resemble World War I on the Western Front.

Mortars of all calibers also played an important role in the bombardment. Two Moerser (mortar) regiments were on hand, the 1st Heavy Mortar Regiment and the 70th Mortar Reg-

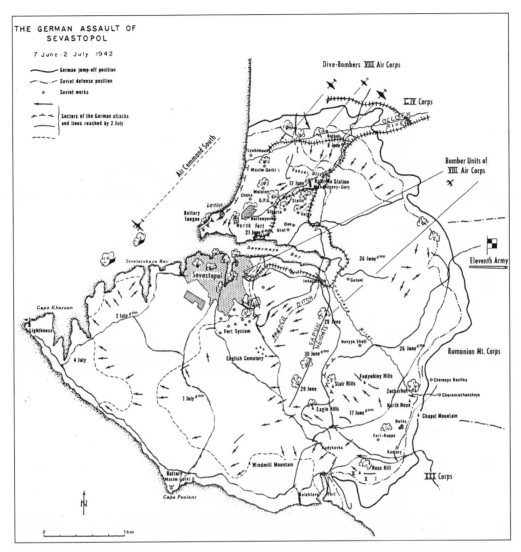

THE GERMAN ASSAULT OF
SEVASTOPOL

7 June–2 July 1942

German jump-off position
Soviet defense position
Soviet works

Sectors of the German attacks
and lines reached by 2 July

Map of the Sevastopol defensive zone showing location of main forts, the principal routes of German advance, and dates lines were reached. *U.S. Air Force*

iment, and the 1st and 4th Mortar Battalions which were concentrated in front of key fortresses. They were under the command of Colonel Niemann, with a total of twenty-one batteries with 576 guns, including the heavy mortars in the 1st Heavy Mortar Regiment.

The continuous rain of shells, bombs, and rockets had a considerable effect on the Russians' morale, as destructive as the shells' physical effects. The constant whooshing of shells and missiles, and the nerve-racking whistle of bombs, combined with the loud detonations, can only be imagined. The explosion of a heavy shell, or several exploding together on a target, often burst the soldiers' blood vessels. Even the men lying a short distance away from the point of impact were demoralized by the deafening noise, flying debris, and paralyzing pressure of the explosions.[11]

A German 21cm *Moerser* 18 at the moment of firing. This howitzer fired a wide range of ammunition and used a carriage similar to the 17cm K18. Maximum range with the standard high-explosive shell weighing 249.17 pounds (113 kg), with charge No. 6, was 18,290 yards (16,725 meters). *From* Infanterie im Osten, *op. cit.*

Other accounts describe the effects of the massive explosions of the huge shells which caused such drastic changes in air pressure, even deep inside the fortifications, that they ruptured eardrums and even the lungs of soldiers far below ground in the concrete chambers and corridors. Terror and fear grew into panic. Only Stukas had been known to produce a similar effect on the usually impassive Russians. On other occasions, the same effect was experienced by German soldiers.[12]

From his observation post high on the hill, von Manstein could plainly see the white flash of explosions from shells and bombs, and the red tracers from antiaircraft and artillery fire. Loud explosions could be heard as big artillery shells and air strikes hit targets over a wide area, but especially in the key northern sector. Soon clouds of smoke and dust rose into the sky from targets struck during the bombardment and from burning buildings in the city. Gradually, the clouds partially obscured the view, but reports from the front constantly kept von Manstein informed.

German gunners were not simply laying down a general barrage, but sought out the enemy forts and emplacements. Shells blasted bunkers and leveled trenches and wire obstacles. Shell after shell struck firing slits and armored cupolas of reinforced concrete gun positions. Von Manstein knew that a conventional preliminary bombardment would be insufficient against Sevastopol's massive defenses. He was well aware of the hundreds of concrete emplacements, the deep belt of pillboxes and bunkers, some built into the rocks and cliff-face, the forts and three defensive lines with 220 miles of trenches, and extensive barbed wire obstacles and minefields. Von Manstein counted on the five days of intensive bombardment by 1,300 guns, and the air attacks, to devastate the Soviet defenses in a hail of steel.

The concentration of German heavy artillery featured several huge cannon that greatly contributed to the capture of Sevastopol. They included three giant 60cm (600mm or 24.2-inch) *Karl Moerser, Geraet 040*. Called a Moerser (mortar) by the Germans, it was referred to as a howitzer in U.S. Army terminology, which classified as mortars only those pieces under 210mm.[13] Transported with its support vehicles and equipment on special railway cars, Karl was an impressive weapon in every way. The gun was mounted facing to the rear on a special self-propelled, tracked chassis and could travel short distances under its own power on reasonably smooth roads or flat ground. Because of its weight, it could not be driven on swampy or rough ground, over tree stumps, or on lightly constructed bridges. The ponderous artillery piece weighed

"This is the 'Thor'! The *Moerser*, like the legendary god that struck with a powerful hammer, thunder and lightning out of the heavens." So says the original caption for this photo of a 60cm Karl self-propelled howitzer crew preparing to load a giant projectile during the siege of Sevastopol in June 1942. *From Artillerie im Osten, op. cit.*

about 120 tons (240,000 kilograms) and fired concrete-penetrating shells called *schwere Betongranaten* that were approximately 8 feet (2.511 meters) long and weighed about 2.4 tons (2,170 kg). Range was 4,000 meters (13,123 feet) or almost 2.5 miles.

Only seven were built, and number VII was used only for testing and development of a similar but longer range 54cm barrel, called Geraet 041. Each Karl-Geraet was given a name from Biblical or Norse mythology. One 60cm piece, with the name "Thor" (the Norse god of war) painted on the side, was photographed at Sevastopol, and Soviet and Western intelligence experts thought that this was the name given to all guns of this type. Each Karl battery was accompanied by a medium Flak battery for protection. Karl Geraet were moved into position only at night, and carefully camouflaged, because their short range required that they be emplaced close to the front line.[14] Additional details are given in Appendix D.

An older but very effective heavy howitzer was the *42cm Gamma-Moerser*. Most sources state that ten of these powerful pieces were constructed for use during World War I from a Krupp design dating back to 1906. It was considered the forerunner of the Krupp 42cm howitzer *"Dicke Berta"* (Big Bertha), named for Frau Berta Krupp, which gained fame during the First World War. After the war, enough parts escaped destruction by the Allied Disarmament Commission to allow a complete gun to be assembled during 1936–37. Gamma was used for ammunition testing until 1942 when it was dismantled and brought to Sevastopol, where it participated in the bombardment.[15]

Gamma weighed a hefty 137.8 tons (140,000 kg) and fired an explosive, concrete-penetrating projectile weighing 2,211 pounds (1,003 kg) to a distance of 46,590 feet (14,200 meters), or about 9 miles. It required a crew of 235 artillerymen to operate and because of its weight, it was very difficult to move and assemble the component parts at the front. Ammunition for big guns like this was hard to transport but, like Karl, the shells from Gamma caused great damage to Soviet concrete and masonry fortifications.

By far the most impressive gun used in the bombardment of Sevastopol was the enormous 80cm (31.5-inch) railway gun called "Dora," the biggest gun ever built.[16] Originally designed in 1937 by the Krupp Works for use against the strongest fortifications of the French Maginot Line, it was not completed until early 1942. Built in secret on Hitler's orders, in cooperation with the *Heereswaffenamt* or *HWaA* (Army Ordnance Office), it was known officially as the *80cm Kanone (E) "Dora,"* (E-Eisenbahn-Railway). It had been referred to earlier as *"Schwerer Gustav,"* the *"Gustav Geraet,"* or the *D-Geraet*. Three of these monsters were ordered, two were built, but only one is known to have been completed and used, during the bombardment of Sevastopol in June 1942.

Dora was a monumental masterpiece of mechanical and metallurgical engineering, but its huge size, weight, and expense, and the logistics and manpower (more than 5,000 men)

Hitler's pride, the monster 80cm Krupp railway gun "Dora," the biggest gun ever built, shelled Sevastopol fortresses with devastating effect. *From OKW*, Die Wehrmacht: Das Buch des Krieges 1941/42 *(Berlin, 1942)*

required for its transportation, erection, and operation made it rather impractical. Nevertheless, Hitler took a personal interest in Dora, as well as the Karl howitzer, and the huge projectiles fired by both guns did cause immense damage to the Russian defenses at Sevastopol.

Dora weighed an incredible 1,170 tons and when ready for action was as high as a two-story building. It therefore required camouflage, a large detachment of antiaircraft artillery, and smoke projectors for protection. With a gun crew of 450 just to operate it, it could fire about three rounds per hour. Because it could not traverse, it fired from a special curved section of double track, which, of course, had to be laid in advance.

Two types of ammunition were developed for Dora: A high-explosive shell weighing 4.8 tons (9,600 lb) or 4,354.4 kg, with a maximum range of 29.2 miles (47,000 meters or about 47 kilometers), and a concrete-penetrating shell of 7.1 tons (14,200 lb), or 6,440.9 kg, with a maximum range of 23.6 miles (38,000 meters or about 38 km). The latter was the biggest artillery shell in the world, but like the gun, not the largest caliber.

Colonel General von Manstein, accompanied by Romanian Marshal Ion Antonescu, were on hand to observe Dora begin its bombardment early on June 5. The main targets were Soviet coastal fortifications and Fort Maxim Gorki, important in the defense of the northern sector. When fired, the sound resembled a thunderclap and could be heard for miles. The shelling of Fort Stalin followed.

Luftwaffe reconnaissance aircraft had found the main Soviet ammunition storage depot, located in a large cave facing the Severnaya Bay, across from Sevastopol's harbor. Bombing was impractical because the armored doors were in the side of the hill and it was out of range of other heavy artillery.

After careful calculation based on aerial reconnaissance, the crew adjusted Dora's position, took aim, and on June 6 began firing on the *Munitionsberg* (Munitions Mountain). The crew managed at this time to reload and fire every 21 to 35 minutes. Rounds 23 through 38 were fired at this target and a giant concrete-piercing shell finally punched through the mountainside and burst in the large chamber containing artillery ammunition. The result was not just a huge explosion, but

Dora at the moment of firing. It was positioned on a curved track in a cut in a small hill north of Sevastopol. Note camouflage screen at left. *U.S. Army Ordnance Museum* more like a volcanic eruption! The gigantic blast was felt and heard for many miles in all directions, especially across the bay in the city of Sevastopol. Anyone at the scene of destruction was killed or injured, and secondary explosions continued for hours. This success was certainly instrumental in causing the defeat of the Red Army in Sevastopol. Firing by Dora continued periodically until June 17, with a total of 48 rounds being lobbed against targets including Forts Siberia, Molotov, and Maxim Gorki II. See Appendix E for additional information.

There was also thunder in the east on the first morning of the offensive as wave after wave of Luftwaffe aircraft took off into the dawn to hammer targets throughout the Soviet defensive perimeter. Bombers from units commanded by Lieutenant Colonel Werner Baumbach joined with aircraft from Colonel General Wolfram Baron von Richthofen's VIII Air Corps for a major effort to destroy key targets and soften up Soviet defenses. Baumbach flew over Sevastopol in his Junkers Ju 88 bomber during the offensive and recounted his impressions in his postwar memoirs:[17]

> In the early morning the sky swarmed with aircraft hurrying to unload their bombs on the town. Thousands of bombs—more than 2,400 tons of high explosive and 23,000 incendiaries—were dropped on the city and fortresses. A single sortie took no longer than twenty minutes. By the time you had gained the necessary altitude you were in the target area. The Luftwaffe flew 1,000, 1,500, and even 2,000 sorties a day.
>
> With all the smoke and dust, amid the roar of the detonations, the battle area is largely invisible to our troops on the ground, though they could see the bombers fly down into the wasps' nest which is the shrinking defense ring. The screaming descent of the Stukas and the whistling of falling bombs seemed to make even nature hold her breath. The storming troops, exposed to the pitiless heat of the burning summer sun, paused for the few seconds which must have seemed an eternity to the defenders.
>
> The Russian Flak was silenced in the first few days so the danger to aircraft was less than in attacks on the Caucasus harbors or Russian airfields. Yet our work at Sevastopol made the highest demands on men and material. Twelve, fourteen and even up to eighteen sorties were made daily by the individual aircrews. It meant tremendous wear and tear for the aircraft and crews, and for the ground staff, those unknown soldiers who could not sleep a wink in those days and nights and were responsible for the safe condition of their machines.
>
> Only when the last Russian soldier had fallen did the end come. Such was Sevastopol, a name spelling something gruesome and horrific to all who were there. Attacker and defender alike fought with a fury which was quite exceptional even for this war.

The VIII Air Corps and other Luftwaffe units, deployed for the operation on airfields mainly north of Sevastopol, included the following:[18]

Two groups, 51st Bomber Wing
Two groups, 76th Bomber Wing
I Group, 100th Bomber Wing
III Group, 1st Air Wing

I, II, III Groups, 77th Dive-
bomber Wing

II, III Groups, 77th Fighter
Wing

III Group, 3d Fighter Wing

3d Squadron, 11th Tactical
Reconnaissance Group

3d Squadron, 13th Tactical
Reconnaissance Group

The main air mission was to continually perform daylight and night bombing attacks against the fortifications and the city of Sevastopol. Since the Luftwaffe had established a clear aerial superiority in the Crimean area, Flak batteries were given ground combat assignments, with the exception of those batteries that were selected

Col. Gen. (later field marshal) Wolfram Baron von Richthofen (left), commander of the VIII Air Corps, explains the air campaign for the siege of Sevastopol to Marshal Ion Antonescu (second from left), and two of his senior Romanian officers. *From* Bessarabien, Ukraine-Krim, *op. cit.*

to protect the super—heavy artillery, including Dora and the Karl guns. Fighter forces were ordered to maintain roving flights over the entire combat area to prevent any hostile air action against German ground or air forces. The few Soviet flyers who, with great courage, went into action in their ground-attack planes were immediately pounced upon by German fighters and sent down in flames.[19]

Luftwaffe Air Command South was assigned the mission outside the area of direct attack to prevent Soviet landings and interdict supply movements by sea along the coastal areas to Sevastopol. Air units attacked and sank a number of Soviet naval and merchant vessels around the Crimean Peninsula.

Final air preparations were made with extreme care. Air support missions were examined in detail by the Eleventh Army, its Corps and divisions, and the Romanian Mountain Corps. On the afternoon of June 1, General von Richthofen gave thorough explanations of the operation to all participating Luftwaffe commanders and assigned missions to the several air units. He advised that good weather was predicted for the next few days

Attacks for the period June 2 to 6 were planned to inflict heavy losses on Soviet forces and to wear down their morale, while those after June 3 were designed to place special emphasis upon the destruction of permanent fortifications, field fortifications, and supply depots. The air operations at Sevastopol constituted one of the heaviest concentrations of aircraft in the eastern theater of operations. The cargoes of death and destruction delivered on Soviet forces, along with the heaviest concentration of massed artillery ever laid down by the Germans in Russia, were no doubt the deciding factor that assured German victory.

From June 2 to 6, the VIII Air Corps committed the following number of aircraft in combat: 723 on June 2, 643 on June 3, 585 on June 4, 555 on June 5, and 563 on June 6. These planes delivered 2,264 tons of explosives and 23,800 incendiary bombs on targets in the Sevastopol area. The core of the fortress was attacked with good success by bombs of all sizes. In one case, the 77th Dive-bomber Wing cut off the city water supply by destroying pumping installations, water reservoirs, and the electric power station. Oil depots on the shore of Severnaya

A Heinkel He IIIH bomber carrying an SB 2500 H.E. semi-armor-piercing fragmentation bomb, the largest bomb in the Luftwaffe inventory. Many of these bombs were dropped on Sevastopol targets during the siege. Of steel construction and weighing about 5,375 pounds (2,400 kg), it was similar to the SC 2500 "Max" which had an aluminum body. Both types had to be carried on external racks because they were too large for the bomb bay. *Smithsonian Photo*

Bay were also set aflame. At the same time, thousands of propaganda leaflets were dropped upon the Russian defenders to shake their spirits and morale.[20]

After five days of intensive bombardment, von Manstein ordered the ground assault to begin. At 3:00 A.M. on June 7, 1942, infantry and combat engineers attacked at points along the front behind an especially heavy, rolling artillery barrage and fierce air strikes.

In the south, the XXX Corps seized points of departure for further attacks and soon, in a surprise drive, pushed on to the foot of the Sapun Heights, a key to the entire central and southern areas. The Romanian units on the central sector also made probing attacks under a heavy artillery barrage to tie down their opponents.

As planned, the main thrust came in the northern sector. Men of the LIV Corps stormed forward against the Russian outpost lines on the south bank of the Belbek River. Infantry and engineers pressed ahead across broken ground shrouded by a dense smoke screen. Many soldiers followed behind assault guns, which fired their 7.5cm cannon at point-blank range to blast trenches, pillboxes, and fixed fortifications. Despite the German barrage, Russian fire, land mines, and barbed wire obstacles took their toll on the attackers.

Flammenwerfer (flamethrowers), a German invention in World War I, fired streams of liquid fire against enemy strongpoints. *Geballte Ladungen* (concentrated explosive charges) blew open entrances to pillboxes and bunkers. *Hindernißsprengroehre* (Bangalore Torpedoes) were used to blast paths through wire entanglements.

In attacking forts and large bunkers, the Germans knew it was a big advantage if engineers could get on top where they could blow open the vents and drop hand grenades and demolition charges down the pipes to explode inside the forts. Such blasts inside the rooms and corridors not only had fragmentation effect but caused tremendous concussion. Some soldiers also died of suffocation when their air supply was cut off. If concrete embrasures could not be blasted from a distance, the men on top of the fort could lower demolition charges attached to poles down the outside that could be exploded directly on the openings.[21] A Bangalore Torpedo was a metal tube or pipe charged with high explosive that was not only useful for cutting breaches in wire entanglements, but was also effective when shoved down the barrel of a cannon or into a firing aperture. Any stunned Russian soldiers who staggered out carrying weapons were gunned down in their tracks. Fanatical Communist Political Commissars often shot any of their soldiers who refused to fight to the death.

The going was slow and costly but the assaults were coordinated with the artillery and air support so that the full fury of the bombardment could be shifted from one target area to another. On June 13, Fort Stalin was captured after a fierce battle by soldiers of Infantry Regiment 16, 22d Division, under command of Colonel von Choltitz. By June 17, German and Romanian troops storming Fort Siberia had occupied this important strongpoint in the defensive perimeter.

By June 17, the troops of the LIV Corps could see Severnaya Bay and by June 26, the determined and continuous attack had won control of the entire fortified area north of the bay and the Gajtani Heights. At the same time both Corps were sup-

The flamethrower was a fearsome weapon often used against concrete fortifications. Although fire was used in warfare in ancient times, the modern portable flamethrower was introduced by the Germans in World War I and added a new dimension of horror. The *Flammenwerfer* 35 in this photo was widely used, including at Sevastopol; it was eventually replaced by the lighter ring-shaped models 40 and 41. *From Eduard Amphlett*, Zeitgeschehen im Farben *(Leipzig, 1943)*

ported on their interior flanks by attacks by the Romanian Mountain Corps under command of Brigadier General Lascar, winner of the Knight's Cross and Oakleaves, who later died at Stalingrad. Among the strongly defended forts taken by direct assault in the northern sector were "Gepen," "Molotov," "Checka," "Volga," "Donetz," and "Urals." These fortresses were taken in storm during battles marked by almost superhuman tenacity and heroism on both sides. The names for the forts around Sevastopol were actually code names given them by the Germans in the fall of 1941.

Fort Maxim Gorki I was one of the key forts in the northern defense sector, where the only good road and railroad led south to Sevastopol. Although not typical of most of the other forts, it deserves a more detailed description. Soviet batteries 30 and 35, both completed in 1933–34, were named Maxim Gorki I and Maxim Gorki II by the Germans. Maxim Gorki I was located about 3.1 miles (5 km) north of Severnaya Bay. Maxim Gorki II was situated on the Chersones Peninsula (sometimes spelled as Khersones or Cape Gersones), 6.2 miles (10 km) southwest of the city.

Although originally intended for coast defense, the two twin-gun turrets could traverse 360 degrees and were used to fire on targets inland during the German assaults. Both forts were extensive in size, had several stories underground, and were among the most modern in the world at that time. The four guns in the two large armored turrets were old 30.5cm M1910–14 cannon originally designed before World War I for use on battleships. Fort Maxim Gorki I consisted basically of a reinforced concrete fort on a hill with the two gun turrets.

Walls were several meters thick. This position, called the *Batterieblock* by the Germans, was connected by an underground concrete tunnel, 1,950 feet (600 meters) long, to the fire direction bunker called the *Feuerleit-und Funkstand* or "Bastion." It was also built of concrete to withstand bombs and shell fire from heavy guns.

Each of the two turrets had an underground command post, communications room, four ammunition storage rooms, and a power generator room. The steel doors featured a gas lock and the two turrets could operate independently. An elevator carried personnel down to the tunnel to the fire control bunker and other underground chambers. Shells were brought up to the gun turrets on a gravity conveyor through an armored hatch in the wall. The powder charges had their own conveyor system since the guns did not use fixed ammunition. Both were brought up to the guns by a hoist. Facilities deep under the Battery Block included a furnace for heating, quarters for the garrison, kitchen, latrines, workshops, storage rooms, and a main power plant. This section was about 495 by 1,148 feet (150 by 350 meters) in size. The entire area outside on the surface was protected by trenches, armed bunkers, barbed wire entanglements, machine gun and mortar positions, and plenty of land mines.

Fort Maxim Gorki I was commanded by a Major Alexander. It first saw action on October 30, 1941, during the initial German advance, and its heavy guns with their long range continued to take a toll on the Germans, especially in the Belbek Valley. During the first German assault, between December 18 and 31, the 305mm guns helped stall the German offensive. For months thereafter, the fire from this fort harassed German supply lines and troop concentrations outside the defensive perimeter.

The second assault on Sevastopol, *Unternehmung Stoerfang*, began with the heavy German bombardment on June 2, 1942, and Fort Maxim Gorki I was a main target. Shells began falling almost immediately from two big German 30.5cm M1 moerser (howitzers), two 60cm self-propelled Karl howitzers, named *Thor* and *Odin*, and the mighty 80cm Dora railway gun. It is estimated that a total of 750 shells rained down on the battery during the siege. A shell from one of the Karl guns struck the western turret on June 6, wrecking one of the 30.5cm guns and putting the other gun out of action.

When the ground assault by the German LIV Corps began on June 7, infantry from the 132d Division had the Maxim Gorki I fort as their main objective. The going was slow and costly because of the strong Soviet defenses, and the first attack on the Bastion on June 11 was repulsed with severe losses. Several more ground attacks were made and finally, on June 17, Infantry Regiment 213, detached from the 73d Division, managed to break

On June 17, 1942, Fort Maxim Gorki I, the main Soviet defensive work in the northern sector, was taken by storm after a heavy bombardment. Here German *Sturmpioniere* (combat engineers) attack a bunker in this strongest and most modern of the Sevastopol forts. *German Official* into the Bastion itself. A combat engineer company set to work blowing up the reinforced concrete fortification with massive explosive charges but soon found that they were in the midst of a Soviet counterattack. The men of the 213th Regiment and the engineers fought a pitched battle and succeeded in driving off the Russian infantry.

The final assault on the other, western end of the fort, with the two massive gun turrets, began with a heavy artillery barrage and attacks by Stuka dive-bombers. A bomb from a Stuka made a direct hit on the eastern turret, knocking out both 30.5cm guns. Then, a 60cm shell from a Karl howitzer struck the western turret, knocking out one gun. The artillery bombardment included five 80cm rounds from Dora that also did severe damage to the fortifications. The infantry and engineers then worked their way through the smoke and dust from the Bastion toward the turret section, despite heavy fire from machine guns and mortars. While the infantry laid down covering fire, the engineers, on their hands and knees, scrambled forward, sheltering in bomb and shell craters. When they were close enough, they threw explosive charges and hand grenades into the openings made in the turrets by the bombardment to kill or drive the defenders underground. They then knocked out the last serviceable gun in the western turret with explosives.

The German after-action report stated that 700 rounds had been fired from the Soviet 30.5cm cannon during the period of the assault. It also said that German losses had been heavy, with almost two thirds of the attackers killed or wounded, but the fort was considered neutralized on June 18.

The Germans had now destroyed the heavy guns and controlled the fortifications and bunkers on the surface; however, the Soviet garrison in the tunnels and chambers below refused the German demand to surrender. The commander of the engineer company did not have plans showing the underground facilities and with

One of the 30.5cm gun turrets of Fort Maxim Gorki I, wrecked in the bombardment by giant German guns during the siege of Sevastopol. Although no *Waffen–SS* troops fought in the Crimea, the label on the back of this official German photo says it was taken by *SS–Kriegsberichter* (SS war correspondent) Gayk. *German Official Photo*

so few men left that were *"K.v." (Kriegsverwendungsfaehig)*, fit for active service, he decided to try to force out or kill the Russians with fire. During the night gasoline was obtained and the next morning a hole was blasted under the western turret and the fuel poured in and ignited with a flare from a 27mm signal pistol. The resulting fire set off powder charges for the cannon and caused a huge explosion and conflagration in the ammunition rooms and stairwell. As the smoke billowed out, two burned and soot-covered Russians staggered out and surrendered. They said their comrades also wanted to give up but were prevented under threat of death by their political commissars.

More fuel and explosive charges were dropped into the underground complex and finally, when a Russian holding a white flag appeared, the defenders were again promised safe conduct. Slowly 117 Russian soldiers and two officers emerged, many wounded or burned, and all blackened and choking from smoke. The Germans learned from the prisoners that over a hundred other Russians were still below, including the major, several officers, and a commissar, about half of them dead or wounded. Oddly enough, the interior lighting system was still functioning as was the telephone connection to Soviet headquarters in Sevastopol.

While the Germans were preparing large demolition charges and more fuel to blast and burn out the remainder of the garrison, the Soviets set off an explosion of their own deep below the western turret, which detonated the German explosives and fuel, killing and injuring an engineer officer and three men. A large charge under the eastern turret was then exploded by the Germans as planned causing a huge fire and a tremendous amount of smoke. Over the next few days small numbers of Russians surrendered from the burning, smoke-filled interior, with the last hold-outs taken prisoner on June 26. According to a German report, Major Alexander was caught trying to escape in civilian clothes with weapons hidden under a coat, and after interrogation was shot.

Soldiers of the German Eleventh Army had to fight for every kilometer of the extensive fortified area around the city and port of Sevastopol, defended tenaciously by the tough veterans of the Red Army. *German Official Photo*

Most forts had to be completely cleared of defenders during the advance to prevent attacks from the rear, and this necessitated entering the dark passages and chambers, some far underground. The assault on each fort depended on the layout of the fort and the number of defenders. The following account is more or less typical of the events during the storming of one of the large forts:

Once the German engineer storm detachments had blasted their way inside the fort, small squads worked their way through the smoky tunnels, scrambling over heaps of bloody corpses, often firing wildly at their desperate foes who were shooting with machine guns from interior firing ports. The rattle of small arms fire and the explosion of hand grenades was deafening in the confined areas, where soldiers often struggled with bayonets, knives, and rifle butts in hand-to-hand combat. Sparks flew as bullets ricocheted off concrete walls and ceilings, some splattered with gore, flinging jagged fragments to rip flesh and bone.

German combat engineers carrying portable flame throwers crept forward, projecting streams of searing fire and clouds of black, oily smoke into rooms defended by Russian soldiers, often led by fanatical commissars, determined to fight to the last man. Illuminated by dancing flames, and reeking with the stench of gunpowder and burning flesh, the battles in the bowels of the fortresses assumed hellish proportions. In this terrifying "Dante's Inferno," the shrieks of men and occasionally women being burned alive unnerved even some of the most battle-hardened German combat veterans. The stress of close combat haunted some soldiers even years later.

German soldiers finish off Soviet defenders in a trench on the Sapun Heights who were holding up the advance. *From* Bessarabien, Ukraine-Krim, *op. cit.*

Once across the Belbek Valley and the formidable antitank ditch, the Germans managed to fight on south through the deeply echeloned defensive system. Infantry, supported by assault guns, picked their way through the barbed wire and seemingly endless trenches and pill boxes, usually under cover of smoke. The Soviets were far from defeated and continued to launch violent counterattacks, supported by artillery fire. The endurance of German troops was visibly diminishing and it was found necessary to take the depleted 132d Infantry Division temporarily out of the line and exchange it with the 46th Infantry Division in the Kerch Peninsula. Its place was taken in turn by the 24th Infantry Division, which had to be released from the left wing of the corps for this purpose. At the same time, Eleventh Army headquarters was under pressure from OKH, the Army High Command, to release the VIII Air Corps for use in the offensive in the Ukraine. Von Manstein managed to convince higher headquarters that the VIII Air Corps was vital to the success of the battle, which was still hanging in the balance.[22]

Great clouds of smoke and dust hung over the northern sector where all available artillery was now concentrated to assist the 24th Division in capturing the forts on the peninsula to the west, dominating the entrance to Severnaya Bay. On June 20, Fort Lenin was taken after violent fighting. Every meter of ground was fiercely contested by the defenders who still had plenty of artillery and even some tanks, mainly type T-26. Field hospitals were kept busy around the clock caring for wounded German, Romanian, and Russian soldiers. Eventually Fort Nord (North) fell, an old but still quite formidable obstacle to the advance.

An aerial view of Sevastopol from the north. The city and harbor are in the upper right-center of the photo, across Severnaya Bay. *From* Bessarabien, Ukraine–Krim, *op. cit.*

Morale rose when the men of the 22d Division, in hard fighting, finally gained control of the cliffs overlooking Severnaya Bay. This was the north shore, and the situation was further complicated when the Soviets launched a strong, surprise counterattack with a brigade that had recently arrived at night aboard a cruiser. The 22d Infantry Division was commanded by Knight's Cross winner Lieutenant General Ludwig Wolff. Meanwhile, the 50th Division managed to fight through an area of thick underbrush to reach the eastern end of Severnaya Bay and gain possession of the heights dominating the mouth of the Chornaya Valley. The north shore of Severnaya Bay was now under German control.

By the morning of June 26, with almost the entire outer belt of fortresses in German hands, the Soviets found themselves pushed back into the inner fortified zone, whose northern front was formed by the precipitous rock-face of Severnaya Bay's southern shore and whose eastern front ran from the heights of Inkerman along the steep Sapun Heights to the cliffs in the south around Balaclava. Balaclava had been the scene of the great battle during the first Crimean War in 1854–56. Von Manstein and the Eleventh Army now had to decide how to break through the inner ring of fortifications and defeat the Soviets once and for all. The Russians had suffered heavy casualties but so had the Germans, and the troops on both sides, fighting for almost three weeks in the stifling summer heat, were almost exhausted. Dead bodies, lying out in the baking sun, were soon bloated and crawling with maggots. Swarms of flies made the gruesome job of disposing of the corpses almost unbearable. Hot as it was, burial details often donned gas masks in an attempt to escape the nauseating stench.

During a visit to a 22d Division observation post on the northern shore of Severnaya Bay, it occurred to von Manstein that if a strong German force could get across the bay in assault boats, they could take the Soviets from the flank and unhinge the strong Sapun defenses blocking an advance from the east. He could see that the south shore was a wall of high cliffs honeycombed with enemy positions, and this would surely be the last direction from which the Soviets would expect a major German attack. Members of von Manstein's staff and some commanders he consulted expressed doubts about staking everything on such a move, one that would depend on absolute surprise. But under the circumstances this seemed to be the only way to bring about a speedy decision. Accordingly, immediate efforts were made to secretly bring up every available assault boat and to position the artillery for supporting fire. During the assault across the bay, the XXX Corps and the Romanians had to simulate an attack by means of artillery fire on the broad front south along the Sapun Heights, then suddenly break into the position on the heights on a small front with heavy artillery and air support. Tension ran high as the urgent preparations proceeded.

The night of June 28–29 was dark and at 1:00 A.M., the first wave of two divisions of the LIV Corps jumped off from the north shore of Severnaya Bay. A hundred boats sped across the dark waters, about a half a mile wide, with all guns silent.

Every available assault boat was pressed into use on the night of 28–29 June to transport German troops across Severnaya Bay to assault the south shore. This daring and risky surprise attack succeeded, and hastened the defeat of the Soviets in their inner defensive zone. The boats in this photo are the *Sturmboot* 39, powered by a large outboard motor. *German Official Photo*

The noise of the outboard motors was masked by heavy bombing raids on the city by planes of the VIII Air Corps. Every piece of artillery was ready to blast the south shore as soon as the assault boats were discovered and came under fire. Much to their relief, all was quiet. The risky crossing was successfully accomplished before the Russians realized what was happening. The Germans were ashore and immediately clearing the surprised Russians from their positions with amazing spirit and resourcefulness.[23]

At dawn, the left wing of the Corps attacked the cliffs of Inkerman and soon captured key positions. Dive-bombers hurtled down into the steep valleys; their flaming explosions rose into the air together with mushroom-like smoke clouds and the sounds of detonations. As the German infantry reached the foot of the cliff, the entire face of the hill exploded. The great caverns in the cliffs, formerly used as champagne cellars, but now loaded with ammunition and wounded Russians, as well as civilian refugees, had been blown up by fanatical Soviet Commissars.[24]

Meanwhile, to the south, at first light, the XXX Corps began their assault against positions on the Sapun Heights. Dive-bombers aided the infantry in capturing an area on the crest, and this was rapidly expanded by troops which threatened to cut off and surround the enemy positions along the front. The Soviets were forced to give up these strong defensive positions and begin a fighting retreat westward into the city and towards the fortifications that cut off the Chersones Peninsula. The 22d Division then broke through, taking the old English Cemetery dating from the original Crimean War. Fresh corpses lay upon the graves from 1854, blasted open by artillery. In the far south the 4th Romanian Mountain Division attacked the Balaclava positions from the rear, capturing 10,000 Russians. The capture of the Sapun Heights also allowed the Germans to lay massive artillery fire on Soviet inner fortifications. Events were now moving rapidly.

On July 1, German infantry, supported by heavy artillery fire and air support, fought their way through defenses on the outskirts and entered the city of Sevastopol, devastated by shelling and a fresh bombing attack. The enemy had evacuated the town during the night but the battle was not yet ended. Stalin had ordered his forces to fight to the last, and the Marshal's orders must be obeyed! The Russians also hoped that at least some of their troops would be evacuated by the Black Sea Fleet from the many deep inlets along the Chersones Peninsula to the west of the city. By noon, the Germans had raised the *Reichskriegsflagge* from the top of a surviving building in the still-smoking city of Sevastopol. There was little satisfaction, as many soldiers now wore gas masks to offset the nauseating reek of bodies rotting in the summer heat.

The harbor of Sevastopol fell into German hands on July 1, 1942, along with the burning city, both devastated by shelling, bombing, and Soviet "scorched earth" destruction. This photo shows the dock area with a wrecked crane and burned-out warehouses. *German Official Photo*

According to the World Almanac of World War II, it is estimated that there were approximately 20 million military and civilian deaths in the Soviet Union between 1941 and 1945. At least twice as many were injured or became ill during the war. When the guns finally fell silent in Sevastopol, hungry and dazed civilians began creeping fearfully out of basements and bomb shelters looking for food and water. The "Hitlerites" had been demonized by Soviet propaganda for a year and the survivors of the siege were greatly relieved when the massacre they were warned about did not occur. Soviet authorities had required civilians in the Sevastopol area to help with the defensive preparations, including digging trenches and gun emplacements, and unloading and transporting supplies and ammunition. Many civilians were even provided with rifles and encouraged to fight.

While the Germans rounded up captured military personnel and marched them off to POW camps, most civilians were searched for weapons and released. Some were soon put to work burying the dead, clearing rubble from the streets, repairing roads, and helping to restore utilities damaged during the siege. A civil administration was established by the German Army within days of the final surrender and included some Russian non-communist civilian advisors and officials.

With the realization that victory was finally within their grasp, the weary Germans summoned their last strength and assaulted the defenses of the Chersones Peninsula in a final push. This pressed the desperately resisting soldiers of the Soviet Coastal Army toward the western cliffs along the Black Sea. Some Russians tried to break through German lines and escape to the hills in the south where they could possibly join with partisans in the Yaila Mountains. The final stand for the Russians was made in large caverns and ravines along the steep banks of the Chersones Peninsula, where they waited in vain for an evacuation that never came. The Luftwaffe at that time was still operating in such strength that it also dominated the sea approaches to Sevastopol. Only General Petrov and a few top commanders escaped by motor-

Fort Konstantinovsky, at the entrance to Severnaya Bay, was damaged in German bombing raids. *From* Bessarabien, Ukraine-Krim, *op. cit.*

torpedo boat. Some commanders and commissars were evacuated by air under cover of darkness.[25]

The last of the major forts to fall was the armor-plated Fort Maxim Gorki II in the far south, on Cape Folient, which was defended by several thousand Russians, including women. The garrison apparently expected to be evacuated by sea. Maxim Gorki II was the strongest and most modern fort in the whole Sevastopol complex. The Germans gave the defenders an ultimatum to surrender and those who refused were buried alive by the Eleventh Army engineers as they demolished the fort and its underground galleries.[26]

At last, after the final firefights on July 4, the weary and hungry Russian soldiers began to emerge from their isolated positions on the rugged Chersones Peninsula and surrender in large numbers. The final count by dusk on July 4 included 30,000 prisoners on the peninsula and a total of 97,000 prisoners throughout the fortress area. The number of Russian dead has never been determined, but was considerably more than the Germans. The Wehrmacht officially claimed the loss of 23,000 of their own troops and 2,500 Romanians. With the guns silent at last, the grim task of the burial parties was resumed. The bodies of many Russians could not be collected and interred because of land mines, booby traps (*Sprengfalle*) and unexploded ordnance. A huge number of Soviet weapons and equipment were destroyed and captured, including 622 guns and 26 tanks.[27] To accomplish this, according to a German report, 562,944 artillery rounds were fired at Sevastopol between June 2 and July 1, 1942.

During the entire offensive, the Luftwaffe flew a total of 23,751 sorties and dropped 20,528.9 tons of bombs. At and around Sevastopol, German air units destroyed a total of 123 Soviet aircraft in the air and 18 on the ground. German air attacks also destroyed 611 motor vehicles, 10 tanks, and 38 guns; silenced 48 artillery batteries; damaged or destroyed 28 barracks and industrial works; detonated 11 ammunition dumps and 10 oil depots; and heavily damaged 2 destroyers, 10 coastal vessels, and 2 cargo ships totaling 12,000 tons. Vessels sunk by German air units included 4 destroyers, 1 submarine, 3 E-boats, 6 coastal ships, and 4 cargo vessels with a total gross register tonnage of 10,800 tons.[28]

German aircraft losses from all causes totaled only 31 planes.

As the smoke cleared from the Sevastopol area, von Manstein could pause and reflect on the great victory achieved by the Eleventh Army. His army had an overall ration strength of about 200,000 men and 70,000 horses. Yet they had destroyed four Soviet armies and conquered the entire Crimea, including Sevastopol, the world's strongest fortress. Von Manstein modestly attributed the victory to the bravery and superior efficiency of the German soldier and the initiative of the leaders and men.[29]

A special German radio communiqué was broadcast, preceded by a triumphal fanfare, announcing the capture of Sevastopol. Shortly thereafter the following message was received by von Manstein over the teletype:[30]

To the Commander-in-Chief of the Crimean Army

Colonel-General v. Manstein

In grateful appreciation of your exceptionally meritorious services in the victorious battles of the Crimea, culminating in the annihilation of the enemy at Kerch and the conquest of the mighty fortress of Sevastopol, I hereby promote you Field Marshal. By your promotion and the creation of a commemorative shield to be worn by all ranks who took part in the Crimean campaign, I pay tribute before the whole German people to the heroic achievements of the troops fighting under your command.

Adolf Hitler

Von Manstein's promotion to the rank of General Field Marshal was effective July 1, 1942. The *Krimschild* (Crimean Shield) authorized by Hitler was classified as a *Waffenabzeichen der Wehrmacht* (Armed Forces Badge), and was awarded to all members of the armed forces, including personnel of the *Ordnungspolizei* (Order Police), who fought in the Crimea between September 21, 1941, and July 4, 1942. It was a bronze metal badge with an outline of the

The guns fell silent on July 4, 1942, and the siege of Sevastopol was finally at an end. While the generals celebrated, a weary German army private takes time out for a meal and a welcome rest. *German Official Photo*

Crimea and its name *Krim*, a German eagle, and "1941, 1942." Officially instituted on July 25, 1942, it was worn on a cloth backing in the color of the uniform on the left sleeve below the shoulder. It was one of only five similar devices officially awarded; the others were for *Narvik* (Norway, 1940), *Cholm* and *Demyansk*, in the Soviet Union (1942), and also for the *Kuban* (1943). Another shield, for Warsaw (1944), was instituted on December 10, 1944, but never produced because an air raid destroyed the dies.[31]

The great victory was celebrated on July 5 by a parade of German and Romanian troops in the city of Sevastopol. General Field Marshal von Manstein and Marshal Ion Antonescu of Romania proudly took the salute. A special celebration was held for the corps, division, and regimental commanders and bearers of the Knight's Cross of the Iron Cross and the German Cross in Gold. Decorations were also presented, and von Manstein gave a short speech in which he thanked all members of his command. Within days, King Michael of Romania and a large contingent of foreign military attachés and officials from neutral and friendly countries visited Sevastopol and toured the battle areas.

The following afternoon, von Manstein had Sergeant Schumann drive him to the German military cemetery near Simferopol, constructed after the first assault on the fortress city the previous December. Here were interred thousands of German soldiers collected across the "deathscape" of the Crimea.

Great thunderheads were building in the summer heat and cloud shadows danced across the rows of freshly dug graves. Von Manstein paused and quietly contemplated the many wooden grave markers, each cut with a top section painted to form a large iron cross on which was painted the name and rank of the deceased. Thousands of young German, Romanian, and Russian soldiers had bravely sacrificed their lives for their countries and, although a patriot and a professional soldier, he could not help but ponder this latest grim example of man's inhumanity to man. Von Manstein raised his hand to his cap in a final, heartfelt farewell to his troops who must forever remain behind, and slowly walked back to the staff car.[32]

Von Manstein soon went on leave in Romania while the troops of the Eleventh Army were enjoying a good rest after the months of extreme exertion and savage combat. There was also plenty of cleaning and servicing of equipment to be done. Everyone expected to participate in Operation Blau, the German summer offensive of 1942, by crossing the Straits of Kerch and advancing southeast along the southern wing towards the Caucasus oil fields.

When von Manstein returned to his headquarters on August 12, he was surprised and perturbed to receive a new directive from the Fuehrer's supreme headquarters which in effect split up the Eleventh Army. Only the Headquarters, XXXXII Infantry Corps, as it was now designated, with the 46th Infantry Division, and certain Romanian units, were to cross the straits. The 50th Infantry Division was to remain in the Crimea and the 22d Division was to be sent to Crete

Parade of the victors in Sevastopol on July 5, 1942. Field Marshal Erich von Manstein and Romanian Marshal Ion Antonescu reviewed the German and Romanian troops as they marched past the reviewing stand in downtown Sevastopol. *From* Bessarabien, Ukraine-Krim, *op. cit.*

in the Mediterranean. The bulk of the Eleventh Army was directed to move to the northern front for assignment to Army Group North and participate in the attack on Leningrad. This was a sad day for von Manstein and his loyal soldiers, and although he vigorously complained, the decision of the Fuehrer was to be obeyed.[33]

As for the men of the XXXXII Infantry Corps and their Romanian ally, they began the long march to the east across the seemingly endless steppe, through dust and danger, to meet their destiny in a city on the Volga called Stalingrad.

EPILOGUE

IT WAS OBVIOUS during the early months of Barbarossa, the German invasion of the Soviet Union in 1941, that the Crimean Peninsula must be conquered and with it the fortress city of Sevastopol, the main Russian naval and air base on the Black Sea. The Crimea constituted a permanent and dangerous threat to the southern flank of the German Eastern Front, as the Wehrmacht pushed east across southern Russia, toward Stalingrad and the vital oil fields of the Caucasus region.

The Soviets had developed Sevastopol into the strongest military and naval fortress in the world. Possession of the port by the Germans not only denied the Russian Black Sea Fleet its main base, but also eliminated the airfields that could be used by the Soviet Air Force for attacking the Romanian oil fields, so vital to the Reichs's conduct of the war.

By the spring of 1942, the city of Sevastopol, like Stalingrad a few months later, had become a symbol of determination and will power on the part of both the Russian defenders and the German attackers. The conquest of the Crimea was a difficult and costly campaign and the siege of Sevastopol proved to be a Herculean task that was one of the most challenging battles waged by the Germans in World War II. The Germans demonstrated bravery and skill in the attack, and despite an increasingly hopeless situation, the Russian defenders fought to the end with remarkable courage and tenacity. The fortress city was conquered only through outstanding leadership and exemplary cooperation between German and Romanian forces, and between ground and air arms.

With the entire Crimean Peninsula, with all its strategic importance, now under German control, the Soviet threat had been eliminated. The Eleventh Army and units of the Luftwaffe were now available for use in the German 1942 summer offensive, Hitler's last chance to defeat the Soviet Union.

What basic facts and conclusions can we draw from a study of Barbarossa or the Crimean campaign?

In retrospect, Germany's defeat in Russia may now appear to have been inevitable, but Barbarossa wiped out most of Russia's original armies and the margin by which the Soviet Union survived was desperately narrow. If Hitler's invasion had been better prepared, with mechanized resources superior to those he had available, and stronger reserves, he might have triumphed by the fall of 1941, or even in 1942. When Hitler launched his great gamble he counted on a superiority of quality—he believed that his generals and troops would enjoy a decisive advantage in skill and organization, benefiting from the experience they had gained in practicing the new Blitzkrieg tactics against Poland, France, and Yugoslavia. Second, Hitler believed that a quick defeat of the Red Army would produce a political upheaval in the Soviet Union and the collapse of Stalin's brutal regime.

Although the reasons that prompted Hitler to invade the Soviet Union in the first place and his conduct of the war are well documented, they are still matters of considerable controversy. It is obvious that Germany was never prepared to fight a war of attrition. Hitler greatly underestimated the strength and will of the Russians, while overestimating his abilities as a supreme commander and the strength of the Wehrmacht.

When the Blitzkrieg failed to destroy the Red Army in the first five months of Barbarossa, and the Soviets managed to withdraw major forces into the vast interior, the Germans had basically lost the war. With no strategic bombers capable of attacking the Russian war industries in the Urals, the prodigious Soviet production, coupled with massive lend-lease aid from the United States and Great Britain, backed by vast Russian manpower reserves, inevitably overwhelmed the Wehrmacht, also heavily committed on other fronts. But this fatal combination of factors was not apparent to Hitler in the victorious summer of 1941. By 1942, the Wehrmacht was significantly weaker because of the losses sustained during the winter, while the Red Army was quickly growing in strength and capability. The German conquest of the Crimea and Sevastopol proved again the Wehrmacht's capability. It was the last major German victory of World War II. Stalingrad and El Alamein in Egypt proved to be the high water mark of Axis conquest. From there on it was downhill for Germany all the way.

On April 10, 1944, the advancing Soviets recaptured Odessa and Field Marshal Ewald von Kleist's Army Group A retreated across the Dniester River into Romania. Worse was to follow for the Germans; on April 11, Lieutenant General F. I. Tolbukhin opened a powerful assault on the Perekop Isthmus and his forces soon broke through the weak German defenses and swept into the Crimea. The remnants of the German and Romanian divisions in the Crimean Peninsula were driven into Sevastopol. The fortress city itself fell to the Soviets on May 9, and though some troops were evacuated by sea, the Axis allies lost thirty thousand prisoners to the Red Army. "Yet another army had been sacrificed to Hitler's strategy of 'holding firm at all costs.'"[1]

Fierce battles would continue on all fronts for another year—in Italy and Normandy as well as Russia, and in the skies over Europe. It took the combined strength of most of the world's major powers to force Germany's ignominious surrender on May 8, 1945, bringing to an end at last Adolf Hitler's Third Reich and his demonic dreams of conquest.

GENERAL FIELD MARSHAL ERICH VON MANSTEIN
"The Victor of Sevastopol"

Erich von Manstein is recognized by most military leaders and historians of World War II as one of Germany's most brilliant and capable commanders. Called "The Allies' most formidable opponent" by British military historian Sir B. H. Liddell Hart, von Manstein gained many laurels during his long and distinguished career.

Born Fritz Erich von Lewinski in Berlin on November 24, 1887, he was the tenth child of General of Artillery Eduard von Lewinski, a member of an old and aristocratic Prussian military family.[2] He was adopted after his christening by Lieutenant General Georg von Manstein and his wife, who had no children of their own. His foster mother was his mother's younger sister, and he eventually took the name Fritz Erich von Lewinski genannt von Manstein, later changed simply to Fritz Erich von Manstein.

Erich entered the Royal Prussian Cadet Corps in 1900 and while in Berlin was a page at the court of Kaiser Wilhelm II. After graduation in 1906, he entered active service with the pres-

Gen. Field Marshal Erich von Manstein, the victor of Sevastopol, 1942. His decorations included the Knight's Cross of the Iron Cross and the Romanian Order of Michael the Brave. *From* Bessarabien, Ukraine-Krim, *op. cit.*

tigious Prussian 3rd Guard Regiment of Foot. As a lieutenant, he attended the War Academy during 1913–14, and at the outbreak of war in August 1914, he was the adjutant of the 2d Reserve Guard Regiment. He took part in the capture of Namur in Belgium and served with distinction during the great German victory at Tannenberg in East Prussia. Seriously wounded in action in Poland in November 1914, he was assigned to various staff jobs as a General Staff officer during his recovery. Even as a young captain he showed exceptional tactical and organizational knowledge and skill. Transferred to the Western Front, he served at Verdun and again on the Russian Front. He was awarded both the Iron Cross Second and First Class for bravery, as well as the Hohenzollern House Order and the Wound Badge in Silver.

During the demobilization after the end of World War I, he was invited to remain in the *Reichsheer*, the 100,000-man army allowed the new German Republic under the peace treaties. He married Jutta Sybille in 1923. Von Manstein gained additional military experience as commander of a *Jaeger* (light infantry) battalion and in various staff jobs, and in 1929 was appointed to a responsible post in the *Reichswehr* Ministry. In his new assignment he was head of Group 1, T1 Section, of the Operations Section, actually the general staff as it was referred to in those days when Germany was not officially allowed to have a general staff. He was promoted to major on February 1, 1927, and lieutenant colonel on April 1, 1932.

Adolf Hitler became Reichs Chancellor in January 1933 and soon consolidated his power as dictator of Germany. To further his ambitious plans for making Germany the dominant nation in Europe, he began a rapid program of rearmament. By March 1935 Hitler felt strong enough to reinstate conscription and announce the formation of the Luftwaffe as a powerful force in being. It was included in the new Wehrmacht, alongside the army and navy. Von Manstein, like many other soldiers, benefited by the expansion of the armed forces. He was promoted to colonel in 1933 and to major general (equivalent to a U.S. Army brigadier general), on October 1, 1936.

In October 1936, von Manstein was appointed to the important post of Quartermaster General of the Army, and Deputy Chief of the Army General Staff. This assignment was under General Ludwig Beck, who had already drawn Hitler's wrath by disagreeing with the Fuehrer's daring gambles such as the remilitarization of the Rhineland. Von Manstein firmly opposed Hitler's precipitous rearmament program and strict racial policies in the army, where Jewish war veterans were no longer permitted to serve in the armed forces.[3] He soon found himself removed from the general staff and assigned as commander of the 18th Infantry Division. Von Manstein's excellent record and reputation within the army probably saved him from being forced into retirement. During this time Hitler began his ambitious program of aggressive diplomacy and purged a number of senior officers who opposed his adventurism, including Field Marshal Werner von Blomberg and General Werner *Freiherr* von Fritsch.

Shortly before World War II began in September 1939, von Manstein was promoted to lieutenant general and appointed Chief of Staff, Army Group South, commanded by General Gerd von Rundstedt. Together with (then) Colonel Guenther Blumentritt, he devised the main battle plan for the conquest of Poland. Von Manstein continued in that position during the buildup against the Western Allies in the winter of 1939–40 and had the opportunity to learn of the proposed plan for the campaign against France.

The original plan was quite similar to the Schlieffen Plan of 1914. This time the invasion featured a frontal attack into northern France through Holland as well as Belgium. Von Manstein believed that this plan was just what the Allies expected and would probably lead to a stalemate on the Western Front such as occurred in World War I. He managed to speak personally with Hitler and presented a daring proposal for a strong, rapid armored thrust through the Ardennes region, a hilly, forested area in the center of the front believed by the French to be impassable for armored forces. His imaginative plan was unorthodox and was opposed by General Franz Halder, Chief of the General Staff, and others. However, it was eventually adopted by Hitler who, of course, took full credit for the remarkable success of the classic Blitzkrieg, which resulted in the speedy defeat of France and the Low Countries, and the evacuation of British forces from Dunkirk.

During the campaign in May and June 1940, von Manstein ably commanded the XXXVIII Infantry Corps, was promoted to General of Infantry on June 1, and was decorated with the coveted Knight's Cross of the Iron Cross. In February 1941, fate smiled on von Manstein when he received just the assignment he wanted—commander of an armored corps.

Von Manstein was not consulted by Hitler or anyone else concerning the plans for the invasion of the Soviet Union.[4] When Hitler launched the great offensive on June 22, von Manstein aggressively led the LVI Panzer Corps during the first weeks of Barbarossa and distinguished himself in the rapid advance on the northern front, through the Baltic States toward Leningrad. Unlike many commanders, he led his troops almost exclusively from the front and usually gave any necessary orders on the spot. He enjoyed the respect and absolute trust of his soldiers who admired him as a caring and resolute leader. Although personally rather reserved, he gained the reputation of being generous and just, and he was said even to take a personal interest not only in his men but in the care and feeding of prisoners of war and the welfare of the civilian population.[5] (Ironically, during his war crimes trial in 1949 he was convicted on charges of neglecting to protect civilian life in Russia.)

Hitler liked von Manstein's style and was aware of his accomplishments. On September 12, 1941, he appointed him commander of the Eleventh Army upon the death in action of Colonel General Eugen *Ritter* von Schobert. Von Manstein's remarkable success in the battles in the Crimea, and the conquest of Sevastopol, prompted Hitler to promote him to Colonel General on January 1, 1942, and to General Field Marshal effective July 1, 1942.

When Field Marshal Walter von Brauchitsch was sacked by Hitler as Army Commander in Chief on December 19, 1941, many young generals hoped that von Manstein would be chosen to succeed him as commander in chief, but Hitler decided to assume the post himself in addition to his other duties. He thought of making von Manstein Chief of the General Staff, but felt he might prove even more difficult than General Franz Halder.[6] Another factor may have been that von Manstein was involved at that time in the complex and difficult battle in the Crimea, including the siege of Sevastopol, which did not end until July 4, 1942.

Autumn 1942 was a crucial turning point for the Wehrmacht on the Eastern Front and in North Africa. Unfortunately for the German Sixth Army, Hitler's over-ambitious and poorly conceived summer offensive in Russia led to the final destruction of German, Romanian, and Italian forces at Stalingrad. Von Manstein was given command of Army Group Don in the fall of 1942, and tried unsuccessfully to relieve the Sixth Army when it became trapped in the city named for Josef Stalin. He was, however, credited with stabilizing the southern front and inflicting defeats on the Soviets in battles along the Donetz and Dnieper, and at Kharkov in March 1943. Von Manstein, a master of maneuver and offensive strategy, had once more regained the initiative for the Wehrmacht.[7] Hitler was greatly relieved; he flew to his headquarters and personally decorated von Manstein with the Oakleaves to the Knight's Cross of the Iron Cross. Von Manstein was respected not only by other senior army leaders, but even Hitler admired his innovative ideas, although increasingly they conflicted with his own.

Von Manstein tried to convince the supreme command in 1943 that Germany should go on the defensive in southern and western Europe and concentrate all possible forces for defeating the Soviet Union. Hitler did not accept this proposal and determined to continue the battle in North Africa by defending Tunisia and even sending reinforcements for that hopeless struggle against British and American forces. He also refused recommendations that the entire line in the east should be pulled back to shorten the front, ease the difficult supply situation, and allow regrouping and rebuilding of German ground and air forces.[8]

In July 1943, "Operation Citadel," the great tank battle at Kursk, which had been drastically delayed by Hitler, was stopped by the Fuehrer after the Allied invasion of Sicily, just as von Manstein was about to defeat the Russians on the southern section of the front.[9] The result was a serious defeat for the Wehrmacht; henceforth Germany lost the initiative and was forced on the defensive. Hitler, a proponent of the offensive, was no longer able to really influence events on the Eastern Front.

Von Manstein's continuing disagreements with Hitler over strategy, command, and organization led to his being relieved of command on March 25, 1944. It is a tribute to von Manstein's ability that Hitler tolerated him as long as he did. His need for eye surgery was announced publicly as the reason for his dismissal, but in actuality Hitler told him that the time for large-scale offensive operations, for which he was justly famous, had passed. What was needed now was a defensive strategy for which Field Marshal Walter Model was better suited. Hitler and Reichsfuehrer-SS Heinrich Himmler's distrust of von Manstein may have been the main reason for his dismissal. Nevertheless, Hitler awarded him the Swords to the Knight's Cross of the Iron Cross with Oakleaves at their final meeting.[10] Perhaps Hitler did not want to add von Manstein to the long list of his known enemies.

The man many considered to be the greatest strategist Germany produced during World War II lived out the rest of the war in retirement near Celle. He was arrested by the British in May 1945 and taken to England where he was interrogated and imprisoned. The vengeful Soviets demanded that he be turned over to them, but this was refused. A Soviet court would probably have sentenced him to hang. After four years in confinement, von Manstein was finally placed on trial before a British Military War Crimes Court at Hamburg in 1948. At the end of the controversial trial, he was convicted of illegal activities in various German high commands, including neglecting to protect civilian life and authorizing forced labor of civilians. He was, however, acquitted of the charges of mass execution of Jews and others in Russia. His prosecution was opposed by several Allied generals and prominent people including B. H. Liddell Hart, who praised him during his trial and described him as an honorable man. Liddell Hart stated that von Manstein was the ablest German general, who combined modern ideas of maneuver and a mastery of technical details with great driving power.[11] Winston Churchill, by then out of office, donated 100 pounds to his defense fund.

Von Manstein was sentenced to eighteen years in prison, but this was later reduced to twelve. He was given medical parole in August 1952 and was released in May 1953. He retired to Irschenhausen, Bavaria, near Munich, where he lived quietly with his wife while writing his memoir, *Verlorene Siege* (Lost Victories), published in Bonn in 1955. Von Manstein was the only Hitler-era field marshal called on as a consultant by the West German government during the planning and formation of the *Bundeswehr*, the modern German armed forces, established under NATO in 1955. Controversy over that role flared in 1967 when he was accused of failing to side with the anti-Nazi plotters against Hitler during the war. Acclaimed German historian Walter Goerlitz countered that von Manstein "was never a political figure." Thus, he contended, the field marshal did not think it possible to take part in a wartime plot against the leader, even though he hated Hitler and would have been glad to see him relinquish power and command of the armed forces.

Field Marshal Erich von Manstein, after a lifetime of preparing for and waging war, died peacefully at Irschenhausen on June 12, 1973, at the age of eighty-five.

CRIMEAN COMBAT REPORT

By Lt. Gen. Guenther Rall
German Air Force (Retired)

After the conquest of the island of Crete in the Mediterranean, in which my squadron, 8./III/J.G. 52 (Eighth Squadron, Third Group, Fighter Wing 52) participated, operating from the south Peloponnesus islands and Maleme on Crete, we were ordered back to Romania to a small airfield at Mizil at the foot of the Carpathian Mountains. It was June 1941 and there we received new airplanes, the Messerschmitt Me 109F, an excellent fighter and better than the Me 109E which we had flown before.

During this time we recognized a tremendous increase in the army forces in the area without understanding the reason. But soon we got the answer: war against Russia! It was a shock; this meant a two-front war against every strategic logic!

On June 23, I was ordered, as squadron commander, to take my squadron to Mamaia, Romania, on the Black Sea just north of Constanta, a chief port. We landed in the evening at this empty grass airfield and found that the Russians had already attacked the oil facilities in the harbor at Constanta with DB-3 bombers. There was no communications at the field, only a telephone and nothing else. At dawn the next morning I sent two Me 109F fighters up to 6,000 meters on patrol over the Black Sea east of Constanta. The remaining members of my squadron were on "cockpit alert" in their airplanes and had their radios turned on. Pretty soon we got the call from the patrol: "DB-3 bombers are coming!" I scrambled with the squadron and engaged the bombers while still over the sea. The DB-3s came without fighter escort and they suffered heavy losses.

The next week they tried to attack every day and the same thing happened; they never reached their target at Constanta. But one day when we were out over the sea engaged in com-

Maj. Guenther Rall in 1944. Rall fought as a fighter pilot on every front from 1940 to 1945 and was credited with an amazing 275 victories. Lt. Gen. a. D *Guenther Rall*

bat with the bombers, three Pe-2 bombers approached the Mamaia Air Base from the west, flying low over the Carpathian Mountains, so they could not be detected. They dropped bombs and destroyed three Me 109Fs on the ground, and we also lost some of our ground crews. Due to heavy losses the Russians stopped their attacks against Constanta.

Subsequently, our *III. Gruppe, J.G. 52*, was transferred to Bjelia Ceskow, south of Kiev in Ukraine. From here on we were in the midst of the most cruel war for the next two-and-a-half years, participating in all important operations. The only interruption for me was my time in hospitals after being shot down and seriously injured. We now encountered the mass of the Soviet fighter and bomber fleet, which was focused on support of the army. Their equipment at that time was not up to Western standards, nor were their pilots experienced and adequately trained. But they had a tremendous fighting spirit.

Then came action in the battle of Kiev, the Dnieper River crossing, Poltava, Kharkov, and across the Ukraine to the Nogai Steppe north of the Crimean Peninsula.

Throughout the centuries the Crimea was a strategic objective and Sevastopol was the predominant fortress and harbor on the Black Sea. In the course of our military operations, it certainly had to be conquered. At our very primitive airfield on the Nogai Steppe just north of the Isthmus of Perekop, a Luftwaffe task force was formed under command of the famous fighter commander, Colonel Werner Moelders. He flew at dawn every day with a Fieseler Fi 156 *Storch* observation plane to the forward lines and by radio dictated the fighter operations, which were concentrated for the battle over the Isthmus of Perekop and the Tatar Ditch. He was acting as one of the first forward air controllers. In the evening we always had a briefing in his tent.

Our opponents in the air at that time were primarily still the I-16 Rata and I-153 fighters, more or less obsolete aircraft compared with ours. After the German breakthrough at the Perekop Isthmus, and over the Tatar Ditch into the heart of the Crimea, we flew fighter sweeps and escort down to Sevastopol, Simferopol, and to Kerch, until late October 1941. At that time my fighter group was transferred to the Mius area, near Taganrog and Rostov, and here the first winter hit us. When temperatures dropped to –40° C. it caused us tremendous problems. We were not prepared for those conditions, not technically and not personally. It was hard to get the engines running until we installed special modifications, like a cold starting system, by switching fuel after the last mission in the evening into the lubrication lines to keep the oil fluid. On November 28, 1941, just before dark, my wingman and I ran into two LaGG or

MiG-3 fighters. It was my thirty-sixth victory, but I was blinded by the flames in the dark and got hit by the second Russian. I crashed and broke my back in three places and was out of action and hospitalized in a body cast for five months.

Upon returning to my squadron in August 1942, and getting familiarized with the situation, I found a different Russian Air Force. They had learned their lessons and trained and engaged their pilots in Western tactics. They had new aircraft of the MiG and LaGG series and soon lend-lease support from their Anglo-American allies. The Spitfire and P-39 Airacobra fighters and A-20 bombers showed up, and the Russian IL-2 Shturmovik played an effective role as well.

The German fighters, with the Italian, Hungarian, Slovakian, and Romanian units, and in the center section of the Eastern Front, the Spanish contribution, were by far too few to cover the huge airspace. Luftwaffe units were therefore used like fire brigades at the focal points of the war. In two years my group operated from forty-four airfields, and most of them were selected as bases from the air! We depended strictly on transport by Junkers Ju 52, and could not use our heavy trucks because of the shortage of, or nonexistence of, usable roads. This was a great problem because of the shortage of transport aircraft caused by heavy losses at Crete, North Africa, and elsewhere. However, by hopping around we were engaged in all the important operations down to the Caucasus Mountains, Stalingrad, and Kursk.

From the summer of 1943 it was only retreat and finally, the following January, we ended up in Bessarabia, Romania. At that time I was already group commander of the III/J.G. 52, and I received the order to fly into the Crimea with my group to assist in the final defensive action of the army. It was clear that German forces had to leave the Crimea after a short time, and this was a problem—it was almost a suicidal action. I gave the order to fly into the Crimea in our Me 109G aircraft which we already had at that time. We received no support and each of us had only one mechanic. We pushed him into the body of the plane, just behind the pilot, when we had to evacuate the Crimea.

The last battle in the Crimea was on Cape Chersones, west of Sevastopol, where we slept in the bunkers from the battles in 1941, and found skeletons in some of them. Every man of my group, including the mechanics, was flown out safely to Romania. It was my last engagement in the brutal war in the east. I got the order to take over a fighter group in Germany for defense against the U.S. Army Air Forces. The USAAF usually executed their air assaults with up to 800 B-17 and B-24 bombers escorted by long-range P-38, P-47, and P-51 fighters.

As mentioned, my last area of fighting in the East was again in the Crimea. Three times I was confronted with the Crimea: the breakthrough of German forces in 1941–42, the offensive from Kerch to the Taman and Kuban bridgehead, and the final battle on Cape Chersones in 1944, which caused unforgettable memories.

Now after more than fifty years we can talk about the events which changed the whole world without too many difficult emotions. But in reading this book by C. G. Sweeting, the memories come back and I am very touched by his detailed, competent, and very fair description of these unforgettable events.

Guenther Rall
Generalleutnant a.D

AUTHOR'S NOTE: Guenther Rall was born in Gaggenau, Baden, on March 10, 1918, and grew up during the difficult years of economic and political crisis in Germany. After finishing school in 1936, he joined the army as a cadet and trained as an infantry officer. While attending the *Kriegsschule* (War College), he developed a keen interest in aviation and transferred to the Luftwaffe in 1937, where he trained as a fighter pilot.

During World War II, Lieutenant Rall scored his first aerial victory on May 12, 1940, during the Battle of France. He fought in the Battle of Britain, the aerial invasion of Crete, and the defense of Romania. After the German invasion of the Soviet Union in 1941, he flew hundreds of missions in the skies over the Crimea and elsewhere in Russia. During this time he suffered severe injuries but always managed to return to flying.

By 1945 Major Rall was engaged in the air defense of Germany. He was credited with an amazing 275 victories and ended the war as the third-highest-scoring ace of all time. Rall was awarded Germany's highest decorations for bravery including the Knight's Cross of the Iron Cross and the Oakleaves and Swords. After the war he joined the West German Air Force, now a part of NATO, and served as a commander until retirement as a lieutenant general in 1974.

As the third-highest-scoring fighter ace of all time, Guenther Rall was awarded Germany's highest decorations for bravery. This is the certificate received upon presentation of the Oakleaves and Swords to the Knight's Cross of the Iron Cross. Lt. Gen. a. D. *Guenther Rall*

APPENDIX B

RANKS, UNIFORMS, INSIGNIA, MEDALS

German Army rank	Literal translation	Corresponding U. S. Army rank (according to function)	German Navy rank	German Air Force rank
				Reichsmarschall.
Generalfeldmarschall.	General Field Marshal.	(None).	*Grossadmiral.*	*Generalfeldmarschall.*
Generaloberst.	Colonel General.	General.	*Generaladmiral.*	*Generaloberst.*
General der Infanterie.	General of Infantry.	Lieutenant General.	*Admiral.*	*General der Flieger.*
Artillerie.	Artillery.			*Flakartillerie.*
Kavallerie.	Cavalry.			*Luftwaffe.*
Pioniere.	Engineers.			*Luftnachrichten-*
Panzertruppe, etc.	Armored Troops, etc.			*truppen, etc.*
Generalleutnant.	Lieutenant General.	Major General.	*Vizeadmiral.*	*Generalleutnant.*
Generalmajor.	Major General.	Brigadier General.	*Konteradmiral.*	*Generalmajor.*
Oberst.	Colonel.	Colonel.	*Kapitän zur See.*	*Oberst.*
Oberstleutnant.	Lieutenant Colonel.	Lieutenant Colonel.	*Fregattenkapitän.*	*Oberstleutnant.*
Major.	Major.	Major.	*Korvettenkapitän.*	*Major.*
Hauptmann.	Captain,	Captain.	*Kapitänleutnant.*	*Hauptmann.*
Rittmeister.	Captain of Cavalry.			
Oberleutnant.	First Lieutenant.	First Lieutenant.	*Oberleutnant zur See.*	*Oberleutnant.*
Leutnant.	Lieutenant.	Second Lieutenant.	*Leutnant zur See.*	*Leutnant.*
Stabsfeldwebel.	Staff Sergeant.	Master Sergeant	*Stabsoberfeldwebel.*	*Stabsfeldwebel.*
Stabswachtmeister.	Staff Cavalry Sergeant.	Regimental Sergeant		*Stabswachtmeister.*
Stabsfeuerwerker.	Staff Ordnance Sergeant.	Major.		*Stabsfeuerwerker.*
Wallstabsfeldwebel.	Staff Fort Sergeant.			
Festungspionierstabsfeldwebel.	Staff Fortification Engineer Sergeant.			
Stabsfunkmeister.	Staff Radio Sergeant.			
Stabsbrieftaubenmeister.	Staff Carrier Pigeon Sergeant			
Stabsschirrmeister.	Staff Maintenance Sergeant.			
Hauptfeldwebel, Hauptwachtmeister.	Chief Sergeant.	First Sergeant.	*Oberfeldwebel.*	*Hauptfeldwebel, Hauptwachtmeister.*
	Chief Cavalry Sergeant.			
Oberfeldwebel.	First Sergeant.	Master Sergeant.	*Stabsfeldwebel.*	*Oberfeldwebel.*
Oberwachtmeister.	First Cavalry Sergeant.			*Oberwachtmeister.*
Oberfähnrich.	Ensign (officer candidate).			*Oberfeuerwerker.*
Oberfeuerwerker.	First Ordnance Sergeant.			*Oberfähnrich.*
Walloberfeldwebel.	First Fort Sergeant.			
Festungspionieroberfeldwebel.	First Fortification: Engineer Sergeant.			
Oberfunkmeister.	First Radio Sergeant.			
Oberbrieftaubenmeister.	First Carrier Pigeon: Sergeant.			
Oberschirrmeister.	First Maintenance: Sergeant.			
Feldwebel.	Sergeant.	Technical Sergeant.	*Feldwebel.*	*Feldwebel.*
Wachtmeister.	Cavalry Sergeant.			*Wachtmeister.*
Feuerwerker.	Ordnance Sergeant.			*Feuerwerker.*
Wallfeldwebel.	Fort Sergeant.			
Festungspionierfeldwebel.	Fortification Engineer: Sergeant.			
Funkmeister.	Radio Sergeant.			
Brieftaubenmeister.	Carrier Pigeon Sergeant.			
Schirrmeister.	Maintenance Sergeant.			
Fähnrich.	(Officer candidate).	(None).	*Fähnrich zur See.*	*Fähnrich.*
Unterfeldwebel, Unterwachtmeister.	Junior Sergeant, Junior Cavalry Sergeant.	Staff Sergeant.	*Obermaat.*	*Unterfeldwebel.*
				Unterwachtmeister.
Unteroffizier, Fahnenjunker-Unteroffizier.	Noncommissioned Officer Cadet	Sergeant.	*Maat.*	*Unteroffizier.*
				Fahnenjunker-Unteroffizier.
Stabsgefreiter.	Staff Lance Corporal.	(None).	*Hauptgefreiter.*	*Hauptgefreiter.*
Obergefreiter.	Chief Lance Corporal.	Corporal.	*Obergefreiter.*	*Obergefreiter.*
Gefreiter, Fahnenjunker-Gefreiter.	Lance Corporal. Junior Cadet.	Acting Corporal	*Gefreiter.*	*Gefreiter.*
				Fahnenjunker-Gefreiter.
Obergrenadier.	Chief Infantryman.	Private, First Class.		
Oberjäger.	Chief Chasseur.			
Oberreiter.	Chief Cavalryman.			
Oberkanonier.	Chief Gunner.			
Oberpionier.	Chief Engineer.			
Oberfunker.	Chief Radioman.			
Oberfahrer.	Chief Driver.			
Oberkraftfahrer.	Chief Motor Driver.			
Grenadier.	Infantryman.	Private.	*Matrose.*	*Flieger.*
Jäger.	Chasseur.			*Kanonier.*
Reiter.	Cavalryman.			*Funker.*
Kanonier.	Gunner.			
Funker.	Radioman.			
Fahrer.	Driver.			
Kraftfahrer.	Motor Driver.			
Pionier.	Engineer.			
Schütze.	Rifleman.			

Ranks in the German Armed Forces

Table of equivalent ranks—German compared to American, mid-World War II. *U.S. War Department*, Handbook on German Military Forces, TM-E-30-451 *(Washington, D.C., 1943)*

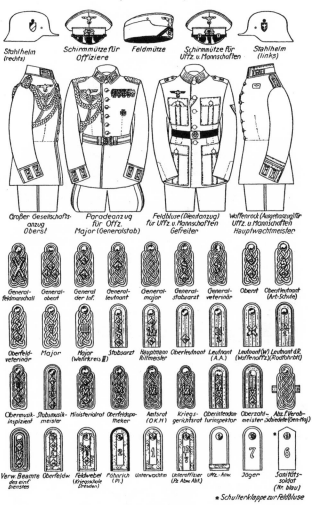

Uniformen des Heeres.

Stahlhelm (rechts) · Schirmmütze für Offiziere · Feldmütze · Schirmmütze für Uffz. u. Mannschaften · Stahlhelm (links)

Großer Gesellschaftsanzug Oberst · Paradeanzug für Offz. Major (Generalstab) · Feldbluse (Dienstanzug) für Uffz. u. Mannschaften Gefreiter · Waffenrock (Ausgehanzug) für Uffz. u. Mannschaften Hauptwachtmeister

Generalfeldmarschall · Generaloberst · General der Inf. · Generalleutnant · Generalmajor · Generalstabsarzt · Generalveterinär · Oberst · Oberstleutnant (Art.-Schule)

Oberfeldveterinär · Major · Major (Wehrkreis II) · Stabsarzt · Hauptmann Rittmeister · Oberleutnant · Leutnant (A.A.) · Leutnant (W) (Waffenoffz.) · Leutnant d.R. (Radfahrbtl.)

Obermusikinspizient · Stabsmusikmeister · Ministerialrat · Oberfeldapotheker · Amtsrat (O.K.H.) · Kriegsgerichtsrat · Oberintendanturinspektor · Oberzahlmeister · Abz.f.Verabschiedete (Gen.-Maj.)

Verw. Beamte des einf. Dienstes · Oberfeldw. · Feldwebel (Kriegsschule Dresden) · Fähnrich (Pi.) · Unterwachtm · Unteroffizier (Pz.Abw.Abt.) · Uffz.-Anw. · Jäger · Sanitätssoldat (Nr. blau)

* Schulterklappe zur Feldbluse

Sturmabzeichen.

Infanteriesturmabzeichen. · Sturmabzeichen (Pioniere). · Panzerkampfabzeichen.

German army and air force uniforms, insignia, and decorations, mid–World War II. *From* Oberstleutnant *W. Reibert*, Der Dienstunterricht im Heere *(Berlin, 1943)*

(on next page also)

Die wichtigsten Uniformen der Luftwaffe

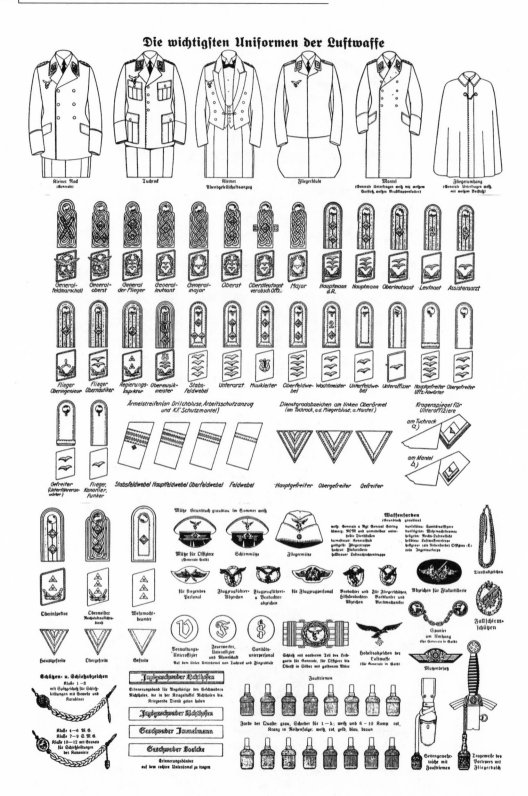

Flieger= ufw. Abzeichen.

Lw.=Flugzeugführerabzeichen
(Silber)

Lw.=Beobachterabzeichen
(Silber)

Lw.=Flugzeugführer=
und Beobachterabzeichen
(Gold)

Lw.=Fliegerfchützenabzeichen

Fallfchirmfchützenabzeichen

Lw.=Segelflugzeugführerabzeichen

Kampfabzeichen der Flakartillerie

Frontflugfpangen.

Aufklärer

Jäger

Kampfflieger

Bronze: 20 Feindflüge
Silber: 60 Feindflüge
Gold: ab 110 Feindflüge

Badges for German Air Force aviators, war badges, and operational flying clasps for observation, fighter, and bomber squadron flying personnel. *From* Oberst *E. Tschoeltsch*, Der Dienstunterricht in der Luftwaffe *(Berlin, 1941)*

Orben und Ehrenzeichen des gegenwärtigen Krieges.

Eisernes Kreuz
II. Klasse
(I. Klasse ohne Band).

Deutsches Kreuz.

Ritterkreuz des
Eisernen Kreuzes
(mit Eichenlaub).

Spange zur I. Klasse
des Eisernen Kreuzes
des Weltkrieges.

Großkreuz
des Eisernen Kreuzes

Spange zur II. Klasse
des Eisernen Kreuzes
des Weltkrieges.

Kriegsverdienstkreuz
I. Kl. (silbern).
(Ohne Schwerter für
Verdienste ohne feindliche
Waffeneinwirkung.)

Verwundeten-
abzeichen.
Schwarz: 1—2malige,
Silber: 3—4malige,
Gold: 5- und mehrmalige
Verwundung.

Kriegsverdienstkreuz
II. Kl. (bronzen).
(Ohne Schwerter für
Verdienste ohne feindliche
Waffeneinwirkung.)

Orders and Decorations of the Present War:

Top row, left to right: Iron Cross II Class (first class had no ribbon) German Cross (Awarded in silver and gold) Knight's Cross of the Iron Cross (with Oakleaves)

Middle row: Bar for I Class Iron Cross from World War I (*if awarded again to same person in World War II*), and Grand Cross of the Iron Cross. (Awarded only to *Reichsmarschall* Hermann Goering)

Bar to Iron Cross II Class from World War I (*If awarded again to same person in World War II*)

Bottom row: War Merit Cross I Class (Silver) (Without Swords for merit not involving combat with an enemy)

Wound Badge. Black, 1–2 wounds, Silver, 3–4 wounds, Gold, 5 or more wounds through enemy action.

War Merit Cross II Class (Bronze) (Without swords for merit not involving combat with an enemy).

Note: A Medal for the Winter Campaign in Russia, 1941–42, with ribbon, was awarded for service between November 15, 1941, and April 15, 1942. German soldiers often referred to it sarcastically as the "Frozen Meat Medal." *From Reibert, op. cit.*

APPENDIX C

WEAPONS OF BARBAROSSA

A weapon was probably man's first invention, and warfare may well be mankind's second oldest profession. Germany has always excelled at both.

When Germany and the Soviet Union, the two great totalitarian nations, clashed in the summer of 1941, both were well armed and equipped for the epic struggle to come. The tremendous victories achieved by the Wehrmacht and the equally remarkable defeats suffered by the Red Army in the first months gave a new dimension to the term *Blitzkrieg*. In considering the weapons of Barbarossa, it is surprising to note the disparity in arms between Germany and the Soviet Union. Hitler nevertheless launched the momentous invasion confident in the superiority of the Wehrmacht over the Red Army. He consistently discounted reports concerning the size, strength, and morale of Soviet forces and the Communist State. As for Russia, no nation in history ever absorbed such great losses in men and materiel and still survived to fight on to final victory. All things considered, without the invasions of southern and western Europe, and the air offensive by the Anglo-American Allies, it is doubtful if the Soviet Union would have, on their own, emerged as the victor in the east.

As for the weapons used in Barbarossa, it was initially German quality against Soviet mass—not so much quality of arms but the quality of the leadership and the troops themselves. The Red Army outnumbered the German Army substantially and fielded thousands more tanks, guns, aircraft, and soldiers. But the armies of the Soviet Union in 1941 appeared more like a huge armed mob than a modern, organized, efficient force. There were, of course, many elite Russian units and the soldiers of the Red Army proved in many instances that they were not only tough and well trained, but had the will to fight tenaciously. Stalin, his generals, and political commissars, callously demonstrated that they could quickly replace their peasant soldiers killed in combat, while the Germans found it far more difficult to replace their better trained and experienced troops lost in action or to the elements.

The same was true to a lesser extent with arms and equipment. The obsolete Soviet weapons destroyed or captured in great numbers in 1941 were soon replaced by crude-looking but quite serviceable arms pouring from factories beyond the reach of the Germans. German armaments, most of higher quality and capability, were more difficult and time consuming to produce, and new, simpler types had to be introduced to replace the heavy losses suffered in the winter of 1941–42. The finely finished German arms, with close tolerances, were generally more accurate, but much more susceptible to dust, mud, and freezing than Russian weapons. German-made arms were tested and proof-marked by the Heereswaffenamt (Army Ordnance Officer).

The Wehrmacht acquired large quantities of arms during the takeover of Austria and Czechoslovakia in 1938 and 1939, and some were kept in production. French weapons, tanks, and equipment were captured in 1940 and more in Poland, Belgium, Holland, and especially the Soviet Union. Most of the modern weapons were pressed into service with the Wehrmacht, its auxiliaries and police during the war, or given to German allies such as Romania, Italy, and Hungary.

Foreign weapons of modern type captured or acquired in quantity were utilized by the Germans either in first-line or more often in second-line formations or police units. Some were modified to chamber German ammunition, but many were issued as is. Whenever possible, approved foreign arms were stamped with the small *Waffenamt* (Ordinance Office) inspection mark of an eagle, "WaA" and the ordnance detachment number, to show that they were approved for issue. The same procedure was followed with ordnance equipment and weapons made in Germany and occupied and friendly countries; for example, WaA261.

All foreign weapons that were issued were given German ordnance nomenclature and a number with a suffix that indicated the country of origin. This facilitated ammunition and parts supply in the German ordnance system. However, the weapon was usually not marked with the German name. Examples include the Russian 7.62mm M1891/30 service rifle designated by the Germans as the *7.62mm Karabiner 454(r)*. The (r) indicates "russisch" (Russian) manufacture. The Russian 7.62mm PPSh-41 submachine gun was very popular with German troops and was designated the *7.62mm Maschinenpistole 717(r)*. The British .303 caliber Bren Gun was called the *7.7mm Maschinengewehr 138(e)*, the (e) showing it was of English origin. The 15cm Skoda heavy howitzer, built in Czechoslovakia for the Czech Army, was kept in production for German forces and carried the German designation *15cm schwere Feldhaubitze 37(t)*, the (t) meaning "tschechisch" or Czechoslovakian. The suffix (p) was assigned to Polish arms, (f) to French weapons, (b) for Belgian, (i) for Italian, (ö) for Austrian, (h) for Holland, (j) for Yugoslavia, etc. The .30 caliber M1903 Springfield rifle of the U.S. Army was given the German designation *7.62mm Gewehr 249(a)* while the U.S. rifle, caliber .30 M1 designed by John C. Garand was given the listing of *7.62mm Selbstladegewehr 251(a)*. Selbstladegewehr means self-loading rifle.

In addition to proof marks stamped on weapons, German arms and items of equipment were marked to indicate the manufacturer. To mask the production of new weapons and war materiel in factories in Germany, and to protect their location in case of war, the actual name and address of the manufacturer were no longer indicated on military weapons or items of equipment after the mid-1930s. Instead, a code letter or number was assigned to each of the main arms plants by the Heereswaffenamt in the fall of 1934. The code number and/or letter were place on the receiver or action of small arms in place of the maker's name or commercial trademark. For example, the Mauser Werke AG at Oberndorf am Neckar was assigned a series of codes including "S" in 1934, "S/42" after 1934, and "42" post-1936. This plant also used code "S/42G"; the "G" may have indicated the date 1935. Other Mauser factories, such as the plant at Berlin-Borsigwalde, used codes 237 and 925. C. G. Haenel of Suhl was issued code 122 and Waffenfabrik Walther at Zella-Mehlis used 480. After the union of Germany and Austria in 1938, Steyr Daimler Puch AG of Steyr was assigned code 660. There were dozens of other factories with these early number codes.

A new and much more comprehensive letter-code system was established for Germany's expanding arms industry in 1941, for plants in Germany and occupied and friendly countries.[1] There were a number of two-letter codes used but more three-letter codes. The Mauser Werke factory at Oberndorf am Neckar received the code "byf," the Mauser factory at Berlin–Borsigwalde was given the code "ar," while the plant at Waldeck bei Kassel was "amo."

Date of manufacture was indicated by two numbers, "41" for 1941, "42" for 1942, etc. It was not until after the war that the U.S. Army was able to obtain a partial list of the hundreds of arms factory codes so that the actual manufacturers of German weapons and war materiel could be fully identified. The set is marked *Geheim* (Secret) and was produced by the *Oberkommando des Heeres, Heereswaffenamt Wa Z2*. A few copies of the five-volume set of manufacturer's codes exist today, including a set at the U.S. Army Ordnance Museum at Aberdeen Proving Ground, Maryland, and a set in the possession of the author.[2]

Here are a few examples of markings on items formerly in the author's collection and now in the Imperial War Museum in London:

- Black leather holster for P. 38 pistol marked "bla," dated "44," with eagle and Waffenamt inspectors mark "WaA158." Code "bla" was E. G. Leuner G.m.b.H. in Bautzen, Germany.
- Kar. 98k rifle made by the Mauser factory in Berlin-Borsigwalde, marked with code "ar," the date "42," serial number 3224a, and inspectors mark of eagle and "26."
- P. 38 pistol made at Carl Walther Waffenfabrik at Zella-Mehlis and marked with the code "ac," the date "41," serial number 7180, and inspector's mark of an eagle and "359."
- Bayonet M84/98, marked "jwh" with inspector's mark of eagle and "WaA261." Code "jwh" was the Staatliche Waffenfabrik, Chatellerault (France), the state arsenal that produced arms under German occupation during World War II.

Rifles

Much of the fierce fighting between German and Russian troops during World War II was carried out using the standard small arms of that period. The basic weapon of every army is the rifle, and the German Army used the *7.9mm Karabiner 98k*, a shortened and slightly modified version of the famous Mauser bolt-action *7.9mm Gewehr 98*, a rifle originally adopted for German forces in 1898. The *Seitengewehr 84/98* bayonet was issued for use with the *Kar. 98k*.[3]

Versions of this excellent rifle were used by armies of many nations, including the United States, which adopted the Model 1903 Springfield, a modified Mauser design, in caliber .30. The German Heereswaffenamt (Army Ordnance Office), placed the Kar. 98k in mass production in 1935, and it continued in use throughout the war despite the introduction of self-loading rifles. A great variety of older German types, and captured rifles and weapons of all kinds, were issued to garrison, occupation, home-defense, police, and other second-line formations for training purposes, as well as to German allies. As can be imagined, the use of so many types and calibers of weapons resulted in a logistic nightmare as the war continued. Ammunition for foreign weapons had to be made in Germany or in occupied countries.

The *Kar. 98k*, like the original *Gew. 98*, was accurate, reliable, and easy to use and maintain, even under unfavorable conditions in the field. There was little difference in performance between the Kar. 98k and its Russian equivalent, the bolt-action 7.62mm M1891/30 Mosin-Nagant rifle. The Mosin-Nagant, a modern version of the rifle originally adopted for the Russian Army in 1891, was longer and less handy than the Kar. 98k, but was equally sturdy and performed satisfactorily at normal ranges. It should be noted that the quality of German weapons declined after 1942 as a result of the great demands on production and the shortages of materials and skilled workers. Although German production actually increased during the war under the direction of Albert Speer, Minister of Armaments and War Production, the relentless Allied bombing of German industry and transportation certainly aided in slowing the flow of weapons to the front.

A sniper rifle version of the Gew. 98 was used in World War I and a sniper Kar. 98k rifle was issued in infantry units in World War II, some fitted with the large *Zielfernrohr 39* (*Zf 39*). The most common Kar. 98k sniper rifle was equipped with the *Zielfernrohr 41* (*Zf 41*), a surprisingly small scope carried in a metal container that could be worn on the belt. The *Gewehr 43* self-loading rifle could also be fitted with a telescopic sight, the *Zf 4*. Sniper rifles were usually specially selected for quality prior to issue.[4]

Although noted for its advanced technical and scientific capabilities, time constraints and priorities during the rapid rearmament in the 1930s apparently did not allow German industry to perfect a self-loading, semi-automatic rifle prior to the war. The Russians actually made more progress in semi-automatic rifle design and development and had issued quantities of the Tokarev SVT 40 7.62mm rifle before 1941. The Germans tested and used captured SVT 40 rifles. The capture of the Tokarev rifle factory in the first months of Barbarossa brought an end to production of the SVT rifle, but the Russians had removed most of the machinery prior to the arrival of the Germans. The Tokarev SVT had a reputation for jamming; however, this may have resulted from the inability of many Russian soldiers to properly handle the cleaning and maintenance of the more intricate gas-operated SVT.

By 1941, Germany was testing two semi-automatic rifles, the *Gewehr 41 (M)* designed by Mauser, and the more successful *Gewehr 41 (W)*; a Walther design. Both operated on a rather complicated gas-expansion chamber at the muzzle. The *Gew. 41 (M)* was discontinued in favor of the *Gew. 41 (W)*; however, it did not prove very successful due to fouling and corrosion caused by its modified Bang system, and only limited numbers were manufactured. The example previously in the author's collection was captured by the British Army in North Africa in 1942. The *Gew. 41 (W)* was discontinued and replaced by the simpler *Gewehr 43*, which incorporated the *Gew. 41 (W)* breechlock with the gas system of the Tokarev SVT 40. All three of the German semi-automatic rifles chambered the standard 7.9mm rifle cartridge.

By 1944, an entirely new shoulder-arm was in production in Germany, the *Maschinenpistole 43*, later renamed the *M.P. 44* and finally the *Sturmgewehr 44* (Assault Rifle 44), after slight modification. Although originally designated as a machine pistol (submachine gun), it was actually a rifle. It was one of the first rifles to be mass-produced from inexpensive stampings and featured single or full-automatic fire. The *M.P. 43* was a revolutionary weapon and the inspiration for all subsequent guns of its type. Some *Gew. 43* and *M.P. 43* rifles were used by German troops defending the Crimea in 1944. The postwar Soviet Kalashnikov AK 47 assault rifle is outwardly similar to the M.P. 43 but different internally; however, the Russian M1943 7.62mm short cartridge used in the AK 47 is a further development of the German *7.9mm Kurz* (short) cartridge of World War II developed for and used in the *M.P. 43, M.P. 44,* and *StG. 44.*

Handguns

Pistols and revolvers played a minor role in World War II and may be considered weapons of last resort. Many different types of semi-automatic pistols in several calibers were employed by the Germans for various purposes. The standard pistol for combat troops during Barbarossa was the 9mm Walther *Pistole 38*, or *P.38*. A sturdy, modern, double-action, semi-automatic pistol with a magazine capacity of eight rounds, it was adopted for the Wehrmacht in 1938 as a replacement for the *P.08*. It was accurate and gave good service under field conditions, and over one million were produced between 1939 and 1945.

The *Pistole 08* or *P.08*, often called the Luger in the U.S. and the Parabellum abroad, is one of the most famous pistols in the world and was the standard handgun of the German Army from its adoption in 1908 until 1938. Originally ordered by the German Navy in 1904, the Army version, the P.08, remained in production until 1943. It was a single-action semi-automatic of unique recoil-operated design with a toggle-lock system that reminded soldiers of the Maxim machine gun mechanism. The P.08 was made with high-precision machined parts and was slow and expensive to manufacture. Although very accurate and a pleasure to handle, it was sensitive to dust, mud, rough handling, and freezing, and had to be protected from damage and the elements while in the field. Both the P.08 and the P.38 were carried in heavy, stiff leather belt holsters which enclosed them and provided good protection as well as a pocket for an additional loaded magazine of eight rounds.[5]

Both pistols, as well as several other substitute-standard handguns, such as the ex-Polish *Pistole 35(p)* and the ex-Belgian *Pistole 640(b)*, commonly called the M1935 GP or High Power, the last pistol designed by John Browning, were chambered for the 9mm Parabellum cartridge. Since its introduction with the P.08 in 1908, this cartridge has proved to be one of the best and most widely used pistol and submachine gun cartridges in the world.

Machine Guns

The machine gun revolutionized warfare. There were many important developments in armaments during the late 1800s and early 1900s, such as smokeless powder, the metallic cartridge, the breechloading magazine rifle, artillery with recoil mechanisms that made it unnecessary to re-aim the gun each time it was fired, indirect fire support, greater ranges and accuracy, improved ballistics, and improved communications, to mention just a few innovations. But thanks to the American inventor, Hiram Maxim, the modern machine gun, capable of full-automatic fire, proved to be one of the most deadly and effective weapons ever developed. It allowed a single, well-positioned soldier to command almost the firepower of an entire infantry company armed with rifles. Several different types were developed and huge numbers were used by the warring powers during World War I, with murderous results. Along with quick-firing artillery, they helped bring an end to the war of movement on the Western Front, forcing troops to dig trenches for protection against the deadly hail of fire.

The Maxim water-cooled, recoil-operated machine gun was adopted by several countries including Germany. It was a rugged, dependable gun that probably killed more people than any other weapon in history. The German Maxim *7.9mm Machinengewehr 08*, the British .303 Vickers-Maxim of 1912, and the Russian Maxim PM 1910 in 7.62mm were quite similar in operation and use. The German *M.G. 08*, also listed as the *s.M.G. 08* (heavy M.G. 08), on its sled mount with fabric belt-feed, was heavy, awkward, and slow firing, but served well through the mud of trench warfare and beyond.

The German 7.9mm MG 34 dual-purpose machine gun. The standard machine gun of the German Army from 1936 to 1942, it was used with a bipod as a light machine gun, and on a tripod mount as a heavy machine gun. Its main features were a high rate of fire (cyclic) of 800–900 r.p.m. (100–200 r.p.m. practical), and a quick barrel change capability. *From U.S. Army Chief of Ordnance*, Catalogue of Enemy Ordnance Materiel *(Washington, ca. 1943–44)*

A lighter German version with a wooden shoulder stock, bipod, and drum magazine was designated as the *L.M.G. 08/15*, and along with the *M.G. 08* served on through the *Reichswehr*, the *Wehrmacht* of the 1930s, and into World War II with second-line troops such as coast defense, guard units, and police.

During Hitler's rapid rearmament program, a new and much improved machine gun for the new German Army was introduced in the mid-1930s. This was the dual-purpose *7.9mm Maschinengewehr 34*, developed by Rheinmetall-Borsig A. G., and incorporating features from other designs. It was considered to be the *Einheitsmaschinengewehr* (Standardized Machine Gun) for ground units of the armed forces. The *M.G. 34* was a fast-firing, light-weight, air-cooled weapon reflecting the new German concept of mobile warfare that evolved into the Blitzkrieg. Also of importance was the quick-change barrel feature, so valuable when continuous fire was required from an air-cooled gun in combat.[6]

An excellent but complex optical sight was provided, the *M.G.-Zieleinrichtung*, made by the firm of Busch in Rathenow. The *M.G. 34* was beautifully made, extremely accurate, and with a cyclic rate of fire of about 800–900 rounds per minute, it was a formidable infantry weapon. However, it was very complex with hundreds of parts, and was expensive, difficult, and slow to manufacture. It worked well in combat during the campaigns against Poland and France, but the close tolerances of the many machined parts made it prone to jamming when exposed to dust, mud, and frost in North Africa and Russia. The constant care and cleaning required was in contrast to the sturdy but slower-firing Russian 7.62mm Degtyarev DP machine gun, which seemed to continue functioning regardless of the elements.

As a light machine gun, the *M.G. 34* could be fired from a bipod (*Zweibein 34*), with a 50-round drum magazine, or from a metal belt-box. For the medium machine gun role it was mounted on a complicated tripod (*Dreibein 34*), also called the *M.G. Lafette 34*. With this mount it fired 7.9mm ammunition from boxes containing 50 or 250 rounds in a disintegrating-link metal belt. A special antiaircraft tripod mount, the *Fliegerdrehstuetze 36*, was also available. The gun was also installed in tanks and vehicles and remained in production by the Gustloff Werke, Mauser Werke, and other firms until the end of the war.

Even before the war began in September 1939, the Heereswaffenamt was aware that the M.G. 34 was too complex and slow to manufacture. Contracts were placed with three manufacturers for development of a much simpler and less expensive dual-purpose machine gun that was easier to mass-produce. A new design by the Grossfuss firm was selected and approved for mass-production in mid-1942 as the new standard machine gun. This was the *7.9mm*

Maschinengewehr 42 or *M.G. 42*. It featured the new technique of manufacturing parts, often by subcontractors, from metal stampings, spot welds, and drop forgings, without sacrificing accuracy and reliability.

The M.G. 42 greatly influenced subsequent automatic weapon design. It was inexpensive and easy to manufacture and like the M.G. 34 was used as both a light and medium machine gun. Its cyclic rate of fire of about 1,200 rounds per minute was even faster than the M.G. 34, which it was intended to eventually replace. And, of course, it featured the quick-change barrel capability. The M.G. 42 soon earned a reputation as an accurate and sturdy gun, much less likely to jam in dusty, muddy, or sub-zero weather conditions.

Like the M.G. 34, the M.G. 42 could be fired from a bipod or a new tripod, called the *M.G. Lafette 42*. It could be used in the antiaircraft mode from the same tripod mount. Although it arrived at the front too late to be used in the siege of Sevastopol in 1942, it was in wide use during the final battles in the Crimea in 1944. A postwar version, the *MG 42/59*, was adopted for use by the German *Bundeswehr* as the *M.G. 1*, and with slight modification, the *M.G. 3*. The M.G. 42 was a success in every way and is considered by many experts to be the best machine gun of World War II, and perhaps the finest machine gun ever developed.

Note that there was one other German light machine gun in use during the 1930s; however, it saw no active combat service during World War II. This was the *7.9mm Maschinengewehr 13*, first procured in 1932 as a provisional weapon for the infantry. The *M.G. 13* was a light-weight, air-cooled gun with a bipod, and saddle-drum or box magazine; externally it resembled the M.G. 34 that replaced it beginning in 1936. Developed from a Dreyse design by Louis Stange, it was made obsolete by the M.G. 34 that had the efficient quick barrel change feature. Most of the M.G. 13 guns were later sold to Spain and Portugal, but a few continued in use for training purposes in garrisons.

Unlike the Germans, the Russians supplied air-cooled heavy machine guns for ground use. The 12.7mm DShK M1938, which had a wheeled tripod mount, was also mounted on armored vehicles. It was comparable in effectiveness to the U.S. .50-caliber Browning M2 heavy air-cooled machine gun, and captured guns were widely used by the Wehrmacht.

Submachine Guns

Trench warfare in World War I, with mass attacks by thousands of troops, required ever-increasing firepower for both the soldiers assaulting and those defending. Machine guns were produced and used in ever-increasing numbers, but even a light machine gun such as the 7.9mm M.G. 08/15, and the Allied equivalents like the British-built .303-caliber Lewis Gun, were more unhandy and difficult to use in the trenches than the long-barreled Gewehr 98 rifle, which was even longer if a bayonet was fixed.

In 1918 a new weapon was introduced for use in the trenches and by German assault troops, the so-called *Sturmtruppen*. This was the 9mm *Maschinenpistole 18/I* or *M.P. 18/I*. Called a machine pistol by the Germans and a machine carbine by the British, it was a short, light-weight, air-cooled submachine gun, firing the same excellent 9mm Parabellum pistol cartridge as the P. 08. This sturdy, blowback weapon was later modified to use a simple box magazine as a replacement for the clumsy 32-round "Snail Drum" magazine, originally supplied with the long-barreled P. 08 with shoulder stock, also intended for use in the trenches. The M.P. 18/I continued to be employed by police well into World War II.

The M.P. 18/I was the first practical submachine gun and greatly influenced later designs such as the German *M.P. 28*, *M.P. 34*, *M.P. Erma*, and *M.P. 35*. These 9mm submachine guns with wooden stocks saw service with German Army, police, and in the case of the *M.P. 35/I*, the Waffen-SS. All of these weapons required expensive machine work, which resulted in rather slow production. The M.P. 18/I and some later types were based on the designs of small-arms expert Hugo Schmeisser of the Bergmann Company.

By the mid-1930s a new and revolutionary design was being developed by Heinrich Vollmer and the Erma-Werke that was lightweight and easy and cheap to manufacture through the extensive use of simple steel stampings and plastics, with little machining. This advanced weapon was the 9mm *Maschinenpistole 38*.[7]

The *M.P. 38*, commonly but incorrectly called the "Schmeisser," was intended originally for use by crews of armored vehicles and paratroopers. With a folding metal buttstock, it became very popular with officers, noncommissioned officers, and troops of every branch that needed a handy, fast-firing weapon. The M.P. 38 had a 32-round detachable box magazine, and because of its fast rate of cyclic fire, 500 rounds per minute, it was often called the "Burp Gun" by Allied soldiers. It was superseded in production in 1940 by a slightly improved model, the *9mm M.P. 40*, which continued in mass production through the war. The total number produced is unknown but over a million M.P. 40 guns were made through the year 1944.

The Russians employed submachine guns in huge numbers during World War II, firing the 7.62mm Tokarev pistol cartridge, and many were used by German soldiers as the war progressed. They included the Degtayarev PPD 1934/38 and PPD 1940, based directly on the German M.P. 18/I design, and the much simpler PPSh 1941 and PPS 1943, designed by G. S. Shpagin and V. Sudarev, respectively. All operated on the original German Bergmann system.

Antitank Rifles

The Germans developed the first gun specifically intended for combating tanks during World War I. This was not an artillery piece but an oversize, single-shot, Mauser bolt-action rifle of conventional design that fired a 13mm armor-piercing steel bullet capable of penetrating the thin armor on the early British and French tanks. Officially named the *Tank-Gewehr* or *T-Gewehr*, it was often called the *Elefantenbuechsen* (Elephant Gun) by the troops, and about 15,800 were produced before the Armistice in November 1918. Its big advantage was that unlike artillery, it could be taken into the front lines and was a great morale-booster for the German infantry confronted with the Allies' roaring, belching, steel behemoths. The T-Gewehr was successful but dangerous to use because of its very heavy recoil which could bruise or even break a soldier's collar-bone. They were confiscated and destroyed by the Allies after the war because the army of the Weimar Republic was not allowed to possess either tanks or antitank guns. Captured examples of the cartridge were used by American ordnance engineers as the basis for developing the .50 caliber machine gun cartridge.

During German rearmament in the 1930s, the *3.7cm Panzerabwehrkanone 35/36* (anti-tank cannon) was produced for the army, and even with its shield it was lightweight and easy to maneuver. However, a small weapon for close-in defense by infantry was also desired, a weapon along the lines of the old T-Gewehr.

A new German antitank rifle was introduced before the war, probably developed by Rheinmetall-Borsig. This was the *7.9mm Panzerbuechse 38*, a rather complex single-shot weapon that did not prove very successful, even in Poland. The *PzB 38* was soon replaced by the *PzB 39*, a much simpler design that also fired the cartridge with a tungsten carbide 7.9mm projectile from a 13mm brass case. During the first months of Barbarossa, the *Panzerbuechse*

39 proved to be ineffective against the heavily armored Soviet tanks and could only be used with any hope of success against obsolescent light tanks. Most of the PzB 39 rifles were modified to fire 30mm grenades by installing a *Schiessbecher* (grenade cup) on the muzzle. Two types of antitank grenades and one antipersonnel grenade could be launched. So equipped, it was called the *7.9mm Granatbuechse 39*, and one of its antitank rounds could disable a light tank or armored vehicle such as an armored car. This weapon was an improvisation and it was not until antitank rocket launchers, such as the *Panzerfaust* and *Panzerschreck*, were introduced later in the war that the German infantryman received a really effective shoulder-fired antitank weapon.[8]

Hand and Rifle Grenades

Hand grenades, small explosive bombs thrown by hand, were first developed and used during the fifteenth century. Ignited by means of a slow match, early grenades often burst prematurely and only the bravest, strongest men were specially trained as "Grenadiers." Grenades, sometimes called "pocket artillery," were used only occasionally over the years, mainly for defense of fortresses, but by the Russo-Japanese War of 1904–05, modern grenades with percussion fuzes were being thrown by both sides.

Hand and rifle grenades of many types saw extensive use in trench warfare during World War I. Two basic types were employed: Defensive grenades could not be thrown beyond their blast area and were usually fragmentation types; offensive grenades could be safely thrown by troops during an advance and depended mainly on blast effect. Grenades with a percussion fuze exploded on impact, and the more common types with a friction igniter and time fuze usually detonated in about five seconds.

The famous German stick-type hand grenade of World War I, often called the "Potato Masher" by Allied soldiers, depended on concussion and blast effect. The egg and ball types of cast iron worked through fragmentation upon exploding. It is easier for Europeans and Asians to hurl a grenade with a handle while Americans, who know how to throw a baseball accurately, favor the egg type.

Germany entered World War II with two basic kinds of grenades: the stick type and the egg type. The stick grenades, *Stielhandgranate 24* and the similar *PH 39*, saw extensive service. In operation, the cap on the end of the wooden handle was removed, the porcelain ball on the end of a cord was pulled, and the grenade thrown to detonate after 4.5 seconds. Although the stick grenade depended mainly on blast effect, it could be made more lethal as an antipersonnel weapon by the use of a serrated steel fragmentation sleeve that could be clipped on the thin, metal explosive head. In 1943, the *Stielhandgranate 43*, with a solid wooden handle, was introduced. The friction primer with the detonator was simply fitted to the top of the explosive head. Chemical grenades, such as smoke, were also available.

The egg-shaped *Eihandgranate 39* was a smaller grenade and easier to carry. Made of thin sheet steel, a friction igniter was employed and the grenade was armed by unscrewing and pulling the round cover on top.

Two types of grenade launchers were available for use with the Kar 98k; the cup-type *Schiessbecher*, with special sight, and the spigot type similar to the U.S. Army model used in World War II. Rifle grenades fired from the cup-type included 46mm and 61mm types with a hollow charge (*Hohlladung*), as well as antitank armor-piercing grenades (*Gewehr Panzergranaten*). A hollow-charge grenade with fins, *Schussgranate P.40*, was fired from the spigot-type launcher.[9]

Flamethrowers

The modern flamethrower was a German invention in World War I. It was especially effective in attacking fortifications. The type introduced for the German Army in the mid-1930s was the *Flammnenwerfer 35*. It was gradually replaced during the War by the *Fla W 40* (Lifebuoy type) and the improved *Fla W 41* and *42* models.[10]

Mortars

The mortar in one form or another has been around for centuries, but they were actually small, smooth-bore, muzzle-loading howitzers, and were rather heavy and difficult to move and aim. The German *Minenwerfer,* used extensively in World War I in several sizes, was the modern development of this type of weapon, which differed little in principle from the old Coehorn mortar used by many nations, including the United States, in the nineteenth century.

The modern mortar was developed by the British in World War I from a design by Wilford Stokes. Often called a "trench mortar," it was a rather simple muzzle-loading, smooth-bore tube and base plate, from which bombs could be rapidly fired at a high elevation, falling almost vertically on the target. This was a very effective weapon for close-in trench warfare, and the high rate of fire compensated for the relative inaccuracy.

The Germans studied captured Stokes mortars and began the design of a similar mortar for infantry use during the 1920s. A model was finally approved in 1932 by the *Reichswehr Ministerium,* and production began in early 1934. This was the *8cm Granatwerfer 34*, which was a sturdy and accurate weapon fitted with the RA 35 dial sight. The *8cm GrW 34* weighed about 140 pounds (64 kg) and was carried in three loads: the barrel, the base plate, and the adjustable bipod. Of conventional design, it was also used in various armored vehicles, and the *8cm GrW 34/1* was a modification especially for mounting on a self-propelled carriage. Range was about 7,880 feet (2,400 meters). Several types of ammunition were developed for this mortar, including a "bouncing fragmentation bomb" called the *Wurfgranate 39*, which bounced into the air after striking the ground and exploded at a height of between 20 and 45 feet. The 8cm GrW 34 was included in the armament of the infantry battalion and served well until the end of the war in 1945.

For the infantry company, a smaller mortar was desired, and as a result of an OKH request, the *5cm leichter Granatwerfer 36* was adopted in 1936 and placed in mass production. This small mortar weighed only 31 pounds (14 kg) and consisted of a tube on a base plate with a telescopic sight. Range was about 1,710 feet (520 meters). Although production ceased in 1941, it continued in diminishing use until 1945.

Heavier mortars were adopted for use at the regimental level or below, and gradually replaced the leGrw 34. They included the *kurzer 8cm Granatwerfer 42*, which resembled the model 34, as did the *10cm Nebelwerfer 35*, originally intended to fire smoke shells but later provided with high explosive bombs. A very powerful mortar with a two-wheeled carriage for towing was copied from the Soviet Model 38. The *12cm Granatwerfer 42*, which not only resembled the Russian weapon but could fire the same ammunition, was widely used during the war.[11] A great variety of foreign and captured mortars of various calibers were also pressed into service, especially the Russian mortars with which the Red Army was liberally supplied.

Artillery

Germany always excelled in the design and manufacture of artillery. The famous Krupp Works was often referred to as "cannon maker to the world" because of its extensive export business. This was not only profitable for the industry and the Reich, but it helped spread German influence abroad.

German artillery in World War I made headlines in August 1914, when the powerful 42cm "Big Bertha" howitzers smashed the Belgian forts along the border during the German invasion. In 1918, the super-long-range 21cm "Paris Guns" shelled the French capital during the final German offensive on the Western Front. However, it was the excellent field guns and conventional heavy artillery that gained the respect and fear of Allied soldiers and commanders, especially during bombardments like that at Verdun.

Unlike other armies, Germany was mainly disarmed in the 1920s and was not saddled with a huge inventory of obsolescent weapons left over from World War I. Hitler's ambitious program to rearm the Reich included the development of a full range of modern, efficient artillery pieces that would make the new army of the Third Reich second to none. Light field artillery was intended to provide direct fire support to infantry units at division level and below. Existing field guns in 1933, such as the *7.7cm Feldkanone 16*, were modernized and used as interim weapons for training and later for coast defense along the "Atlantic Wall." With a new 7.5cm barrel, it was designated the 7.5cm *FK 16 n/A* (n/A; neuer Art; new model). The same was true of the other mainstay of the German Army in World War I and after, the *10.5cm leichte Feldhaubitze 16*, which was relegated to reserve units and coast defense after replacement with the modern *10.5cm leichte Feldhaubitze 18*, adopted and produced beginning in 1935.

During the 1920s when Germany was prohibited by the peace treaties and Treaty of Versailles from producing or possessing most types of heavy weapons, artillery design and development was secretly conducted in German factory subsidiaries or under contract in other countries such as Sweden, Holland, and Switzerland. Among the new weapons placed in production in Germany after Hitler's rise to power were the *10cm schwere Kanone 18* and *15cm Kanone 18*, and the *15cm Feldhaubitze 18* and *18M*, as well as 17cm and 21cm guns and howitzers. Another type of very heavy artillery built in limited numbers was the railway gun (*Eisenbahn Kanone*) of 15cm, 17cm, 24cm, 28cm, and 38cm.[12]

The 1930s was a transition period when motorization and mechanization of the German Army was emphasized.[13] Most new types of artillery were designed with wheels and axles that allowed them to be towed either by horses or behind a motor vehicle. Several types of military cars and trucks and powerful prime movers with tracks were developed to tow heavy weapons on the battlefield and across rough terrain. Unfortunately for the Wehrmacht, they never had enough of these special vehicles, and most of the army still depended on the horse and *Knobelbecher* (Jackboot) for transportation.

The great need for additional weapons during World War II caused the Heereswaffenamt to press into service dozens of types of captured foreign artillery pieces, especially Russian guns. Some captured guns acquired in various countries were originally manufactured in Germany.

It should be noted that work on new artillery designs began in the 1920s and surreptitious production started in 1933, soon after Hitler was firmly in power. The new designs were at first given misleading model numbers (usually M 18) to suggest that they were much older models dating from World War I.

A note on ammunition: A number of different types of small arms, mortar, and artillery ammunition were employed by the warring powers during World War II. Shells included high-explosive (HE), armor-piercing (AP), illuminating, incendiary, smoke, and other chemical types, and most are still in use today. A type that is not used today is the shrapnel shell. It was invented in 1784 by Lieutenant (later Major General) Henry Shrapnel (1761–1842) of the British Army. It was a projectile containing a large number of lead or zinc balls; when fired, a time fuze set in the base set off a powder charge which in turn scattered these balls to make an effective antipersonnel round. Shrapnel shells became the standard projectiles for field artillery in the nineteenth century when troops usually fought in the open. It was of less use in trench warfare during World War I and was superseded by the high-explosive shell, although some old stocks were used up by the French and by the British as late as 1943.

When modern high-explosive shells explode, they produce fragments or splinters, not shrapnel. Obviously, shrapnel can come only from a shrapnel shell and cannot come from a modern explosive shell, bomb, or grenade. Although commonly used today, the term "shrapnel" to mean fragments, or to refer to a "shrapnel wound," is incorrect.[14]

Infantry Guns

Artillery had been used for centuries for direct fire support of infantry formations. Guns were up front with, or even ahead of the infantry, until the end of the war of movement on the Western Front in late 1914, which saw the widespread use of machine guns in the front lines. From then on artillery, in ever increasing numbers, was located behind the lines and used for indirect fire support. This left the infantry in the trenches with the need for more firepower such as that provided by the small French 3.7cm Infantry Gun M1916, a true "trench gun." With the arrival of Allied tanks on the front, the German Army realized that they required direct-fire weapons in the front lines to supplement the *Granatwerfer* (mortars) then in use with their high angle of fire. Moving some field guns forward was not a satisfactory solution.

During the 1920s, German tacticians and veterans, who studied the experiences of the Army in World War I, confirmed that the infantry needed a light infantry gun that could accompany the troops into the front lines. The result was the development of the *7.5cm leichtes Infanteriegeschuetz 18*, and production began even before Hitler became Reichs Chancellor in January 1933. Originally equipped with spoked iron-rimmed wheels to be drawn by horses, the *leIG 18* weighed only 880 pounds (400 kg). With axles, disk wheels, and pneumatic tires for towing by motor vehicle, it weighed 1,279 pounds (570 kg). With its protective shield, it could be relatively easily manhandled by its usual six-man crew and was used extensively until the end of World War II.

The *15cm schweres Infanteriegeschuetz 33* was the most powerful of all German infantry guns but could not always be taken into the front lines. Like the *leIG 18*, it was produced from 1933 to 1945.[15]

Field Guns

The term *field artillery* generally refers to guns and howitzers of 75 to 105mm, with a crew of about six men, capable of being easily moved by towing with a light motor vehicle or by a team of six horses. One of the first successful field guns with a hydraulic recoiling barrel mechanism was built by Heinrich Ehrhard, cofounder of the Rheinmetall Werke. It entered service with the German Army in 1904. A recoiling mechanism was important because it allowed the gun to remain in position so it did not have to be reaimed after each shot. As mentioned previously, the German Army successfully used the *7.7cm Feldkanone 16* and *10.5cm leichte Feldhaubitze 16* for direct fire during World War I, and these dependable cannon even saw limited service in World War II.[16]

The *7.5cm FK 16 n/A* (the updated gun), was officially replaced by the improved *7.5cm leichte Feldkanone 18*, beginning in 1938. It combined the best features of a Rheinmetall-designed gun with a Krupp carriage. Much more extensive use was made during World War II of the *10.5cm leichte Feldhaubitze 18*, a modern Rheinmetall design adopted as the standard field howitzer by the German Army in 1935. In 1940, the *10.5cm leFH 18* was modified to fire a more powerful round by improving the recoil system and adding a muzzle brake. This gun was designated as the *10.5cm leFH 18M* (M-Muendungsbremse), and other modifications were made during the war based on experience. Another gun in limited production until 1943 was the *10cm Kanone 18*; from 1942, the *10cm Kanone 42*. The guns, with different wheels, were capable of being towed by either horses or motor vehicles. More captured field guns were used by the Wehrmacht than any other type of foreign artillery.[17]

Medium and Heavy Guns

Field artillery of 75mm to 105mm generally provided direct fire support to German divisional units while medium artillery of 105mm to 155mm was intended to furnish long-range fire on rear areas and fortifications. Heavy artillery in the German Army included all guns above 155mm, but there were a few exceptions.

German designers at Krupp and Rheinmetall excelled in artillery design that gained a reputation for excellence as early as the Franco-Prussian War of 1870–71. German *15cm* (150mm) *schwere Feldhaubitze 13* guns used in 1917–18 were obsolete by 1939 and were mainly replaced by the powerful *15cm schwere Feldhaubitze 18*, and from 1942 the *15cm sFH 18M* with muzzle brake. The *15cm Kanone 18* was also standard equipment from 1938, but the gun considered to be the best heavy artillery piece was the *17cm Kanone 18 in Mrs Laf.* (In Moerserlafette — in a howitzer carriage).

German 15cm *schwere Feldhaubitze* 18 (sFH 18), a 150mm (5.9-inch) heavy field howitzer introduced in 1934, was the standard German gun of its type in World War II. Its high-explosive shell weighed 94.7 pounds (43.5 kg) and had a range of 14,572 yards (13,325 meters). *From British War Office*, German Weapons Illustrated *(London, 1943)*

In the heaviest category, the old *langer 21cm Moerser* (howitzers) dating back to 1916 were modernized during the 1930s but were replaced during the war by the *21cm Moerser 18*, introduced in 1939. It in turn was superseded in production in 1942 by the *17cm Kanone 18*. The *24cm Kanone 3* first entered service in 1938 and was used in small numbers. Some additional types of guns in 21cm and 24cm were employed in small numbers along with many captured foreign guns of large caliber, especially in defense of the English Channel and the Atlantic coast.[18]

As described in Chapter V, heavy artillery pieces of almost every type in the German Army inventory were brought to Sevastopol for the final offensive that began in June 1942. Even obsolete heavy guns such as the *42cm Gamma Moerser* from 1906, used before the war for ammunition testing, was dismantled, shipped in on ten special railroad flat cars and reassembled, a task that took a large crew over two and a half days to accomplish. A number of captured guns of

German *17cm Kanone in Mrs. Laf.*, a 170mm (6.7-inch) cannon on the 210cm *Moerser* 18 howitzer carriage, proved to be the best German heavy gun. Its 149.8 pound (68 kg) high-explosive shell had a maximum range of 30,621 yards (28,000 meters). The AP shell weighed 156.4 pounds (71 kg). *From* German Weapons Illustrated, *op. cit.*

large caliber, with their ammunition of various caliber, were also used in the siege. Among the most remarkable heavy guns were the big self-propelled *60cm "Karl" Moerser*.

Railway guns were a unique method of getting very heavy long-range artillery to the front and moving such guns rapidly from one place to another. This was practical in much of Europe but was difficult in Russia because of its limited railway system and different rail gauge. The huge guns on rail lines and spurs were difficult to aim and almost impossible to effectively camouflage, making them vulnerable to air attack.

Heavy railway guns saw service during the western campaign against France in 1940, and were then used for shelling the southeast coast of England. A few were used occasionally at other locations during the war. For example, *Eisenbahn Artillerie Regiment z.b.V 679* bombarded Leningrad with a *28cm Kanone 5 (Eisenbahn)*. Two similar 28cm railway guns were used in Italy. One gun, named "Leopold," but called "Anzio Annie" or the "Anzio Express" by the Americans, emerged frequently from the safety of a railroad tunnel to hurl 562-pound (about 255 kg) shells into the Allied beachhead at Anzio in 1944. "Anzio Annie" was eventually captured in northern Italy and taken to the United States for study. It is currently on display at the U.S. Army Ordnance Museum at Aberdeen Proving Ground, Maryland. And, of course, the most remarkable German railway gun of all, the giant *80cm "Dora,"* helped destroy the Soviet defenses at Sevastopol in June 1942.[19]

Mountain Guns

Mountain artillery was a specialized type for use by highly trained mountain troops. Such guns had to be as small and light as possible and had to be capable of being broken down into small loads for horse and human transport in steep, mountainous terrain. The leIG 18 was modified for mountain service as the *7.5cm leichtes Gebirgsinfanteriegeschuetz 18* and was never fully replaced by the improved *7.5cm Gebirgsgeschuetz 36*, which could be dismantled and carried in eight loads weighing about 1600 pounds (727 kg). The *l0.5cm Gebirgshaubitze 40* entered service in 1942 and could be broken down into four loads that were intended to be towed by the *SdKfz 2k Kettenkrad*, a unique motorcycle half-track made by NSU. Many other older German and captured mountain guns were employed during World War II.[20]

Antiaircraft Guns

Germany fielded the first gun specifically intended to attack an "aircraft." This was the *4cm Ballonkanone,* hurriedly produced by the Krupp Works in 1870 to shoot down balloons escaping from besieged Paris during the Franco-Prussian War of 1870–71. It was a giant single-shot rifle with a shoulder stock attached to a swivel on top of a post mount, which was installed on a four-wheel cart.[21] Antiaircraft guns, known as *Flugabwehrkanone* or *"Flak"* guns in Germany, were first produced in earnest in the early 1900s concurrent with the development of the military dirigible and airplane. World War I saw the use of many types of antiaircraft guns including machine guns on improvised or special post mounts, and the further development of light, medium, and heavy guns by the warring powers, some on the backs of trucks.

The Germans were not permitted to manufacture or possess antiaircraft artillery (AAA) after the Armistice, but secretly continued experiments in Holland and Switzerland during the 1920s on high-velocity guns with flat trajectories. During rearmament in the 1930s, great numbers of new Flak guns were designed and produced, including the *2cm Flugabwehrkanone 30,* followed by the improved *2cm Flak 38* and the *2cm Flugabwehrkanonevierling 38,* a successful four-barrel version on a modified carriage. Other guns were the *3.7cm Flak 18, 3.7cm Flak M42, 3.7cm Flak 43,* and *5cm Flak 41.* Combat tests by the German Condor Legion during the Spanish Civil War (1936–1939) determined that these and larger guns were very effective against ground targets, including tanks, a fact apparently overlooked by foreign military attaches, observers, and reporters. When the famous "88" gun, the *8.8cm Flugabwehrkanone 18,* was used against British tanks in the North African desert in 1941–42, it was at first thought to be a new German secret weapon.[22]

The "88" is probably the best-known artillery piece of World War II and saw service in both the AAA role and in ground combat on every front. The U.S. Army even published a 183-page illustrated manual on the gun so that captured 88s could be properly utilized.[23] Despite its height and bulk, this gun showed that it could knock out even the heaviest tanks, usually before the enemy could get in range with their own guns. In 1943, an antitank version of the *Flak 41* with a low profile was introduced, designated the *8.8cm Pak 43.*

The *8.8cm Flugabwehrkanone 18,* or *Flak 18,* was an original design developed in 1931 by Krupp engineers working in Sweden. It was placed in production in Germany in 1933 and tested in Spain along with its efficient fire control equipment. The

The famous German "88," probably the most effective and versatile gun of World War II. The Luftwaffe's 8.8cm Flak 36 and later versions were in action on every front in both the anti-aircraft role and against tanks and ground targets. With a normal crew of seven, it had a practical rate of fire of 15 rounds per minute. A muzzle velocity of 2,690 feet per second gave it a flat trajectory, long range, and excellent accuracy. The Flak 18, 36, and 37 were the main types used in Barbarossa, with the Flak 41 entering service in 1943. Some captured guns were used by the Allies. *From U.S. War Department,* German 88mm Antiaircraft Gun Materiel, TM E9–369A *(Washington, 1943)*

Flak 36, and *Flak 37* guns were slightly improved models featuring the three-sectioned barrel liner of the Flak 18, and all remained in service through World War II. The *8.8cm Flak 41* was a more powerful version first introduced in 1943 and used mainly for air defense in Germany. The Flak 18, 36 and 37 guns could be equipped with a large shield for defense against enemy fire, an especially useful feature when used in the dual-purpose role. Most antiaircraft guns, even in the ground combat role, were assigned to the German Air Force. At Sevastopol, the *"Acht-Acht"* (88) as the German soldiers often called it, was brought forward by Luftwaffe crews to blast Soviet fortifications and positions in the rocky cliffs and hills.

Allied airmen learned the hard way about the effectiveness of heavier caliber German Flak guns in the German radar-equipped air defense system. They included the *10.5cm Flak 38* and *Flak 39,* the *12.8cm Flak 40,* and the *12.8cm Flugabwehrkanonezwilling 40,* a remarkable twin-gun on a fixed mount used mainly for the air defense of Berlin. In addition, many Russian and other captured AA guns were pressed into service for the air defense of Germany as well as troops and targets behind the fronts. Ammunition for many of these foreign guns was produced during the war when the original supply of ammunition ran out.

Antitank Guns

The introduction of the first tanks on the Western Front by the British Army in 1916 presented the Germans with a dilemma: How to combat these lumbering steel monsters that frightened the infantry and threatened to break through German lines. The first expedient was the use of fire from massed field guns which had some success against the clumsy, slow-moving tanks operating on the muddy, shell-torn battlefields. This was followed shortly by the issue of special armor-piercing 7.9mm cartridges with steel bullets that could be fired from the Gewehr 98 service rifle. This ammunition proved rather successful when fire could be concentrated on the early tanks with thin armor of low quality. More heavily armored tanks with stronger armor plates were countered with fire from the 13mm Tank-Gewehr, as described earlier under antitank rifles. None of these measures were the final answer to the question of how to defeat tanks.

Germany was not permitted to possess tanks after World War I, but the design and manufacture of a lightweight antitank gun was eventually permitted, resulting in the *3.7cm Panzerabwehrkanone L/45,* introduced in 1928. This gun could be drawn by horses and man-handled for short distance by its crew wearing harnesses. A modernized version, the *3.7cm*

The 3.7cm Pak 35/36 was the best German antitank gun until 1941, when more powerful guns entered action. Its service life was extended during the war by the use of *"Stielgranate* 41," large hollow-charge stick shells with fins inserted in the muzzle. The caption on this photo says: *"Panzerjaeger* in defensive battle in Soviet Union." *German Official Photo*

Pak 35/36, with a new axle and magnesium alloy wheels with pneumatic tires, was developed in 1934 for towing by motor vehicles. It was used successfully during the first two years of World War II, but more modern tanks with heavier armor eventually made the 37mm gun obsolete.[24]

A new *5cm Panzerabwehrkanone 38 (5cm Pak 38)* was designed and produced in time for use during the German offensive in the west in May 1940. It also had a shield and a low silhouette like most antitank guns. With tungsten-core ammunition it could penetrate all Allied tanks in 1941 except the heaviest Soviet models and the sloping frontal armor of the T-34 medium tank.

One of the best and most powerful of the standard German antitank guns was the high-velocity *7.5cm Pak 40*, used on all fronts from 1941 to 1945. It was also mounted on several types of self-propelled carriages. However, when it came to supreme stopping power, nothing could compare with the 8.8cm Flak guns with their long range and flat trajectory. It had the disadvantage of having a high profile, especially when equipped with a shield. An *8.8cm Pak 43* with a low profile and shield was introduced during 1943 and was probably the best all-around antitank gun produced by any nation. It featured a semiautomatic breech and electrical firing circuit for rapid fire and proved to be a deadly foe of even the heaviest Allied tanks. As with other weapons, numerous Russian, French, and other captured guns were extensively employed by the Germans during World War II.

During the first months of Barbarossa, the Wehrmacht was almost constantly on the move or attacking, so land mines, both antitank and antipersonnel, were seldom used by the Germans. However, great numbers of Soviet mines were encountered and caused many German casualties despite the best efforts to avoid or neutralize them. The situation was reversed when the Germans went on the defensive. Mines were most troublesome for both sides during the winter because snow hid the mines and the ground was often frozen so hard that holes could not be dug to implant them or remove them.

Tanks and Armored Vehicles

Morale was high among *Panzermaenner* (tankers) during the first few heady weeks of Barbarossa. The Russian landscape was soon littered with wrecked and burning Soviet tanks and guns, and hundreds of thousands of Red Army soldiers were being herded into huge POW camps. With their talented and experienced commanders such as Generals Heinz Guderian and Herman Hoth, excellent radio communications, aerial reconnaissance and close air support, German tank crews were outmaneuvering and soundly defeating the Soviets. Many believed in the summer of 1941 that they were close to achieving final victory on the Eastern Front. Although great battles had been won, there was growing concern as they plunged ever deeper into the vastness of the Soviet Union. And after the first weeks of confusion, the Russians seemed to be fighting back harder than ever.

After weeks of heavy fighting and movement over long distances, the troops of the Wehrmacht were tired, and their tanks, guns, and vehicles badly needed repair and maintenance. In addition, the ever-increasing distances and poor roads made it increasingly difficult to obtain fuel, ammunition, and rations, let alone spare parts. The Fuehrer had said that it would be a short, victorious campaign but now the Blitzkrieg seemed to be slowly running out of steam. Another troubling fact was the seemingly endless number of Russian tanks, guns, and troops encountered, far more than had been predicted. When the Wehrmacht destroyed a dozen Soviet divisions, the Reds brought up twelve more. But most ominous was the fact that the rainy season and winter were coming and to the east lay the endless expanse of forests and barren steppe, drawing them ever farther into a cold, harsh, and primitive world with no end.[25]

The German Panzer (armored) divisions, with their excellent mobility and heavy firepower, formed the spearhead for most of the Blitzkrieg offensives from the Polish campaign in September 1939 to the offensive against the West in 1940 and in the Balkans and North Africa in 1941. The Germans had gained invaluable experience at all levels of command, and during Barbarossa the armored forces were the heart of the German Army's offensive power, contributing greatly to the remarkable victories in the battles of encirclement in 1941.

The principal German tanks in action in Russia in 1941–42 were the *Panzerkampfwagen IIJ* (*PzKw IIJ*), weighing 9.5 tons and armed with a 2cm KwK/180 gun; the *PzKw IIIH*, 21.6 tons, with a good 5cm KwK L/42/99 gun; and the *PzKw IVF-1*, 22.3 tons, with a short-barreled 7.5cm KwK L/24/80 gun. The *PzKw IVF-2* was up-gunned with the more powerful long-barreled 7.5cm KwK 40 L/43 gun and entered action in early 1942. It became the mainstay of the Panzer divisions. The *PzKw V "Panther,"* weighing about 44 tons, with the 7.5cm KwK 42 gun, did not enter service until the summer of 1943. The famous *PzKw VI "Tiger"* heavy tank of 56 tons with the powerful 8.8cm KwK gun first saw action on the Eastern Front in September 1942.[26]

The Czech-built *PzKw 35(t)* light tank of 9.7 tons was used in Barbarossa, armed with a 3.7cm gun. Captured French Somua medium tanks of 18 tons, armed with a 4.7cm gun, were used by some Panzer units, occupation and police forces. Many other captured tanks and vehicles were also pressed into service with second-line units, and police forces, or converted to self-propelled artillery.

The *Sturmgeschuetz* was actually the brainchild of (then) General von Manstein prior to the war, who envisioned them as self-propelled close-support artillery for the infantry divisions. The organic assault gun units were equipped with 7.5cm short-barreled guns built on the PzKw III, and IV chassis. Like the PzKw IV, they were equipped with the long-barreled 7.5cm gun beginning in 1942. Assault guns were under the control of the divisional artillery, not the Panzer arm. The Eleventh Army was not provided with tanks but made good use of the assault guns in the Crimea and at Sevastopol.

Sturmartillerie played an increasingly important role in combat on the Eastern Front. Guns of various calibers were built on the chassis of PzKw II, III, and IV tanks, as well as Czech and captured French tank chassis. There were also tank destroyers, *Panzerjaeger* or *Jagdpanzer*, usually guns built on the PzKw III and IV chassis. German antitank guns or foreign guns were mounted, or the powerful 7.5cm long-barreled gun, and by 1943 the 8.8cm guns were mounted on PzKw III/IV and other chassis. Half-track vehicles were very versatile and were employed in ever-increasing numbers. Called *Schuetzenpanzerwagen*, they served as armored personnel carriers and communication vehicles, and as gun carriers they wrote an entirely new chapter in armored warfare as a partner for the tanks. They were eventually armed with a variety of antitank, field, and flak guns.

Other specialized vehicles included modified tanks for commanders with special radio equipment, armored cars, and ammunition carriers. The main problem was that the Wehrmacht never had enough armored vehicles in reserve to cover losses, even in the first months of Barbarossa, let alone after the Soviet production in the Ural region accelerated in 1942 and Allied lend-lease began arriving in quantity. It should be remembered that from 1942 on, German industry and transportation were subjected to increasing Allied air attack.

Soviet armored warfare capability in 1941 suffered from two main problems: inferior equipment and inexperience. Stalin's purging of the officer corps in the 1930s deprived the Red Army of many of its most experienced and capable commanders. The Russians had thousands of tanks at the beginning of the war but most were obsolete or proved rather ineffective in use because of leadership deficiencies. The Russian light tanks such as the T-40 with a 2cm gun were inadequately armed and armored, and the heavy tanks, such as the KV II with a 15.2cm M-10 howitzer, were slow, unwieldy, and difficult to maneuver on rough terrain.[27]

Russian tanks in 1941 also suffered from lack of adequate communication equipment, and many had no radios at all. Trying to use signal flags hampered Russian command and control during combat. Soviet experience during the war with Finland disclosed the failings of Russian armored vehicles. This, along with the urgency of the situation developing in Europe, prompted swift action to introduce improved tanks such as the superb T-34 medium tank with sloping frontal armor plate.[28] When this new tank with its 7.62cm gun entered action in July 1941, it came as a surprise to the Germans and brought a fear hitherto unknown into the hearts of the Panzer troops. Developing improved tanks immediately became an urgent priority in Germany.

Among the odd tracked vehicles used by the German ground forces during World War II were the *Ladungstraeger*, remote-controlled tracked demolition vehicles. They were designed for attack on fortified positions or enemy tanks, and all were identified as B-IV devices. Type A, also known as *Modell 1*, was the *schwere Ladungstraeger* or heavy charge or load carrier. It was 12 feet long, 4 feet 6 inches high, weighed 4.5 tons, and resembled a small tank. A soldier drove this vehicle en route to the objective, then got out so that the vehicle could be radio controlled to its target, where it was detonated. Apparently only a limited number were ever used.

The Type B (or *Modell 2*) was called *Goliath* and saw much more extensive use. It was smaller and resembled a World War I tank with all-around tracks. Goliath was carried to the release point on a two-wheeled handcart or small trailer. It was 5 feet 3 inches long and 2 feet high, and weighed about 800 pounds depending on the size of the explosive charge. Powered by either a 703cc motorcycle engine or an electric motor, depending on the manufacturer, it was controlled to the target by a wire up to a distance of 50 yards (45.7 meters). The rear compartment contained the wire and reel, the engine and control gear was in the center section, and either a 150-pound (68 kilogram) or 200-pound (90.6 kg) high-explosive charge was located in the front compartment.

A number of Goliaths were used in the siege of Sevastopol, operated by *Panzer Abteilung 300*. During the attack on the southern front, Goliaths entered action as a substitute for artillery fire. They were sent up a road in a steep-sided valley that restricted artillery fire, ahead of the assault troops, and exploded against Russian pillboxes and strong points with some success.

The third model, Type C, was the N.S.U. Springer. It was of intermediate size and was not encountered in action. All things considered, the Ladungstraeger as a secret weapon did not prove to be very practical.

Aircraft Armament

As discussed in Chapter II, Germany built the Luftwaffe, including its elaborate infrastructure, from practically nothing in 1933 to the most powerful air force in Europe in 1939. For details on German aircraft of World War II see the U.S. Army Air Forces Informational Intelligence Summary No. 44–32, *German Aircraft and Armament*, dated October 1944, reprinted by Brassey's Inc. in 2000 with a foreword by Walter J. Boyne.

Concurrent with the rapid development of aircraft and engines was the design and production of aircraft armament. The standard flexible air-cooled machine gun adopted for the new airplanes was the Rheinmetall-Borsig *7.9mm Machinengewehr 15*, a dependable, compact, recoil-operated weapon that could be fitted in various handheld mounts on a variety of aircraft. A fixed version was also used initially. The rate of fire was 750 rounds per minute and the fixed gun could fire about 200 RPM faster. Several improvements were soon made in the fixed version and the modified weapon was produced as the *7.9mm M.G. 17*. Beginning with the new Messerschmitt Bf 109 single-seat fighter, and the two-place, twin-engine Bf 110, the Oerlikon FF 20mm aircraft cannon was installed in the wings or as an engine gun, and later as a flexible gun in bombers. The cyclic rate of fire was about 550 shots per minute.[29]

Germany started the war in 1939 with few types of guns in order to standardize manufacture and achieve large-scale production. When the new generation of bombers, such as the Heinkel He 111, were introduced in the mid-1930s, they were as fast or faster than the biplane fighters in use by Germany and the major European powers. As a result, most German bombers were armed with only three M.G.15 guns; in the nose, in the upper dorsal position in the rear of the fuselage, and below facing the rear. None had power-operated gun turrets. During the Battle of Britain, German bombers faced fast, modern eight-gun Spitfire and Hurricane fighters, and it was soon obvious that defensive armament must be drastically improved. The faster-firing *7.9mm M.G. 81* with a cyclic rate of 1,000 shots per minute was built by Mauser and used as a flexible gun, sometimes in a twin-mount. Soon *the 13mm Mauser M.G. 131* appeared, as a single or as a twin gun in turrets and later as a fixed gun. The *Oerlikon FF 20mm* was replaced on some planes by the Mauser *M.G. 151* in 15 or 20mm. These were not the same gun with a different barrel as was believed during the war, but two different guns with several variations in design. They soon became the basic gun in turrets and fixed mountings.

Fighter armament was increased and synchronized rifle-caliber guns were replaced on some aircraft with 13mm M.G. 131 guns, such as on the Bf 109G models.

The *Maschinenkanone 101* (*M.K. 101*) of 30mm, an automatic cannon, saw some service, and later the *30mm M.K. 108* automatic cannon became the main weapon for the Bf 109G, Me 163, and Me 262 fighter-interceptors. There were other guns, mainly experimental, and heavier guns of 5cm such as the *B.K. 5*, *5.5cm MK 112*, and *MK 114*. Rockets of several types and sizes were employed ending with the advanced *R4M* air-to-air rocket installed under the wings of the Me 262 jet in 1945.

For "tank busting" a Rheinmetall *3.7cm Flak 18* cannon could be specially mounted under the wings of the Junkers Ju 87G Stuka dive bomber. It was used by Colonel Hans-Ulrich Rudel to knock out over 500 Soviet tanks between 1942 and 1945.

A new family of aircraft bombs was developed for the Luftwaffe.[30] Unlike most bombs used by other nations, German bombs normally had two fuzes set in pockets in the side of the bomb body, instead of in the nose or tail. The three principal types of demolition bombs available in various weights and sizes were *Spreng Cylindrisch* (*SC*) high-explosive cylindrical general purpose, *Spreng Dickenwand* (*SD*) semi-armor-piercing and fragmentation, and *Panzer Cylinderisch* (*PC*) armor-piercing. *Sprengbomben* (*SP*) were antipersonnel high-explosive bombs, and there were also bombs with a hollow-charge called a *Hohllandung* (*HL*). *Splitter Beton* (*SBe*) were concrete fragmentation bombs. Rocket-assisted armor piercing bombs were indicated by *PC-RS* and had propellant in the rear of the body. Aircraft torpedoes were employed against shipping, especially on the route to Murmanesk in northern Russia. Dinort rods were secured to the nose of some SD type bombs and used to obtain a "daisy cutter" effect on impact. When attached to the nose of a bomb they were called a *SC Stabo* bomb and caused the bomb to explode above the ground for maximum blast effect. SB bombs were types for maximum blast effect and came in various sizes.

General purpose bombs came in various sizes including the *SC 50* of 50.5 kilograms (about 112 pounds); *SC 250*, 236 kg (about 500 pounds); *500 SC*, 500 kg (1,188 pounds); *1000 SC*, 1,000 kg (2,250 pounds); *1200 SC*, 1,117 kg (2,475 pounds); *1800 SC "Satan,"* 1,800 kg (4,000 pounds); *2000 SC*, 1,950 kg (4,350 pounds); and the *2500 SC "Max,"* 2,400 kg (5,300 pounds). Max was the largest type of conventional bomb employed operationally by the Luftwaffe. It was 12 feet 9 inches long and 2 feet 8 inches in diameter and was too large to fit in the bomb bay of any German bomber, so it was carried on an external fuselage rack. The 2500 SC "Max" bomb was carried on the Heinkel He 111H bomber and dropped on Sevastopol during the siege.

Incendiary, smoke, and practice bombs were also available, and during the war guided bombs and missiles were developed for aircraft use.

INFANTRY WEAPONS

Type	Calibre	Weight	Practical rate of fire rpm	Maximum practical range yards	Weight of projectile	German name of ammunition fired	Muzzle velocity f.s.	Remarks
Pistols								
(a) Pistol 08 (Lüger) ...	9 mm (·35″)	1 lb 14 oz	—	50 to 100 yds	123 grains	Pist Patr 08 (ball)		Self-loading — One of the standard service pistols.
(b) Pistol 38 (Walther) ...	9 mm (·35″)	1 lb 15 oz	—	50 to 100 yds	123 grains	Pist Patr 08 (ball)		Self-loading. Another standard pistol.
(c) Grenade pistol (Walther) (Kampfpistole)	27 mm (1″)	1 lb 9½ oz	—	100 yds (approx)	5 oz	Sprenggranate Z (HE) Nebelgranate Z (smoke) Deutgranate Z (indicating)		A modification of a standard signal pistol with a rifled barrel and small dial sight.
Rifles								
(a) Rifle 98 (bolt-operated) ...	7·92 mm (·31″)	About 9 lb	—	Sighted for 100–200 metres	198 grains 194 grains	Patr SS (ball) Patr Sm K (H) (AP with tungsten carbide core)	2,510 2,860	Several types in use, the latest being a short rifle (length 44¼ in) Gewehr 98/40.
(b) Rifle 41 (W) (self-loading)	7·92 mm (·31″)	10 lb 14 oz	—	Sighted for 100–1,200 metres	,,	,,	,,	Reload automatically after each shot. Magazines hold 10 rounds.
(c) Rifle 41 (M) (self-loading)	7·92 mm (·31″)	10 lb 4 oz	—	,,	,,	,,	,,	
Rifle grenades (fired from discharger cup fitted to rifle (a) or anti-tank rifle (b))								
(a) Anti-personnel	3-cm (1·2″)	9 oz	10–15	250	9 oz	Gewehr Spreng-granate 30	—	(a) Can be thrown by hand, with 4½ sec delay. Functions when fired on impact; self-destroying after 11 sec should fuze not function.
(b) Small anti-tank ...	3-cm (1·2″)	8·8 oz	,,	100	8·8 oz	Gewehr Panzer-granate 30	—	Functions on impact on hollow charge principle. Penetration approx 30 mm.
(c) Large anti-tank ...	3-cm (1·2″)	13·5 oz	,,	100	13·5 oz	Gross Gewehr Panzergranate 40	—	Has a larger bursting charge than (b).
Hand grenades								
(a) Stick grenade	—	{ 1 lb 5 oz { 1 lb 6 oz	—	About 50	{ 1 lb 5 oz { 1 lb 6 oz	—	—	There are two types, model 24 and PH 39. HE may be replaced by smoke composition, and in this case is sometimes fitted with an adaptor for throwing without the stick.
(b) Egg grenade	—	8 or 10 oz	—	About 25	8 or 10 oz	—	—	Relies on blast for effect as (a) above. 5 sec delay.
Anti-tank rifles								
(a) A tk rifle (Pz B 39) ...	7·92 mm (·31″)	27 lb 4 oz	6–8	Up to 300 yds	225 grains	Patr 318	3,800 (approx)	Fires an AP tracer bullet with a tungsten carbide core and a small lachrymatory pellet. Penetration 33 mm at 100 yds at normal.
(b) A tk grenade rifle (Granatbüchse 39)	7·92 mm (·31″)	23 lb 2 oz	—	—	—	—	—	Fitted with discharger cup and fires rifle grenades described above. Bulleted blank cartridge.

FLAMETHROWERS

Type	Weight (charged)	Quantity of fuel carried	Range	Duration of continuous discharge	Remarks
	lb.	*gals.*	*yds.*	*secs.*	
Small, model 35	79	2·2	25	10—12	The equipment with which the army was equipped at the outbreak of war. This is a one-man load, though it usually has a crew of two. The equipment is carried on the back. Ignition is by means of a ring of burning hydrogen gas round the nozzle of the projector.
Small, model 40 (Lifebuoy)	47	1·5	25	8	This is a lightweight flamethrower, made in the form of two lifebuoy like rings—a large outer one for fuel and a smaller concentric one for hydrogen. In respects other than the pack layout, this equipment resembles the one above.
Small, model 41	44½	1·5	25	8	This flamethrower has a pack of two horizontal cylinders, the lower (larger) one for fuel and the upper one for nitrogen. The projector is the same as that used in the earlier models, with a long, thin cylinder (for hydrogen) mounted on the top.
Small, model 42	about 42—44	1·5	25	8	The model 42 flamethrower is the same as the model 41 except for the projector, which is a new design. The projector is shorter, has a large trigger lever on the side (instead of a short one on the top) and incorporates a new method of fuel ignition.
Medium	225	6·6	25—30	25	This is carried on a two-wheeled trolley and is simply a larger model of the small portable flamethrower model 35.
Flamethrower tank Pz Kw II (F) Sd Kfz 122.	—	2 × 35	35	3–4 mins	This equipment has two projectors, one on the front of each track guard. Each projector has a 180° traverse from 9 to 3 o'clock.

NOTE.—To assist maintenance in the field, a recharging trolley is provided. This has two tyred wheels, is drawn by two men and carries fuel oil, a cylinder of nitrogen, charged hydrogen cylinders and spare parts. Total weight 680 lb.

Wehrmacht weapons and equipment data. *From British War Office*, Pocket Book of the German Army 1943 *(London, 1943)*

INFANTRY WEAPONS—*contd.*

Type	Calibre	Weight	Practical rate of fire rpm	Maximum practical range yards	Weight of projectile	German name of ammunition fired	Muzzle velocity f.s.	Remarks
Machine carbines Schmeisser MP38/40	9 mm (·35″)	9 lb	Cyclic 520–540	Up to 250– 300 yds	123 grains 98·5 grains	Pist Patr 08 (ball) Pist Patr 08 m.E. (semi-AP)	1,260	The standard weapon. Vertical box magazine 32 rds. The following other types are in service : (a) Schmeisser 28ᴵᴵ. Straight box magazine in left side of weapon—32 rds. (b) Bergmann MP18ᴵ. Snail type magazine on left side. (c) Bergmann MP34ᴵ. Straight box magazine on right. (d) Steyr-Solothurn MP34 (δ). Straight box magazine on left. Fires long Mauser pistol ammunition (Pist Patr M 34 (δ)).
Machine guns (a) MG 34	7·92 mm (·31″)	26·5 lb (weight tripod 42 lb)	150 as MMG 300 (cyclic 800–900)	1,650 as MMG 3,750	198 grains 178 ,, 157 ,,	*For LMG* Patr s.S. (ball) Patr s.m.K (A.P.) Patr s.m.K.L'sp (A.P/T)		These MGs may be used as light or medium MGs according to type of mounting provided (bipod or tripod). Belts of 50 are fired and two or more may be joined. Barrel changing after 250 rds more or less continuous fire. Single and twin AA mountings are also provided.
(b) MG 42	7·92 mm (·31″)	23·75 lb (weight tripod 43¼ lb)	150–160 as MMG probably 400 (cyclic about 1200)	1,650 as MMG 3,750		*For MMG* Patr s.S. or S.m.E. (semi-A.P.) Patr S.m.K. Patr S.m.K.L'sp		
Mortars (a) 5-cm (l.Gr.W.36) (equivalent of 2″)	—	30·8 lb	Max 45	515	2·2 lb	5-cm Wgr 36 (HE)	262	The standard light mortar. Has one charge only
(b) 8-cm (m.Gr.W.34) (equivalent of 3″)	—	12·5 lb	Max 45	2,078	7·75 lb	8-cm Wgr 34 (HE) ,, ,, 38 (airburst) ,, ,, 39 (,,) ,, ,, 34 (Nb) (smoke) ,, ,, 34 (Deut) (indicator)	499	Divides into three parts, each weighing about 40 lb. The crew consists of one NCO and five men. Has five charges.
(c) 12-cm (4·7″) See Remarks. (i) Russian ... ... (ii) French " Brandt " (iii) Finnish " Tampella "	 12-cm (4·7″) 12-cm (4·7″) 12-cm (4·7″)	 5½ cwt 16 cwt 5 cwt	 6 6 12	 6,500 8,000 7,550	 35 lb 37 lb 27½ lb	(i) 12-cm Wgr 378/1 (r) ,, ,, 378/2 (r) ,, ,, 378/3 (r) all HE	 — — —	Certain German units are being equipped with 12-cm mortars. These are certainly the Russian (i) (Gr.W.378 (r)), and may also be the French " Brandt " (ii) or the Finnish " Tampella " (iii) 12-cm mortars.

CLOSE-SUPPORT GUNS

Type	Calibre	Weight	Practical rate of fire rpm	Maximum practical range— yards	Weight of projectile	German name of ammunition fired	Muzzle velocity fs	Remarks
INFANTRY GUNS								
(a) 7·5-cm (2·95-in) inf gun		880 lb	5–10	3,880 3,780	12 lb 13·2 lb	7·5-cm Igr 18 Do. do.	730 690	
(b) 15-cm (5·91-in) inf gun		1·5 tons	4	5,140	83·6 lb	15-cm Igr 33 and 38	790	
ASSAULT GUNS								
(a) 7·5-cm (2·95-in) assault gun		19·9 tons		6,758 5,668 1,635 3,270	12·6 lb 9·68 lb 14·96 lb 13·64 lb	HE Hollow charge APCBC, Smoke	1,378 1,476 1,263 1,387	On Pz Kw III chassis
(b) 15-cm (5·91-in) assault gun		11 tons	4	5,140	83·6 lb	15-cm Igr 33 and 38	790	On Pz Kw II chassis

ARTILLERY WEAPONS—MOUNTAIN, FIELD, MEDIUM, AND HEAVY

Type	Weight in action	Weight of shell	Muzzle velocity— feet per sec	Maximum range— yds	Degrees elevation	Degrees depression	Degrees traverse	Remarks
7·5-cm (2·95-in) mountain gun (Geb K15)	·62 tons	12 lb	Normal third charge— 1,000 Super fourth—1,270	5,890 7,250	50°	−9°	7°	Obsolescent equipment
7·5-cm (2·95-in) mountain gun (Geb Gesch 36)	74 tons	HE—12 lb 10 oz or 12 lb 13 oz Hollow charge shell— 9 lb 12 oz	1,558 (HE) 1,280 (hollow charge)	10,115 (HE) 1,094 (hollow charge shell)	70°	−1° 53′	40° (trails open) 4° (trails closed)	Indicator shell (K Gr rot Deut für Geb G36)
7·5-cm (2·95-in) light field gun (lFK18)	1·1 tons	13 lb (HE) 13·6 lb (smoke) 11 lb (hollow charge) 15 lb (APCBC tracer)	590 (small charge) 1,180 (medium charge) 1,590 (large charge)	2,980 8,070 10,310	45°	−5°	30°	Very light equipment, on wooden spoked artillery wheels ; but travels well behind a fast truck
10·5-cm (4·14-in) guns (s10 cm K18)	5·5 tons	33·5 lb (HE) 31·25 lb (AP) 34·62 lb (APCBC)	1,805 (small charge) 2,264 (medium charge) 2,740 (large charge)	13,900 (small) 17,200 (medium) 20,800 (large)	45°	−1°	60°	Standard equipment. Being replaced by 10-cm K42
10·5-cm (4·14-in) gun howitzer (lFH18, and lFH18M)	1·9 tons	32·6 lb (HE) 31·25 lb (AP tracer) 25·9 lb (hollow charge) 32·4 lb and 30·8 lb (smoke shell)	Normal fifth charge— 1,280 Super sixth charge— 1,540	11,670	40°	−6°	56°	lFH18M fitted with muzzle brakes, fires a special long range shell with long range charge. MV= 1,772 f/sec. Max range= 13,470 yds. An lFH42 has also been reported
10·5-cm (4·14-in) mountain howitzer (Geb H40)								
15-cm (5·91-in) howitzer (sFH18)	5·4 tons	95·7 lb (HE anti-concrete shell, AP shell, smoke shell)	1,705	14,570	45°	−1°	60°	A model with muzzle brake, sFH 18/40, has been reported, also an sFH42 details of which are not known
15-cm (5·91-in) gun (K16)	10·7 tons	113·5 lb (HE)	2,485 (large) 2,280 (medium) 1,820 (small)	24,100	42°	−3°	8°	Believed to be still standard equipment. Improved 15-cm K16 KP of last war
15-cm (5·91-in) gun (K18)	12·6 tons	99 lb (HE APCB and APCBC)	2,920	27,200	5°	−4°	60°	Believed to be new equipment to replace K16. This gun is also provided with a platform weighing 5·9 tons
17·25-cm (6·79-in) medium gun (17-cm K18 in Mrs Lafette)	17·5 tons	150 lb (charge 1–3) 138 lb (charge 4)	2,034 2,428 2,821 3,035	20,013 32,371	50°	0°	16° (360° on platform)	Carriage interchangeable with 21-cm Mrs18. Can be used against AFVs at ranges up to 1,640 yds
21-cm (8·27-in) howitzer (Lg 21-cm Mrs)	9 tons	264 lb	1,350	11,220	70°	6°	4°	Obsolete equipment
21-cm (8·27-in) howitzer (Mörser 18)	16·4 tons	267 lb (HE—21-cm Gr18) (Anti-concrete—21-cm Gr 18 Be)	1,854	18,263	72°	0°	360°	New equipment

ARTILLERY WEAPONS—ANTI-AIRCRAFT

Type	Calibre	Muzzle velocity in f/s	Max horizontal range yds	Ceiling* ft	Time of flight to ceiling secs	Wt of projectile	Rate of fire Theoretical	Rate of fire Practical	Wt in action	Remarks
2-cm Flak 30	20 mm (·79-in)	2,950	5,230	7,215	6·0	4·2 oz (HE) 5·2 oz (AP)	280	120	9·25 cwt	AA/A tk. Fitted with Flakvisier 35 (course and speed sight). MT drawn or on SP mounting. Accurate engagement unlikely above about 3,500 ft.
2-cm Flak 38	20 mm (·79-in)	2,950	5,230	7,215	6·0	4·2 oz (HE) 5·2 oz (AP)	420–480	180–220	8 cwt	(a) AA/A tk. Fitted with Flakvisier 38 (tachymetric sight). MT drawn or on SP mounting. Accurate engagement unlikely above about 3,500 ft. (b) A mountain version also exists.
2-cm Flakvierling 38 (four-barrelled)	20 mm (·79-in)	2,950	5,230	7,215	6·0	4·2 oz (HE) 5·2 oz (AP)	1680–1920	700–800	1·48 tons	AA/A tk. Fitted with Flakvisier 40 (tachymetric sight). MT drawn or on SP mounting. Accurate engagement unlikely above about 3,500 ft.
3·7-cm Flak 18 & 36	37 mm (1·45-in)	2,690	7,080	13,775	14	1·4 lb (HE) 1·5 lb (AP)	140	60	1·53 tons	(a) AA/A tk. Fitted with Flakvisier 33 (course and speed sight). MT drawn or on SP mounting. There is also a new type shell self-destroying at 7–10 secs at 9,185–11,480 ft. Accurate engagement unlikely above about 5,000 ft. (b) A new gun, the 3·7-cm Flak 37, with identical performance and fitted with Flakvisier 37 (tachymetric sight) has recently been introduced. (c) There is also a 3·7-cm Flak 43, about which nothing is known at present.
8·8-cm Flak 18 & 36	88 mm (3·46-in)	2,690	16,200	32,500	—	20 lb (HE) 21 lb (AP)	—	15–20	4·92 tons	AA/A tk. Telescopic sight, ZF20E, fitted for engagement of ground targets. MT drawn. Effective ceiling: 26,250 ft (see note).
8·8-cm Flak 41	88 mm (3·46-in)	3,280	22,000	39,400	—	20·68 lb (HE) 22·44 lb (AP)	—	20		AA/A tk. MT drawn. Particulars of this gun are at present incomplete. Effective ceiling is estimated at about 35,000 ft (see note).

*Note.—Ceilings quoted for *light guns* denote heights at which self-destruction takes place at maximum QE; heights up to which accurate engagement is likely are given in " Remarks " column.
Ceilings quoted for *heavy guns* are based on maximum fuze range; effective ceilings (based on 20 secs engagement of directly approaching aircraft flying at 300 mph, last round being fired at QE 70°) are given in " Remarks " column.

SMOKE MORTARS AND MULTIPLE ROCKET PROJECTORS

N.B.—The smoke mortars, properly so called at Serials 1 and 2, should not be confused with the rocket projectors at Serials 3 and 5 where the term "smoke mortar" is merely a convenient rendering of the misleading German term "Nebelwerfer." All are potential CW weapons.

Serial	Equipment	Weight in action	Weight of projectile	Type of projectile	Max range	Rate of fire	Transport	Remarks
1	SMOKE MORTARS 10·5-cm (4·14-in) smoke mortar 35 (10-cm Nebelwerfer 35)	231 lb	16 lb	HE Smoke	3,300 yds	12–15 rpm	2-wheeled handcart	Standard smoke/CW weapon.
2	10·5-cm (4·14-in) smoke mortar 40 (10-cm Nebelwerfer 40)	15–25 cwt	19 lb	HE Smoke	6,780 yds (min range 550 yds)	8–10 rpm	2-wheeled rubber-tyred carriage	Breech-loaded.
3	MULTIPLE ROCKET PROJECTORS 15-cm (5·91-in) smoke mortar 41 (15-cm Nebelwerfer 41 or Werfer 41; formerly Nebelwerfer d)	10½ cwt	71 lb	HE Smoke	6,670 yds	6 rounds every 90 secs	Mounted on pair of rubber-tyred wheels and split trail	Weapon resembles small gun and has six barrels arranged in circle like the chambers of a revolver.
4	15-cm (5·91-in) rocket projector (15-cm DO Gerät 38)		Probably as for Serial 3	Probably as for Serial 3				Equipment, designed for dropping by parachute, comprises bipod and projector frame in form of rectangular metal framework 7–8 ft × 6 ft.
5	21-cm (8·26-in) smoke mortar 42 (21-cm Nebelwerfer 42, formerly Nebelwerfer e)	245 lb		HE				A larger version of the 15-cm (5·91-in) smoke mortar 41.
6	Heavy projector 40 (schweres Wurfgerät 40)		183 lb 174 lb	28-cm (11-in) HE 32-cm (12·6-in) incendiary	1,090–2,080 yds 1,090–2,180 yds Indications of development of new projectile said to have range of 6,000 yds	Four HE or incendiary projectiles in rapid succession		Consists of a stand in the form of a wooden ramp, which is transported to firing position and then dismounted for firing.
7	Heavy projector 41 (schweres Wurfgerät 41)		183 lb 174 lb	28-cm (11-in) HE 32-cm (12·6-in) incendiary	Ditto	Ditto		Similar to heavy projector 40, but stand is made of metal.
8	Heavy projector 40 on armoured semi-tracked vehicle (Schwerer Wurfrahmen 40 am mgp Zgkw—Sd Kfz 251)	Ditto	Ditto	Ditto	Ditto	6 rounds in 10 secs		Consists of six projector frames, mounted on medium armoured semi-tracked vehicle, three on each side. Frames can be elevated, but not traversed.
9	28/32-cm (11/12·6-in) smoke mortar 41 (28/32-cm Nebelwerfer 41)		183 lb 174 lb	28-cm (11-in) HE 32-cm (12·6-in) incendiary				Fires same ammunition as Serials 6, 7 and 8. Possibly multi-barrelled.

ANTI-TANK AND TANK GUNS

Serial	Type of Weapon	Practical rate of fire rpm	Weight of gun in action	Weight of Projectile	Types of Ammunition and Penetration Performance	Ft per sec Muzzle Velocity	Comments
1	2-cm (·79-in) AA/A tk gun (2-cm Flak 30)	120	1,036 lb	1. HE 4·2 oz 2. AP 5·2 oz 3. AP incendiary 5·2 oz 4. AP 40 shot 3·6 oz	HE incendiary (with or without tracer), AP, AP incendiary, AP self-destroying and AP 40 shot. The AP shell penetrates 31 mm of homogeneous armour plate at 30° at 100 yds and 25 mm at 30° at 400 yds. The AP 40 shot penetrates 49 mm at 30° at 100 yds and 37 mm at 400 yds.	1. 2950 2. 2625 3. 2625 4. 3270 (AP 40)	MT drawn or on SP mounting.
2	2-cm (·79-in) AA/A tk gun four-barrelled (2-cm Flakvierling 38)	700–800	1·48 tons	See Serial No. 1	See Serial No. 1	See Serial No. 1	Four 2-cm Flak 38 guns mounted together with a dual AA/A tk role. Normally transported on Trailer 52 (Sd Ah 52), but is also carried on semi-tracked vehicles. Provision is made for single shot or continuous fire on each weapon.
3	2-cm (·79-in) AA/A tk gun (2-cm Flak 38)	180–220	906 lbs, but in draught is about 14¾ cwt	See Serial No. 1	See Serial No. 1	See Serial No. 1	This is the single version of the Flakvierling 38 above. The performance of the gun does not differ materially from the older 2-cm Flak 30 apart from a higher rate of fire. There is a mtn version (2-cm Geb Flak 38), exactly the same, but on a light mounting—7 cwt.
4	2-cm (·79-in) Tank gun (2-cm KwK 30)	120	Weight of gun 142·5 lb	See Serial No. 1	See Serial No. 1	See Serial No. 1	The piece is the same as the 2-cm Flak 30 (Serial No. 1 above). It was formerly the principal armament of the Pz Kw II and stands in a similar relationship to the later 2-cm KwK 38 as does the 2-cm Flak 30 to the 2-cm Flak 38.
5	2-cm (·79-in) Tank gun (2-cm KwK 38)	180–220	Weight of gun 142·5 lb	See Serial No. 1	See Serial No. 1	See Serial No. 1	This gun is essentially identical in design with the 2-cm Flak 38, save that the magazine holds only 10 rds against 20 in the case of the 2-cm Flak 38. It is the latest model of the 2-cm KwK 30, whose functions it assumed.
6	2·8-cm (1·1-in) A tk gun 41 (2·8-cm Pz B 41)	8 to 10	501 lb	AP 4·6 oz HE 3·02 oz	HE and AP. The AP shell penetrates 69 mm of homogeneous armour plate at 100 yds at 30° and 53 mm at 30° at 400 yds	AP 4580	Tapered-bore gun. Splits up into loads of under 132 lb. Normally it is towed portee on a trailer equipped with ramps. It may be mounted on a lorry, split into a five-man load or transported by air. There is also a specially light parachutists' version.
7	3·7-cm (1·45-in) A tk gun (3·7-cm Pak)	8 to 10	890 lb	1. HE 1 lb 6 oz (shell) 2 lb 10 oz (round) 2. AP 1 lb 8 oz (shell) 3 lb 2 oz (round) 3. AP 40 shot 12·5 oz 2 lb 4. 3·7-cm (1·45-in) – muzzle stick bomb (Mun 3·7-cm Pak Stiel Gr) 13 lb.	HE, AP and AP 40 shot. AP penetrates 42 mm of homogeneous armour plate at 200 yds at 30°, 36 mm at 500 yds at 30°. AP 40 shot penetrates 68 mm at 100 yds at 30°, 49 mm at 400 yds at 30°	AP 2,625 AP 40 3,450	This was formerly the chief German anti-tank gun, but is now being extensively replaced by the 5-cm (1·97-in) A tk gun 38. It is towed on its own wheels, or mounted in an armd tp carrying vehicle and can be air-borne.
8	4·2-cm (1·65-in) A tk gun (4·2-cm Pak 41)			AP ·796 lb	AP estimated penetration 93 mm homogeneous armour plate at 30° at 200 yds, 55 mm at 30° at 1,000 yds. HE also fired.	4,600	Tapered-bore gun.
9	4·7-cm (1·85-in) SP A tk gun (4·7-cm Pak)		7·5 tons complete with chassis	1. HE 5·1 lb 2. AP 3·6 lb 3. AP 40 1·8 lb	AP, HE and AP 40. AP penetrates 59 mm of homogeneous armour plate at 30° at 300 yds, 55 mm at 500 yds at 47 mm at 1,000 yds at 30°.	AP 2,540 HE 1,300	Mounted on the Pz Kw I tk chassis, and has a three-sided armour plate shield. With the gun are 74 rounds AP and 10 rounds HE. The gun itself is of Czech origin. It has a crew of three.
10	5-cm (1·97-in) A tk gun (5-cm Pak 38)	12	2,016 lb (18 cwt)	1. HE 3·9 lb 2. APC 4·56 lb 3. AP 40 2 lb	APC penetrates 65 mm of homogeneous armour plate at normal at 500 yds, and 52 mm at 1,000 yds at 30°. Fires HE, APC, and AP 40.	APC 2,700 AP 40 3,445 HE 1,800	Mounted on a split trail carriage and normally towed by a semi-tracked tractor. Can be air-transported.
11	5-cm (1·97-in) Tk gun (5-cm KwK)		Weight of gun, 489 lb	1. HE 3·9 lb 2. APC 4·56 lb 3. AP 40 2 lb	Fires HE, APC and AP 40. APC penetrates 68 mm of homogeneous armour plate at normal at 500 yds and 54 mm at 1,200 yds. AP 40 shot penetrates 83 mm of homogeneous armour plate at 30° at 200 yds, and 69 mm at 500 yds.	APC 2,250 AP 40 3,445 HE 1,476	Mounted in the older Pz Kw III tank.

TANKS

Name	Type	Weight	Country of origin	Crew	Armor (maximum)	Armament	Ammunition	Engine	Road speed	Radius	Suspension system
Pz.Kw. I (Sd. Kfz. 101).	Obsolete, but may still be used as reconnaissance, liaison, and command vehicle.										
Pz.Kw. II (Sd.Kfz. 121).	Light	9 tons	Germany	3	40-mm	One 20-mm Hv MG, one LMG.		6-cyl Maybach air-cooled.	25 mph	125 miles	5 wheels; older type has 4 small bogies, 3 connected by girder.
Pz.Kw. IIF (Sd. Kfz. 121) aus A.	Light	12 tons	Germany	3	30-mm	One LMG, two flame-throwers mounted on each track guard.	1,800 rds. of SAA, 35 gals of oil.		34 mph	155 miles	large bogies, 4 return rollers.
CZDV8H Pz.Kw. 38 (t)	Light medium.	16.5 tons	Czechoslovakia.	4	36-mm	One 47-mm gun, one Hv MG coaxially mounted, one Hv MG to left of driver.	90 rounds for 47-mm gun, 3,000 for Hv MG's.	245 hp V8	27 mph	77 miles	9 bogie wheels, 1 independent; 4 pairs of bogies each with semi-elliptic leaf springing connected by outside bearer girder.
Pz.Kw.III(Sd.Kfz. 141).	Light medium.	18–20 tons	Germany	5	50-mm	One 50-mm gun, one LMG coaxially mounted, one LMG in hull.		320 hp V121 water-cooled	28 mph	100 miles	(a) Latest type with 6 small rubber bogies, independently sprung. (b) 8 small bogie wheels. (c) 8 small bogies in 4 pairs with leaf springings, but all have 3 return rollers.
Pz.Kw.IV(Sd.Kfz. 161).	Medium	22 tons	Germany	5	60-mm	One 75-mm gun, one LMG coaxially mounted, one LMG on ball mount to right of driver.		320 hp V121 water-cooled	25 mph		8 small bogie wheels, 4 pairs with leaf springing.
Somua (S. 40)	Medium	18 tons	France	3	40-mm	One 47-mm, one MG.		190 hp water-cooled.	29 mph	140 miles	9 small bogies protected by armor plating with 2 return rollers.
Pz.Kw.VI("Tiger").	Heavy	56–62 tons	Germany	5	102-mm	One 88-mm, two MG's, one MG to right of driver, others mounted coaxially, three smoke grenade dischargers.		680 hp	22 mph	75 to 85 miles	8 axles, 24 Christie-type wheels on each side.

Characteristics of tanks.

RESTRICTED

AIRCRAFT

Aircraft manufacturer and model	Engines, model and hp rating	Weight (gross lbs)	Speed (maximum mph)	Service ceiling (ft)	Cruising range (miles)	Armament (caliber in mm)	Bomb load (lbs)
Focke-Wulf, F.W. 190A, Fighter or Fighter-Bomber.	BMW 801D 1 x 1,695 hp at S. L. (fully rated).	8,580 to 10,803 maximum.	392 at 17,250 ft.	36,500	Normal 380. Maximum 960.	2 x MG 151/20+2 x MG 17/7.9+2 x FF/20 MG 17 and FF Oerlikon may be omitted on fighter-bombers.	Normal 1 x 550 or 1 x 1,100. Maximum 1 x 2,200 (overload).
Messerschmitt, Me. 109 G, Fighter or Fighter-Bomber.	DB 605 1 x 1,425 hp at 21,300 ft.	8,000 to 8,500. (estimated)	385 at 25,000 ft.	40,000+ (estimated)	Normal 400. Maximum 1,020 (fighter with external tanks).	3 x MG 151/20+2 x MG 131/13.	550.
Messerschmitt, Me. 110 TE, Fighter-Bomber.	DB 601A 2 x 1,150 hp at 2,400 rpm.	15,360	365 at 19,000 ft.	33,300	Normal 920. Maximum, 1230.	Normal 4 x MG 17/7.9 +2 x FF/20+1 x MG 15/7.9.	Normal, none. Occasionally 615.
Messerschmitt, Me. 210 TE, Fighter-Bomber.	DB 601F 2 x 1,400 hp at 14,500 ft.	20,250 (estimated)	365 at 20,000	33,000 (estimated)	1,300 with 1,100 lb bombs at 323 mph.	2 x MG 151/20+2 x MG 17/7.9 at 2 x MG 131/13 in Barbettes.	Normal 1,100. Maximum 3,300.
Henschel, Hs. 129, Ground-Attack Dive Bomber.	Gnome-Rhone, 14M 2 x 820 at 10,500 ft.	12,000	275 at 11,000 ft.	25,300	Normal 460. Maximum 520.	2 x MG 151/15+2 x MG 17/7.9 and 1 x MK 101/30.	Maximum 770. When MK 101/30 is carried load is 2 x 110 or 45 x 4.4.
Junkers, Ju. 88 C 6 TE, Fighter-Bomber Night Fighter.	BMW 801 Dz 2 x 1,650 at 15,000 ft.	24,000	345	32,500	Normal 820, maximum 1,660 with fuel overload.	3 x FF/20+3 x MG 17/7.9. (May vary.)	Normal, none. Maximum 1,100.
Junkers, Ju.89 A-4, Bomber and Dive Bomber.	Jumo 211J 2 x 1260 at 12,500 feet.	29,300	300	19,500 to 30,000.	Normal 1,130; maximum Bombers 680. Maximum fuel 2280.	4 to 5 MG 81/7.9	Normal 4,400. Maximum 6,600.
Junkers, Ju. 87D, "Stuka" Dive Bomber.	Jumo 211J 1 x 1260 at 12,500.	9,400 to 10,500.	245 at 15,000 feet.	24,500	425 to 950	2 x MG 17/7.9+2 x MG 81/7.9.	Normal 1,100. Maximum 3,100 or 1 x 2,200 rocket bomb or 1 x 3,000+4 x 100.
Heinkel, He. 111 H6, Bomber	Jumo 211F 2 x 1,200 at 13,300 feet.	25,300 to 31,000.	255 at 16,000 feet.	26,500	840/900 to 1,760/1,900 maximum.	1 x FF/20+2 x MG 15/7.9+2 x MG 81/7.9+1 x MG 17/7.9.	Normal 4,400. Maximum 6,200 bombs or torpedoes.
Focke-Wulf, FW. 200K, Bomber and L. R. Recn.	Bramo-Fafnir 323R 4 x 940 at 12,000 feet.	50,500	250 at 13,000 feet.	21,500	1,250 to 2,430.	2 x MG 131/13+2 x MG 151/20+1 x MG 15/7.9. (May vary.)	Normal 3,300. Maximum 11,000. May carry mines or torpedoes.
Dornier, Do. 217E2, Bomber and Dive Bomber.	BMW 801A 2 x 1,650 at 15,300 ft.	32,000 to 34,000.	325 at 17,000 ft.	22,500	1,090 to 2,150 maximum.	3 x MG 131/13 + 2 x MG 81/7.9. (May vary.)	Normal 4,400. Maximum 6,600. May carry torpedoes.
Heinkel, He. 177, Heavy Bomber.	DB 606 2 x 2,300 mounted in pairs =4 x 1,150.	6,700 (estimated)	270/300 at 18,000 ft. (estimated)	21,000 ft (estimated)	3,400 maximum. (estimated)	3/6 MG 131/13 + 1 x MG 151/15 or 20.	Normal 13,200. Maximum 16,000 or 8 torpedoes.
Junkers, Ju. 52. Transport.	BMW 132A or T 3 x 660 hp. at S L.	23,100 maximum	165 mph	16,000	Maximum load 530. Maximum fuel 4,000 lb. load 790.	2 to 4/7.9 MG	22 fully equipped troops or 5,000 lb. freight.
Messerschmitt, Me. 323, Transport.	Gnome-Rhone 14 M 6 x 820 hp at 10,000 ft.	65/70,000. lbs. (estimated)	140 at S L (estimated)	? Low flying.	?	6 MG	(Estimated). 120 fully equipped troops, motorcars or small tanks 20/25,000 lb. freight.

Characteristics of German airplanes.

SOVIET WEAPONS

The basic mission of an army in wartime is to break things and kill people. During World War II the Soviet Army not only became very proficient at this but eventually became one of the world's foremost military powers. Soviet willingness to destroy was evident in 1941 when Josef Stalin ordered the "scorched earth" policy of demolishing everything of value that could not be evaluated ahead of the advancing Germans, including industry, shelter, and foodstuffs.

As a vast continental land power, Russia always relied on a mass ground army for both defensive and offensive military purposes. Traditionally less advanced industrially than Western European nations, huge manpower reserves tended to compensate for shortages and deficiencies in arms and equipment. This was particularly evident during World War I when limited production capacity contributed to the defeat of the armies of the Czar at the hands of German and Austro-Hungarian forces.

With the success of the Bolshevik Revolution, V. I. Lenin and his radical supporters established one of the most repressive totalitarian regimes, controlled by an aggressive political party that intended to eventually communize the world. For this the Party needed strong and well-armed military and police forces for internal security, for defense, and to support the expansion of its political ideology abroad.

The Red Army (its previous name, officially replaced by *Soviet Army* in 1946) was created on February 23, 1918, during the chaotic period of the Revolution.[31] During the 1920s the Red Army underwent extensive reorganization and expansion and by 1934, the Army was well on its way toward mechanization and modernization. A huge arms industry was created as part of the industrialization process, at the expense of the consumer industry. By the time of the German invasion in June 1941, the Army was abundantly equipped with weapons of all types, but was again involved in a reorganization and rearmament as a result of weaknesses in the cumbersome Soviet military machine revealed by the Finnish War (1939–40).

The first disastrous year of war with Germany and her allies resulted in changes in organization from the high command down to tactical units. The large stores of modern and obsolescent weapons were adequate to replace the tremendous combat losses and equip new formations while the arms factories were being moved to central Russia ahead of the Germans. They were reestablished in a remarkably short time and developed an amazing capacity for mass production of improved weapons and equipment. By late 1942, both a substantial increase in war production and changes in organization had largely been carried out, just as Germany's ability to provide the strength necessary to fight on all fronts was weakening.

Generally speaking, Soviet weapons were characterized by designs that were simple, sturdy, and effective. While not always as efficient as German and European

These Soviet infantrymen are carrying the standard 7.62mm (about .30 caliber) Moisin-Nagant M1910/30 bolt-action rifle with the angular bayonet that was always fixed to the gun. *U.S. Army*

weapons, they were able to operate in dusty, muddy, and severe winter weather conditions, and the massive firepower of the Soviet forces compensated for most shortcomings. Because of the huge quantities of war materiel destroyed and captured by the Germans during the initial months of Barbarossa, the U.S.S.R. was forced to replace the weapons lost with arms of still simpler design. For example, new submachine guns that were roughly welded, and featured cheap stampings, were easy to produce and supplemented the rifle, thereby increasing infantry fire power. The fact that the loss in effective range brought on heavier casualties was accepted.[32]

Soviet weapons generally were more remarkable for the tactical concepts they were built to fulfill than for the technology that went into their design and construction. Simple weapons were cheaper and easier to produce. Originality was not a prime characteristic of Soviet arms, but they were able to exploit the best features of foreign designs to provide rugged weapons that were easily understood and maintained by peasant soldiers with limited education and training. Especially during World War II, little effort was made to polish or finish weapons that was not essential to their functioning. Weapons therefore often appeared crude, with plenty of tool marks, but they were properly finished where it counted.

Mass armies, armed with automatic and fast-firing weapons, necessarily put astronomical demands upon ammunition supply. As a result Soviet ammunition—particularly that for small arms and artillery, tended to be unsatisfactory from the German and Western point of view. However, the Russians were capable of improvisation and even very advanced thinking. During World War II, the Soviets were the first to introduce the use of mass rocket fire, and their employment of tanks later in the war set the pace for the Germans and other armed forces.

Rifles and Carbines

The only thing unusual or noteworthy about the rifle, adopted in 1891 as the standard weapon of the Imperial Russian Army, was its bayonet. The angular bayonet issued without a scabbard was intended to remain fixed to the rifle at all times, except when cleaning the barrel. This was probably intended to motivate the infantry with the spirit of attack, and perhaps to impress troops of other armies with the élan and determination of the Russian soldier. This tradition was continued in the Red Army. The bolt action of the M1891 was developed by Colonel S. I. Moisin of the Russian Army and the single-line box magazine by a Belgian engineer, Emile Nagant, hence the name Moisin-Nagant.[33] Chambering the standard 7.62mm cartridge, it was a fairly good rifle, with an overall length of 51.37 inches and with bayonet, 68.2 inches. This proved to be rather unhandy during the Russo-Japanese War of 1904–05 and in World War I, especially in the trenches, and in 1930 the rifle finally received several improvements. These included modified sights and a minor reduction in length to 48.5 inches, with bayonet 65.4 inches.

The Moisin-Nagant M1891/30 was the standard rifle of the Soviet Army during World War II. Other models introduced included a dragoon model issued to mounted troops about 1900, a 40-inch carbine without bayonet adopted in 1910 mainly for cavalry use (they carried a saber), and an improved M1938 carbine model that entered service in 1939. There was also a sniper version of the M1891/30, usually fitted with the PE 4-power telescopic sight. The last Moisin-Nagant model adopted was the Carbine M1944 with a 40-inch overall length and featuring a folding bayonet that was permanently attached near the muzzle and could be folded down the right side of the stock when not in use.

There were many experiments with self-loading rifles during the interwar years. Both S. G. Simonov and F. W. Tokarev produced 7.62 mm self-loading rifles.[34] The Simonov M1936 or AVS36 was made in small numbers for testing but recoiled badly and had mechanical problems, so production was discontinued. The Tokarev M1938, or SVT38 self-loading rifle, was more successful and was adopted in 1938. When some parts proved fragile Tokarev modified his design and produced the M1940 or SVT40. Both rifles were tested during the Russo-Finnish War. The SVT40, like the Simonov, was gas-operated and had a magazine capacity of 10 rounds. A sniper version with a telescopic 3.5X PU scope was rather widely employed, including at Sevastopol. Production of the SVT40 ceased in 1943, but it continued in use throughout World War II and even for some years after until replaced by the AK 47 assault rifle and other more modern shoulder arms.

Handguns

With the introduction of large numbers of submachine guns during World War II, pistols and revolvers no longer had any great combat significance in the Soviet Army. Plenty were available and they were still carried by some armored vehicle and aircraft crews, staff officers, and many service troops and police.[35]

The venerable M1895 7.62mm Nagant revolver continued in use with rear echelon and service troops after being replaced in most combat formations by the 7.62mm TT M1933 semiautomatic pistol. The old M1895 revolver was designed by the Nagant brothers in Belgium, who had a good working relationship with the Russian arms industry. It was produced in Belgium and at the Tula Arsenal in Russia. The M1895 was made in both single-action and double-action versions. A rather unusual feature was that the 7-shot cylinder moved forward before the hammer fell and the forward end of the chamber aligned for firing telescoped the barrel.[36] This was a true "gas-seal" revolver, the most reliable of all time.

The 7.62mm TT M1933 Tokarev pistol was made at Tula and designated the "TT" for "Tula-Tokarev." It was a modified Colt-Browning design that replaced the similar TT M1930 pistol made in limited numbers. A basic design without a safety catch, it had a magazine capacity of eight rounds. Many other pistols were imported from abroad over the years for use by Army and police units, including the Mauser M1920 "Bolo" semiautomatic pistol, the Schwarzlose M1898 in 7.63 Mauser like the M1920, and small foreign pistols for use by high-ranking officers. Captured German pistols were always popular.

Machine Guns

The first machine guns in regular use by the Russian Army were Maxim guns made in England by Vickers' Sons and Maxim Machine Gun Company. Some of these were the first to be used in modern combat during the Russo-Japanese War of 1904–05. Production of a Russian-built model began at the Tula Arsenal about 1905, and this was the 7.62mm PM1905 (PM—Pulemet Maxim, or Maxim machine gun), sometimes also designated the SPM. It was a heavy piece, belt-fed and fitted with a bronze water cooling jacket. In 1910, a somewhat improved model was adopted, the PM1910, which featured a steel barrel jacket and modified feed mechanism. This Russian Maxim was similar to the German MG 08 and can be seen in World War I photographs equipped with a fluted water jacket, protective steel shield, and installed on a wheeled mount designed by Sokolov. Although a slow-firing gun at 500–600 cyclic RPM, it served, with minor alterations, in the Soviet Army through World War II. During the 1930s many were installed on a new dual-purpose mount, the M1931. The PM1910 was also modified in the mid-1920s for use as an aircraft gun and designated the PV-1.

SMALL-ARMS

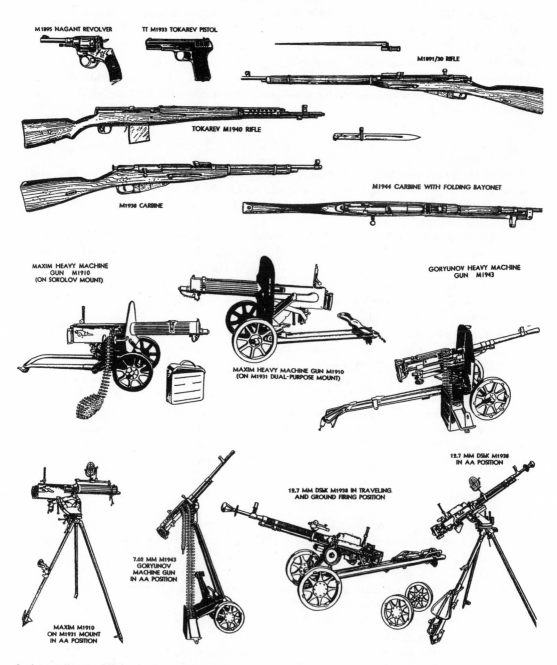

M1895 NAGANT REVOLVER

TT M1933 TOKAREV PISTOL

M1891/30 RIFLE

TOKAREV M1940 RIFLE

M1944 CARBINE WITH FOLDING BAYONET

M1938 CARBINE

MAXIM HEAVY MACHINE GUN M1910 (ON SOKOLOV MOUNT)

MAXIM HEAVY MACHINE GUN M1910 (ON M1931 DUAL-PURPOSE MOUNT)

GORYUNOV HEAVY MACHINE GUN M1943

12.7 MM DStK M1938 IN AA POSITION

12.7 MM DStK M1938 IN TRAVELING AND GROUND FIRING POSITION

7.62 MM M1943 GORYUNOV MACHINE GUN IN AA POSITION

MAXIM M1910 ON M1931 MOUNT IN AA POSITION

Soviet small arms: Rifles, pistols, heavy machine guns. *U.S. Army*

Just before the war, an attempt was made to replace the Maxim with the 7.62mm gas-operated, air-cooled M1939 Degtyarev, but a more successful replacement appeared in 1943, the M1943 Goryunov or SG43. These outwardly similar guns were belt-fed, had a wheeled dual-purpose mount, with shield, and a higher rate of fire than the Maxim at 600–700 RPM. The M1943 also featured an air-cooled barrel that was replaceable and continued in service long after the end of World War II.

Another Degtyarev design was the 12.7mm DShK M1938 heavy machine gun. Gas operated and air-cooled, like other Degtyarev models, it remained the standard Soviet HMG through the war and after, both for infantry use and as secondary armament on large tanks and patrol boats. For ground use it was equipped with a wheeled mount which could be quickly converted into a tripod mount for antiaircraft fire. Vasily Degtyarev (sometimes spelled Dyegtyaryev) was an arms genius.

Some foreign light machine guns were used by the Russians in World War I, such as the U.S. Colt M1895, the Lewis gun, and the M1902 Madsen LMG. Soviet designers experimented with light machine guns, and the first machine gun of original design to be adopted was the 7.62mm DP (Degtyarev Pekhotniy or Infantry) of 1926. The DP1926, the DP1928, and subsequent modifications were gas-operated, air-cooled light machine guns with a drum magazine and bipod. A sound, simple, and rugged design, the last modification of this excellent gun was the DPM M1944.

Variations included the DT (T for tank) for use in armored vehicles with a larger 60-round drum in place of the 47-round drum magazine of the DP. It had an adjustable stock and lacked the DP quick-change barrel. An aircraft version was produced as the DA.

Submachine Guns

The submachine gun became almost synonymous with the Red Army in World War II. Development actually began in the early 1930s, and the first Russian design was produced by the design team headed by Vasily A. Degtyarev, the talented machine gun designer. The first model adopted was the PPD1934 or PPD-34, and a somewhat improved model replaced it in production in 1938 with the designation PPD1934/38. These guns were blowback types based on the Bergmann system used in the German MP18/1 and MP28II. They fired the rather weak 7.62mm Russian pistol cartridge from a 25-round box magazine or a 71-round drum.[37] The cyclic rate of fire was about 800 rounds per minute (RPM), the stock was of wood, and the barrel was protected by a slotted housing. An improved version, the PPD1940, appeared in the spring of 1940, similar in general design and function to the PPD1934/38, but using only the drum magazine. It was still heavy at 13 pounds, and although all of these guns functioned adequately they required considerable milling of metal parts and could not be reproduced in sufficient quantity to meet the great demands of World War II.

Another similar looking 7.62mm SMG was developed by George S. Shpagin and eventually replaced most of the Degtyarov guns during the war. It was simpler and less expensive to produce, and by the late 1940s over five million PPSh-41 guns had been manufactured.[38]

A submachine gun even easier and cheaper to manufacture reached the troops in 1942. No doubt influenced by the German MP 38 and MP 40, the PPS1942 was designed by A. I. Sudarev while surrounded by the Germans in the city of Leningrad. The PPS1942 fired the same 7.62mm cartridge from a 35-round box magazine at 700 RPM, weighed only 7.40 pounds, was made of metal except for the pistol grips, and had a folding metal stock.

Combat experience indicated that mechanical improvements were required in this gun,

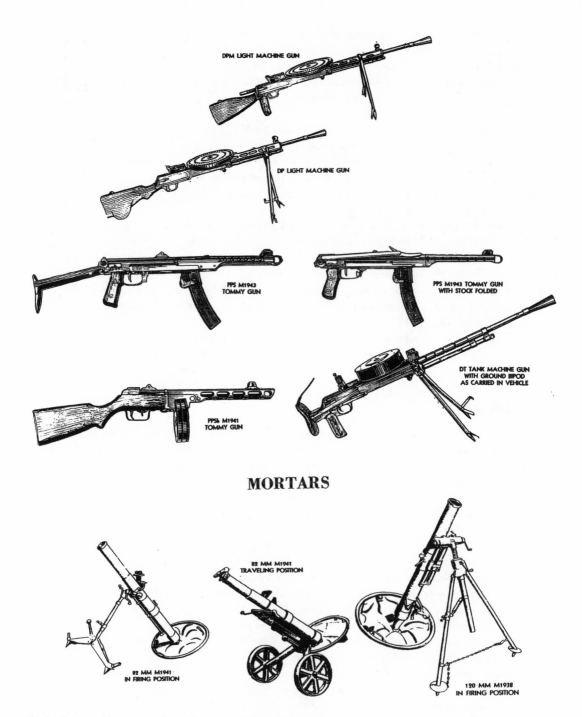

DPM LIGHT MACHINE GUN

DP LIGHT MACHINE GUN

PPS M1943 TOMMY GUN

PPS M1943 TOMMY GUN WITH STOCK FOLDED

PPSh M1941 TOMMY GUN

DT TANK MACHINE GUN WITH GROUND BIPOD AS CARRIED IN VEHICLE

MORTARS

82 MM M1941 TRAVELING POSITION

82 MM M1941 IN FIRING POSITION

120 MM M1938 IN FIRING POSITION

Soviet light machine guns, submachine guns, mortars. *U.S. Army* and a much-modified version was placed in production and designated the PPS1943. This was the last wartime model developed and remained in service until finally replaced by the assault rifle for most purposes after the end of World War II.

Widely issued to infantry as well as vehicle and weapon crews, submachine guns apparently were, in part, a wartime easier-to-make substitute for rifles.[39]

Antitank Rifles

The Soviet infantry was still equipped with antitank rifles long after they were no longer effective against modern medium tank armor. They were finally replaced after the war with Russian copies of the German *Panzerfaust* AT rocket.[40] However, obsolete weapons were seldom scrapped by the Soviets but sold or given to satellite armies. Both the PTRS-41 and the PTRD-41 AT rifles were captured by American forces during the Korean War (1950–53), where they were still effective against trucks and soft targets.

Two long-barreled, single-shot, 12.7mm antitank rifles, patterned after the German *T-Gewehr* of 1918, were dropped from production in 1939 as no longer effective and replaced two years later by two new guns, a Simonov and a Degtyarov.

The Simonov PTRS1941 in 14.5mm was simply a forty-four-pound scaled-up version of the Tokarev rifle. It was a powerful semiautomatic, gas-operated gun with a 5-round magazine and a vicious "kick."

The Degtyarov 14.5mm PTRD1941 was a handier 35-pound single-shot, bolt-action rifle and was semi-recoil operated. It could punch through 30mm armor at 100 meters (109.3 yards) and like the PTRS1941, was equipped with a bipod mount and muzzle brake to reduce the heavy recoil. Greased ammunition was required, and an examination of a PTRD1941 disclosed that it was sighted for 100 to 1,500 meters (109.3 to 1,640 yards).

Hand and Rifle Grenades

Hand bombs have done their destructive work for centuries, but the first Russian combat experience with modern hand grenades occurred at the siege of Port Arthur and Mukden, Manchuria, during the Russo-Japanese War in 1904–05.[41] Grenades were considered an important weapon by the Soviets and issued in great quantities. The M1914 stick-type hand grenade of World War I was basically an explosive charge and igniter with a handle. It was continued in production for the Red Army and eventually modified and issued as the M1914/30. The same year, a rifle grenade was developed, the VGD1930, fired from a special rifled launcher attached to the barrel of the M1891/30 rifle. The projectile resembled a small artillery fragmentation shell.

A new type of stick hand grenade soon appeared, the RGD1933, which, like the 1914/30, could be employed either as a defensive or offensive grenade by attaching a fragmentation sleeve. The first standard "egg" type grenade, the F-1, looked like the British Mills bomb and the U.S. Mk. II. It was a defensive fragmentation type with a serrated iron body that had to be thrown from cover. Like similar grenades, to operate it a safety pin was pulled, the safety handle was released when it was thrown, and the grenade exploded after a 4.4-second delay. The RG1942 was a heavier offensive stick hand grenade.

The RPG1940 was the earliest antitank hand grenade used by the Soviets and had a handle not unlike the RGD1933. Courageous soldiers often attacked German tanks from their foxholes with grenades like this during World War II. Magnetic mines were also used in the same way and led to the Germans coating armored vehicles with a plaster-like substance called "Zimmerit."

Other grenades used by the Red Army during World War II included the VPG-S-1941 rifle grenade with a hollow shaped-charge head for antitank use. It was launched by inserting a rod at the base into the bore of the rifle and firing a bulletless blank cartridge in the rifle. The grenade detonated upon impact and had an armor penetration of 1.18 inches. It was also effective against concrete and masonry buildings or fortifications. The RPG1943 was an antitank stick grenade with a powerful shaped-charge head and had to be thrown from cover because of its secondary fragmentation effect.

Lastly, the famous "Molotov Cocktail" was a frangible incendiary grenade made from Vodka or beer bottles containing gasoline and thrown by hand. It was named for Vyacheslau Molotov, the ruthless Soviet foreign minister. Frequently improvised with a wick, an igniter was normally secured to the side of the bottle and lighted before the bottle was thrown. There was also a special cup-type grenade launcher developed to project this type of grenade to greater distances.

Mortars

The first modern mortars used by the Soviets were of French or other foreign manufacture, but after considerable experimentation, an 8.2cm (82mm) mortar of Russian design was adopted in 1937. The M1937 was a close copy of the rather simple French Stokes-Brandt "trench" mortar, adopted by many nations, and consisting basically of a smooth-bore tube, base plate, and bipod legs. "Company" mortars of 5cm were also produced in quantity, the M1937 and M1939, but they were superseded as insufficiently powerful by larger mortars of increased caliber.

A simplified 8.2cm mortar, the M1941, had an ingenious mount that permitted quick attachment of wheels for rapid movement over relatively even ground. One man could pull the M1941, but it was phased out of production in favor of the M1943 that was similar but had bipod legs that did not fold, and the wheels were not removable. The wheels were, of course, raised from the ground when the M1943 was placed in firing position on its characteristic round base plate.

Mortars played a very important role in Soviet wartime operations. They represented a cheap, quickly produced substitute for the masses of artillery materiel lost in the Soviet debacles of 1941–42. Mortars could easily accompany infantry at the front over almost any terrain and provide vital fire support. Up to 1943 they played a greater part (for the Soviets) than artillery.[42]

The Soviets considered mortars of 8.2cm and above artillery and produced larger models of similar design in several sizes. These were the 10.7cm M1938 mountain mortar, the 12cm M1938, the improved M1943, and the 16cm M1943. These larger, heavier types had carriages with bigger wheels and rubber tires, and all could be manhandled by their crews and easily towed by vehicles.

It should be noted that mortar ammunition is relatively easy to manufacture, and this ammunition has the highest ratio of explosive content to total weight of any type of projectile.[43]

Artillery

By tradition the Soviet Army favored a large and powerful artillery arm.[44] In 1939, the Soviets held a parade to celebrate the 550th anniversary of the introduction of artillery into the

Army. Since the era when Peter the Great armed the Imperial Army with thousands of muzzle-loading cannon, the artillery branch had received continued emphasis and attention. However, in World War I severe shortages of equipment developed, especially of field artillery, which resulted in staggering losses that shook the framework of the state.[45]

Soviet artillery development began in 1927 with the first Five-Year Plan. Numbers of Czarist models dating from World War I were modernized, and new designs, including antitank, antiaircraft, and heavy artillery pieces were produced. Russian artillery designers were greatly influenced by foreign artillery developments and were quick to recognize and try out promising new ideas. They improved their work as they acquired experience during the 1930s and World War II in the design and mass production of modern artillery. After the great losses in the defensive battles of 1941–42, new production allowed mass artillery fire to play an important role in Soviet ground operations. In line with the Soviet emphasis on offensive striking power as the primary battlefield tactic, artillery was used to annihilate defensive positions to open the way for their rapid-moving armored and motorized rifle units.[46]

Regimental Guns

The widely used box-trailed 7.6cm howitzer M1927 was the first piece of original Soviet design. It was referred to by the Soviets as a regimental gun, but was actually a howitzer, and along with mortars provided close support for the infantry. The Germans referred to close support weapons like this as infantry guns. The 7.6cm howitzer M1943 (also called a gun by the Soviets), never quite replaced the dependable M1927 in service during and even after World War II.

A table of artillery characteristics is included in this section with details on these and many other artillery pieces used by the Red Army during World War II.[47]

Division Artillery

Division or field artillery played an important role in Soviet defensive and offensive tactics. Thousands of obsolete guns were destroyed or captured by the Germans during 1941, including the updated 7.6cm Gun M1902/30. The Putilov-built M1902 provided excellent service during World War I and was considered for its day superior to the famous French "75." Another widely used weapon issued during the war as standard divisional artillery was the 12.2cm howitzer M1938, intended to supersede the 12.2cm M1910/30 howitzer.

Corps Artillery

Heavier artillery was classified as corps artillery by the Soviets; the 10.7cm gun M1910/30 and its intended replacement, the 10.7cm gun M1940, provided excellent service during World War II and beyond. The 12.2cm gun M1931/37 and the 15.2cm gun-howitzer M1937 with muzzle brake were companion pieces mounted on the same type of carriage, and were fitted with either hard rubber or pneumatic tires. The 15.2cm howitzer M1938 entered service before the war but was found to have several flaws, and a new model was developed incorporating a German-type double-baffle muzzle brake and mounted on the better carriage of the 12.2cm howitzer M1938. The new piece—the 15.2cm howitzer M1943—largely replaced the M1938 by the end of the war.

The missions for the 10.7cm gun and the 12.2cm gun were counterbattery, antitank, and destruction of field fortifications. The 15.2cm gun-howitzer was the outstanding wartime So-

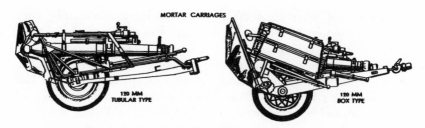

MORTAR CARRIAGES

120 MM
TUBULAR TYPE

120 MM
BOX TYPE

Mortar Characteristics

Mortar	Weights (lbs.)		Maximum Range (yds.)	Rate of Fire (rpm.)	Weight of Round (lbs.)	Effective Radius of Fragmentation (yds.)
	Firing Position	Traveling Position				
.. M1937	121	134	3,325	Up to 25	HE—7.3; Smoke—7.63	33 vs. standing targets; 20 vs. prone targets
.. M1941	99	111	3,325	Up to 25	HE—7.3; Smoke—7.63	33 vs. standing targets; 20 vs. prone targets
.. M1943	128	128	3,325	Up to 25	HE—7.3; Smoke—7.63	33 vs. standing targets; 20 vs. prone targets
n., M1938	575	¹ 1,874	6,900	Up to 15	HE—17.64	44 vs. standing targets; 22 vs. prone targets
n., M1938	617	¹ 2,425	6,240	Up to 12	HE—35.05; Smoke—36.38; Incend. 38	55 vs. standing targets; 22 vs. prone targets
n., M1943	606	¹ 2,414	6,240	Up to 12	HE—35.05; Smoke—36.38; Incend. 38	55 vs. standing targets; 22 vs. prone targets
n., M1943	2,381	2,480	5,500	3–4	HE—88	

¹With limber and loaded caisson.

ARTILLERY

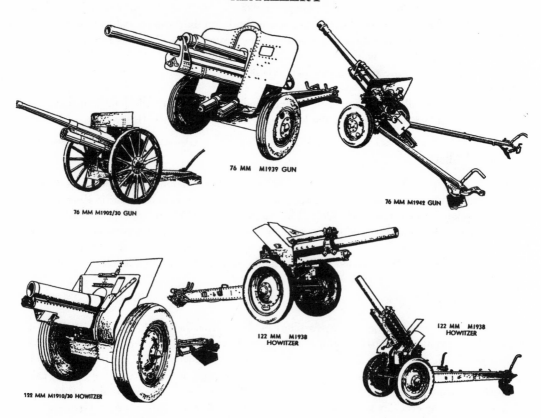

76 MM M1939 GUN

76 MM M1902/30 GUN

76 MM M1942 GUN

122 MM M1938 HOWITZER

122 MM M1938 HOWITZER

122 MM M1910/30 HOWITZER

Soviet mortar carriages and artillery. *U.S. Army*

viet counterbattery weapon, and its missions included the suppression of distant targets, destruction of field fortifications, and even antitank use.

Heavy Artillery

All Soviet heavy artillery pieces in World War II used the same unique tracked carriage. This allowed better cross-country movement than wheels. The barrels were removed for long hauls and placed on separate limbers. The 15.2cm gun M1935 had an exceptional range of 27,000 yards and the 20.3cm howitzer M1931, a ballistically modern piece, had a range of 19,700 yards. The huge 28cm M1939 piece was classified as an artillery mortar (i.e., a high-trajectory howitzer) by the Soviets because of its short range of 11,500 yards. Its mission was the same as for the 20.3cm: destruction of concrete fortifications; neutralization of key or well protected artillery; and fire on key objectives. All of these guns had to be towed.

Super-heavy artillery was also part of the Soviet inventory, but in limited numbers. The Germans destroyed or captured a number of these guns in 1941 and they were never replaced. The Skoda-type 21cm gun and the 30.5cm howitzer used the same basic carriage which, although affording 360-degree traverse, was difficult to transport and took considerable time to place in firing position. These excellent guns, and the 28cm mortar M1939, were broken down into three loads for transport. Artillery of all types was employed in the defense of Sevastopol.

Red Army artillerymen prepare a 20.3cm (203mm) howitzer for firing. The man on top is laying the gun with the panoramic sight. The M1931 was a ballistically modern gun with a range of 19,700 yards. Note the tracked carriage used on all Soviet heavy artillery pieces. *U.S. Army*

Antiaircraft Guns

Aircraft played a rather minor role on the vast Eastern Front in World War I. Developments in aviation in the 1930s made the Soviet Army very conscious of the need for antiaircraft protection of field forces. Great attention was paid to protection of even small units against strafing—an effort which proved invaluable during World War II. The Germans' neglect of strategic bombing after the sporadic raids of 1941–42, however, made it unnecessary for the Russians to parallel German and Western Allied development of heavy AA guns and highly efficient AA fire-control systems. Soviet antiaircraft weapons were undistinguished in design. The most common guns of Soviet manufacture—those above 2cm (20mm)—closely followed Bofors designs.

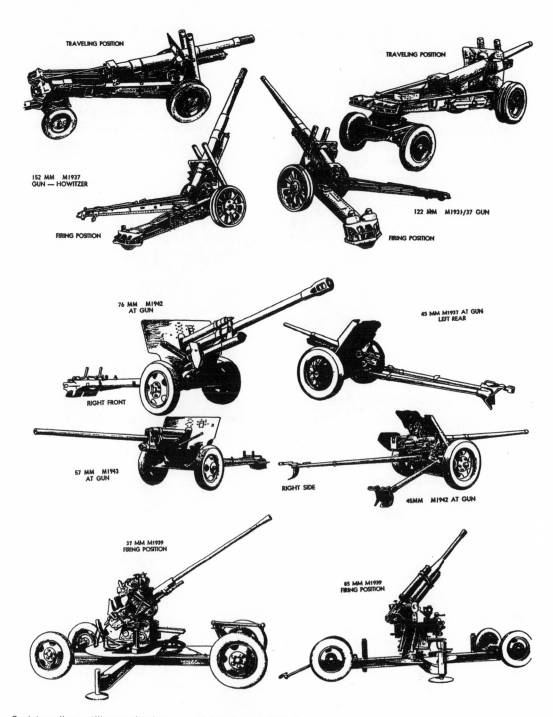

Soviet medium artillery, antitank guns, antiaircraft guns. *U.S. Army*

Infantry were instructed to fire on enemy planes with everything they had. Light AA guns included the old 7.62mm Maxim machine gun M1910 on a dual-purpose M1931 mount or M1929 AA tripod, or in a twin or quad configuration. They were followed during the war by the 7.62mm Goryunov machine gun M1943 for which a dual-purpose mount was standard. The 12.7mm DShK M1938 machine gun could be truck-mounted or use the dual-purpose mount along with front speed ring and rear aperture sights.

Large numbers of medium antiaircraft guns were in service during the war. These included the M1931 and M1938 7.62cm guns and the 8.5cm M1939 with Bofors-type muzzle brake. Only limited numbers of the 10.5cm heavy AA gun M1934 were produced and placed mainly around Leningrad, Moscow, and Sevastopol. Captured German 10.5cm and 12.8cm guns were also pressed into use with their excellent fire-control systems.

Antitank Guns

Credit must be given to the Soviets for their early policy of outgunning the antitank artillery of other nations by introducing a 4.5cm M1932 antitank gun of their own design. It was similar in appearance to the lighter weight 3.7cm German Rheinmetall gun of 1928, which was also built in the early 1930s in limited numbers. The 4.5cm M1932 AT gun was tested in combat during the Spanish Civil War and modernized with a faster-operating, semi-automatic breech. It was placed in production as the 4.5cm M1937, and both the M1932 and M1937 were the first modern weapons to be mounted on tubular steel trails. The 4.5cm M1942 model had a strengthened breech and a longer tube length to obtain increased muzzle velocity and penetration.

The 5.7cm M1941 and M1943 AT guns were followed by the 8.5cm M1945 and finally the 10cm M1944 AT gun toward the end of the conflict. The more powerful AT guns were introduced to defeat heavier German tanks, and following the example of the German 8.8cm Flak guns, light field guns and the 7.62cm and 8.5cm antiaircraft guns were designed to be capable of use in the antitank role. All of these antitank guns had lightweight, low-silhouette carriages, and the final models had the recoil mechanisms behind the shield.

Antitank rifles are discussed under small arms in this section.

Note that the Germans had a high regard for Soviet artillery and placed many of the modern guns in use with the Wehrmacht and their allies.

ARTILLERY CHARACTERISTICS

Weapon	Maximum Horizontal Range (Yards)	Maximum Vertical Range (Feet)	Maximum Armor Penetration in mm. at 550 Yards	Weight of Projectile (Pounds)	Rate of Fire (RPM)
25-mm. AA Gun M1940	6,600	14,850	—	0.64	240–250
37-mm. AA Gun M1939	8,800	19,800	46	1.6	160–180
45-mm. AT Gun M1937	9,750	—	SC 57	HE 4.7 AP 3.1	25
45-mm. AT Gun M1942	8,700	—	SC 79	HE 4.7 AP 3.1	25
57-mm. AT Gun M1943	9,200	—	SC140	HE 9.2 AP 6.9	25
76-mm. Howitzer M1927	9,350	—	57	13.6	12
76-mm. Gun M1902/30	14,300	—	SC 92	14	10
76-mm. AA Gun M1938	15,730	31,000	96	14.5	15–20
76-mm. Mountain Gun M1938	11,110	—	—	13.6	14
76-mm. Gun M1939	14,300	—	SC 92	13.8	25
76-mm. Gun M1942	14,300	—	SC 92	13.8	25
76-mm. Howitzer M1943	4,620	—	57	12.6	12
85-mm. AT Gun M1945	17,000	—	125	20	15
85-mm. AA Gun M1939	17,000	34,600	111	20	15–20
85-mm. AA Gun M1944	17,600	39,400	125	20	15–20
100-mm. Gun M1944	22,900	—	152	34.5	8
105-mm. AA Gun M1934	19,800	42,900	—	33	12
107-mm. Gun M10/30	17,900	—	130	36.3	6
107-mm. Gun M1940 M60	19,100	—	130	36.3	6
122-mm. Howitzer M1910/30	9,800	—	100	47	6
122-mm. Gun M1932	22,400	—	157	55	5–6
122-mm. Gun M1931/37	22,400	—	157	58	5–6
122-mm. Howitzer M1938	12,900	—	100	47	6
152-mm. Gun Howitzer M10/34	19,360	—	124	84–86	1–2
152-mm. Gun M1935	27,000	—	—	107	1–2
152-mm. Gun Howitzer M1937	19,360	—	124	84–88	2–3
152-mm. Howitzer M1938	13,650	—	—	88	2–3
152-mm. Howitzer M1943	13,650	—	—	88	2–3
203-mm. Howitzer M1931	19,700	—	—	220	1 in 3
210-mm. Heavy Gun SKODA	33,000	—	—	297	—
280-mm. Mortar M1939	11,500	—	—	632	1 in 3
305-mm. Howitzer SKODA	17,500	—	—	728	—

Land Mines

The land mine was one of the Soviets' principal weapons in World War II for: (1) safeguarding defensive positions; (2) channeling hostile attacks; and (3) demoralizing enemy troops.[48] Many new types of mines were developed and employed throughout the war but there was less use of mines by the Soviets after they began advancing west against the retreating Germans. There were exceptions, of course, as during the great tank battle at Kursk in July 1943.

Soviet antipersonnel mines during the war were mainly small wooden boxes containing an igniter assembly and a small charge, depending on blast for their lethal effect. Many such mines were improvised using captured artillery shells, and metal objects could be added for fragmentation. During the war, the Soviets made considerable use of remote-controlled mines detonated by radio. Huge mines were often set in buildings during the retreat to the east, and Kiev was virtually destroyed by these mines in 1941, forcing the Germans to withdraw temporarily after first occupying the city. Such mines were normally detonated by timers.

Antitank mines were simple, if not crude, in design and operation, generally wooden or metal cases filled with 8 to 22 pounds of trotyl (TNT) or amatol. They detonated when 400 to 600 pounds of pressure was applied to the top of the mine by a vehicle. The M1938 AT mine consisted of a square, field-gray, sheet-metal case with a hinged lid which acted as a pressure plate. It contained six pounds of TNT blocks and the igniter assembly.

Soviet forces were capable of ingenious, if not actually wild, experiments. During World War II, for example, the Soviets trained and equipped dogs for use as mobile attack mines. A special harness fitted on the dog's back carried a block of explosives on each of his flanks. Atop the animal's back was a springloaded lever, which detonated the igniter upon being depressed. The dogs were trained to obtain food only between the tracks of tanks; they were then loosed against German

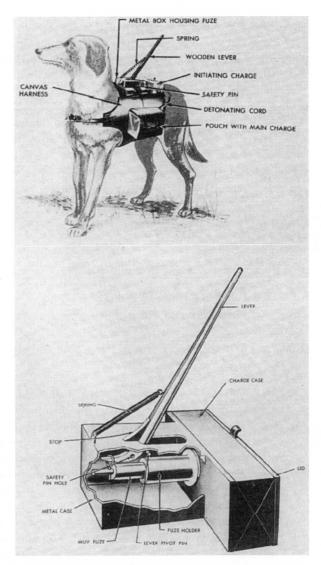

A Soviet antitank dog mine of World War II. In theory, the dogs would run under an enemy tank, detonating the explosive. Tactical use of dogs proved to be of very limited value. *U.S. Army*

armored vehicles. This program was discontinued when some of the dogs, probably frightened by the din of battle, ran back to the Soviet lines and blew up their own tanks.[49]

Tanks and Armored Vehicles

Soviet tanks have been discussed in comparison with German tanks in the Preface, Chapter I, and the German section of this appendix. Soviet interest in tanks began in the early 1920s when KS light tanks, copies of the World War I French Renault, were built, but the lack of suitable manufacturing facilities for engines and transmissions hindered production. The first Five-Year Plan of 1927–32 finally gave the Soviets the necessary industrial base for the production of modern armored vehicles. An intensive study was made of the best armored vehicle designs of other countries, and good features of the Vickers models and experimental American Christie tanks were adopted. Production of tanks increased, and by 1938 tanks of Soviet design were equipping the Red Army with a variety of models. Maneuvers disclosed some of the weak points in design, and unsatisfactory characteristics were corrected.

Russian tank designers wasted considerable time and effort before the war building tanks with more than one turret before concentrating on the more practical designs with one turret. The two-turret concept was also tried in the United States in the 1930s with the M2A2 tank. While Russia, German, France, England, Italy, and Japan were rearming and building thousands of light, medium, and heavy tanks, most armed with cannon, the United States was building only small numbers of light tanks, armed only with .30 and .50 caliber machine guns. On the eve of war in 1941, the U.S. "armored might" comprised under 400 tanks, the vast majority light tanks.[50]

Soviet light tanks were used for scouting and infantry support and proved in 1941 to be quite vulnerable to even the German 3.7cm antitank gun. Among these were the obsolescent T-26 variations weighing about 9.4 tons and armed usually with a 3.7cm gun, the T-40 amphibious tank of only 5.5 tons with a main armament of a DShK 12.7mm machine gun, and the T-60 modification of 1940 with a ShVAK 2cm cannon. The T-70 of 10.2 tons was armed with a 4.5cm antitank gun and had improved armor protection, but was easily dealt with by the Germans.

Medium tanks were produced in quantity before the war, especially those in the BT series armed with a 3.7cm or 4.5cm antitank gun. The BT-7M of 14.65 tons had a powerful 7.62cm gun. Some were equipped with a radio instead of the usual signal flags. The T-32 medium tank of 19 tons had a 7.62cm dual purpose gun and a radio. The T-28 medium tanks were built in quantity and featured the main turret with a 7.62cm gun and two subsidiary turrets armed with machine guns. On most of these tanks the armor was too thin and not well positioned. After the battles in the Karelian Isthmus during the Russo-Finnish War, the armor of the T28B was increased from 50mm to 80mm and the sides and rear to 40mm. This was accomplished by "screening" the tank by attaching additional armored screens, but this was still not considered the perfect tank design.

Soviet experience and experimentation paid off with the approval on December 19, 1939, of the design for the new T-34 medium tank. The advent of the excellent T-34 tank of 30.2 tons, mounting the 7.62cm gun in the turret, came as a most unwelcome shock to the Germans in 1941. So effective was the T-34 that it served as the spearhead of the Red Army armored units throughout the rest of the war. During four years of combat, significant modifications were limited to the improvement of the main armament, which was increased to a gun of 8.5cm. This tank was maneuverable and afforded a high degree of armor protection with its considerably sloped front plate. Soviet medium and heavy tanks used the same Diesel engine, thereby adding greatly to standardization, production, and maintenance, and Diesel fuel greatly reduced the fire hazard.[51] The T-34 tank with the 7.62cm gun was often referred to as the T-34/76, and the later model with the 8.5cm gun as the T-34/85.

Many of the burned-out hulks littering the landscape of European Russia in the summer and fall of 1941 were obsolete Soviet heavy tanks destroyed by the advancing German Panzers. Tanks in the prewar T-35 series weighed about 45 tons and were armed with the 7.62cm gun. The ponderous T-100/SMK heavy tank variations weighed either 45 or 56 tons, the heavier had a main upper turret armed with a 7.62cm gun and a smaller turret below with a 4.5cm gun. They performed poorly during the war with Finland, and the small number of these unwieldy tanks still in service in 1941 did not last long during Barbarossa.

The KV-I heavy tank was a big improvement, providing increased armor and firepower without increasing weight that would have reduced mobility.[52] When it appeared in late 1939, it was enthusiastically approved by Stalin, who insisted on involvement in weapons design, and placed in mass production. The KV-I was named for Marshal Kliment Voroshilov, People's Commissar of Defense in 1939. The KV-I, at 46.35 tons, with a 7.62cm gun in a single turret, had three-inch armor and was a most advanced tank for its day. Hundreds of KV-I tanks were encountered during World War II and in the Crimea in 1942; they were worthy opponents.

Also in 1940, an artillery version of the KV tank was produced, the KV-II, with a huge turret armed with a 15.2cm howitzer. This behemoth proved to be too slow, heavy and unmaneuverable at almost 57 tons; it was dropped from production. Those met by the Germans in 1941 were easily recognized from a distance by the high silhouette of the massive 12-ton turret. They were destroyed mainly by 8.8cm Flak guns and other heavy artillery.

New and improved heavy tanks appeared later in World War II, including the Josef Stalin series, the JS-I (IS-I), JS-II, JS-III etc., with heavier guns and even better armor. These were the tanks that were faced by the West in the early years of the Cold War.

It was not until the Germans demonstrated the utility of self-propelled guns in 1941 with their *Sturmgeschuetz* that assault guns were appreciated by the Soviet high command. Some makeshift Russian self-propelled guns appeared in 1942 but it was not until 1943 that factory-built types began to appear at the front. The SU-76, with a 7.62cm gun, was built in quantity during the war for infantry support on the T-70 light tank chassis. It remained in service for years and was encountered by U.S. forces during the Korean War.

Armored cars entered mass production in 1930. The BA-10 heavy armored car was based on the GAZ-AAA

The Soviet KV-IIA was an artillery version of the KV tank with an impressive 15.2cm (152mm) M1938/40 L/20 howitzer in a high box turret. Built on the hull of the KV-I, it was found to be operationally ineffective during Barbarossa because of its weight of 57 tons, which made it slow, and a high silhouette of 13.7 feet compared to 8.75 feet for the KV-I. *U.S. Army*

six-wheeled commercial truck chasis. A turret mounted on the rear of the armored vehicle had either a 3.7cm gun or a 12.7mm machine gun. With six wheels, it had fair cross-country capability and a unique feature—tracks could be attached to the four rear wheels to improve performance. The Soviets found that armored cars were quite useful for internal security. Other variations and improved models appeared, and during the war gutted BA-10 and BA-32 armored cars were used as armored personnel carriers. The last new armored car model to see action was the BA-64 of 1943, which was based on the German Sd Kfz-222 series armored cars, which it closely resembled. It was fast at 55 mph but was only armed with machine guns. The Red Army used armored cars mainly for liaison.

Artillery tractors such as the Komintern full-tracked artillery tractor were also built; trucks such as the VZ semi-track and the GAZ-60 semi-track were also constructed with tank tracks and suspension in the rear and wheels in the front. They were used mainly as supply vehicles and prime movers on the muddy and snowy Russian roads.

Aircraft Armament

In 1917 the Bolsheviks inherited a vast empire and a small air force.[53] Out of the chaos of the revolution, the small Red Air Fleet, as it was called, was formed from the remnants of the Imperial Russian Air Force. During the Civil War, the Communist leadership articulated a basic air doctrine which emphasized the tactical use of air power in support of the Red Army. After consolidating political power, efforts began to build the industrial base to support an aviation industry and a powerful air arm. With the clandestine cooperation of the German Army of the Weimar Republic, progress was made in building an efficient Soviet Air Force, the VVS, always a semi-autonomous branch of the Army.

Under the rule of Stalin, the VVS was greatly expanded and equipped with a new generation of modern aircraft, including fighters and bombers. The Soviet Union, along with Germany and Italy, gained valuable combat experience during their involvement in the Spanish Civil War, 1936–39. Experience in the war with Finland during 1939–40 revealed deficiencies, and in 1941 the VVS was again in the midst of a reorganization and reequipment with new aircraft of more modern design.

Until 1932 all aircraft guns were derived from the PM1910 Maxim machine gun, firing rimless ammunition in 7.62mm caliber.[54] The DA 7.62mm gun adopted in 1928 was designed by Vasely Degtyarev, the famous Russian small arms designer. DA was an abbreviation of *Degtyarev Aviatsionnyi* (Degtyarev Aviation). It was usually installed on a flexible, hand-held mount while the modified Maxim guns were used in fixed, forward-firing positions on fighter planes. All were, of course, air cooled.

The 7.62mm PV-1 gun or *Pulyemet Vozdushnyi* (Air Machine Gun), was also introduced in 1928 and was used in fixed, synchronized, or flexible mountings. The designers and engineers continued their development work, and the 7.62mm ShKAS machine gun was adopted in 1932 and proved to be an excellent, fast-firing gun that replaced the old Maxims on new Soviet fighter planes such as the I-15 and I-16; it was also used in flexible installations. It was not until 1950 that a 12.7mm machine gun, the UB or *Universal'nyi Beresin*, was introduced, considered by the Russians to be better than the U.S. .50 caliber Browning guns received under the lend-lease program during World War II. Designed by M. Ye. Beresin, it was also designated as the UBS for synchronized gun, the UBK for wing gun, and the UBT for turret gun.

With their emphasis on ground attack and close air support, the Soviets began developing the first of a long line of aircraft cannon. The 2cm ShVAK gun, adopted in 1936, had a rapid rate of fire of 800 RPM and good muzzle velocity. A 2.3cm cannon, the VYa, MP-23, also appeared in 1940, but after the Soviets began receiving American Bell P-39 Airacobra fighters with 37mm cannon, they quickly introduced the NS-37, a powerful 37mm cannon. It could penetrate almost 40mm of armor and was considered superior to both American and German guns of its type.[55] These were followed by the NS-45 4.5cm cannon and the OKB-16-57 of 5.7cm in 1944, an improved 2cm, the B-20, and the NS-23 2.3 cm gun, both in 1945. Several more advanced aircraft cannon for jet aircraft would follow in the Cold War of the post-war period. Aircraft ammo was made to higher standards.

Aircraft rockets of 7.5, 8.2, and 13.2cm were in service by 1939 and were used by the thousands during World War II, especially against German tanks and other ground targets.

Aircraft bombs used by the Soviet Air Force were the least developed of their aircraft armament.[56] Up to the end of 1942, Soviet bombs were mainly pre-war stock with nose and/or tail fuzes which had been designed and manufactured with little thought for ballistic qualities. Also, in contrast to German bombs, the workmanship was essentially crude, because of Soviet dependence on unskilled labor and lack of qualified personnel. This changed by the end of 1943 when modern bombs of good quality were finally available. This greatly improved accuracy and reduced the number of duds. Many German bombs captured during their retreat, as well as electrical fuzes and equipment, were used during the latter part of the war. The following are the principal types of bombs employed by the Soviet Air Force.[57]

General Purpose	Incendiary
Semi-Armor Piercing	Smoke
Armor Piercing	Flare
Antitank	Propaganda
Fragmentation	Cluster Container (Molotov Breadbasket)

It is believed that the largest Soviet bomb used in World War II was the 990-kg (2200-lb) FAB-1000. It was of welded construction, contained TNT, had a nose and tail fuze, four fins for stability, and was classified as a general purpose (GP) bomb.

Rockets

The Red Army during World War II employed fin-stabilized, solid fuel rockets on a larger scale than any other army. These relatively cheap substitutes for artillery undoubtedly had adverse morale effects upon German soldiers who called them "Stalin Organs." However, they were inaccurate and were mainly effective only for close-in massed fire against static positions—a type of operation which characterized Soviet offensives of World War II.[58] Like the German Army *Nebelwerfer*, Soviet rockets were employed on a variety of mounts, including wheeled launchers, and special racks on 6 × 6 trucks, armored vehicles and river craft. The M-13 rocket launcher, the famous *Katyusha*, can often be seen in wartime photos mounted on the back of Studebaker trucks supplied by the U.S. under lend-lease. The main Soviet artillery rocket used during World War II was the 8.2cm, and 36 to 48 could be fired from the M-8 launcher. Sixteen 13.2cm rockets were fired from the M-13 launcher and 30cm rockets were launched from a 12-rail rig mounted on the back of a large GAZ-AA truck. None of these artillery rockets contained a guidance system.

THE "KARL" *GERAET* SUPER HOWITZER

The small group of German and Italian officers watched as the three Junkers Ju 52/3m transports landed on schedule at the airstrip near Terespol. The town was in former Polish territory near the fortress of Brest-Litovsk, recently captured from the Soviets during Operation Barbarossa. The escort of four Messerschmitt Bf 109 fighters circled the field a few times and then flew off to refuel at their own airfield and wait for orders to accompany the transports back to Wolfsschanze, Hitler's secret supreme headquarters in East Prussia.

Among those emerging from the lead aircraft were the world's foremost Fascist dictators, Adolf Hitler and Benito Mussolini. On hand to greet Mussolini was his aviator son, Vittorio, who was serving on the Eastern Front with the Italian Expeditionary Force, fighting with the German Army.

Hitler and Mussolini had flown here to view the results of the bombardment of the Soviet fortress at Brest-Litovsk by the giant 60cm (600mm) *"Karl" Moerser (Geraet 040)*, a self-propelled gun called a mortar by the Germans and a howitzer in U.S. Army terminology. The visiting leaders soon climbed into staff cars and *Kuebelwagen* and were driven to the fortress where Karl gun detachment members were waiting to provide details to the Fuehrer.

An artillery officer explained the workings of the remarkable gun and its special support vehicles and described the first use of this fearsome secret weapon in action. Hitler had taken a special interest in the development of this gun, originally intended for bombarding the fortifications of the French Maginot Line along the Franco-German border. He asked a number of surprisingly technical questions, and the officers from the Karl detachment explained how the two 60cm guns, number III and IV, and a crane, were shipped from their base in Germany and unloaded at the train station at Terespol, under cover of darkness, and quietly moved into their firing positions. This was just forty-eight hours before the German invasion of the Soviet

Union began at dawn on June 22, 1941. The firing positions outside of town were about 4,702 yards (4,300 meters) from the fortress.

The other vehicles, including the ammunition carriers and support personnel, were unloaded at the train station in the town of Biala — Podlaska, about 24.8 miles (40 kilometers) west of Terespol and arrived at night by road. On command, on the morning of June 22, the guns began firing their huge concrete-piercing projectiles, which were lifted onto the loading tray behind the gun breech with the crane mounted on its special tracked vehicle. The complete round of ammunition, ready for firing, consisted of the projectile, separate bags of gunpowder, and a strong steel shell case to seal the breech.

The crew of a Karl howitzer, the 60cm *Geraet* 040, has removed the canvas cover from the gun and is preparing the giant self-propelled behemoth for firing. *From* Artillerie im Osten, *op. cit.*

The fortress of Brest-Litovsk consisted of an old but massive brick and masonry citadel, with protective grass-covered earthworks, and a north fort of similar construction. The *Zitadelle* was positioned on a hill overlooking the Bug River that separated Terespol from the town of Brest and formed part of the border between German- and Russian-occupied Poland.

According to a German after-action report, the *Karl batterie Nr. II, schwere Artillerie-Abteilung 833* (Heavy Artillery Detachment 833), was ordered to commence firing early on the morning of June 22. (*Batterie Nr. I* was in action against other targets along the border). Gun number III, nicknamed "Odin," fired four rounds, and gun number IV, called "Thor," three rounds, before both developed difficulties in loading the 60cm projectiles into the breech because of defective copper driving bands. On June 23, gun no. III could not fire because of a short in the electrical firing mechanism, but gun no. IV lobbed seven rounds on the fortress.

Early on June 24, "Odin" fired six rounds and "Thor" eleven rounds, for a total of 31 rounds. All struck the target accurately and proved more destructive than even the 21cm guns also bombarding the fortress. The shells demolished large sections of the fortifications including the strong brick walls, 6.56 feet (2 meters) thick, which were blown apart. Shells that struck in the courtyard inside the fort blasted craters about 49.2 feet (15 meters) wide and 16.4 feet (5 meters) deep.

Hitler and Mussolini found the work of the Karl howitzers very impressive, and the Fuehrer was pleased to learn that the *Heereswaffenamt* (Army Ordnance Office) considered the guns to have performed satisfactorily during their first baptism of fire. The shelling had a drastic effect on the morale of the Soviet garrison. Hitler gained grim satisfaction from the description of the gruesome effects of the bombardment on the soldiers of the Red Army. Many men were blown apart or crushed by debris. Even deep inside the massive Citadel, the tremendous concussion of the shells produced such great changes in air pressure that they ruptured the lungs and eardrums of many of the hapless defenders. The fortress was also shelled by other artillery and attacked by Junkers Ju 87D Stuka dive-bombers, but nothing could compare with the thunderous detonations of the Karl shells. The fortress was finally occupied by the troops of the German 45th Infantry Division on June 25.

After seeing the destruction caused by the giant guns at first hand, Hitler and Mussolini picked their way through the rubble inside the Citadel, returned with their entourage to the airstrip, and flew back to Wolfsschanze.

The Karl guns were developed and deployed in secrecy, and even with the passage of time there are still gaps in the history of this extraordinary weapon.[1] The development of super-heavy artillery was included in Hitler's ambitious program for the rearmament of Germany. Contracts were signed by 1935 for the design and manufacture of several types of large railway guns and other heavy artillery that Germany had been prohibited from possessing by the Treaty of Versailles. Hitler believed that France would be the main obstacle to his plans for German hegemony over Europe, and he knew that if war came the Wehrmacht would require very heavy artillery to defeat the Maginot Line of fortifications along the Franco-German border. Railway guns were important, but their use was limited by the extent of the rail system. The size of bombs carried by aircraft of that period was also limited. The answer was determined to be a super-heavy mortar, actually a howitzer according to U.S. Army nomenclature of World War II, which classified as a howitzer any mortar over 210mm.[2]

The Artillery Design Department of the *Heereswaffenamt, Waffen Pruef 4*, initiated discussions with the firm of Rheinmetall-Borsig in late 1935, and initial design proposals for a very heavy gun with a high angle of fire was codified in a development contract in late 1936. As first conceived, the gun was to be 80cm and built in sections to be carried to a prepared position near the front in tracked vehicles, where it would be assembled and fired.

It was decided after further study that this design was too cumbersome and assembly too time-consuming. It was therefore not in accordance with the new German concept of Blitzkrieg, then being formed, which featured mobile warfare to avoid the stalemate and war of attrition that characterized conflict on the Western Front in World War I.[3] Eventually, Rheinmetall submitted a new design to the *H.Wa.A., WaPru 4*, for a smaller 60cm (23.6 in) gun to be mounted on a special self-propelled, tracked vehicle. This gun was intended to be ready for firing in thirty minutes after reaching its firing position, instead of almost eight hours for the original design.

This new design was approved for further development in early 1937, and work on the proposed weapon system continued as a secret project. Controlling the size and weight of the gun presented a number of problems. Extensive tests and studies had to be completed, not only on the weapon itself, but on the tracked, self-propelled chassis, special loading mechanism, and other essential components. Trials of the prototype chassis, which later evolved into the chassis of the *Pz. Kpfw. IV tank*, took longer than anticipated, and proceeded in conjunction with the development of the gun, ammunition, and other accessories.

The first gun prototype and test ammunition were finally finished in May 1939 and test firing began in June. The weapon system was referred to by the cover designation *Geraet 040* (Equipment 040). The gun had a short barrel with a rather low muzzle velocity of 220 meters a second. It had a sliding block breech and was fired electrically.

The gun was mounted on a chassis that was basically a steel box with tracked suspension. The engine was located in the front compartment, the gun mounting was in the center section, and the batteries and reduction gear drive were in the rear compartment. This gear was coupled to the torsion bar suspension mounts and allowed the bars to be rotated to lower the hull to the ground and thus relieve the suspension of the shock upon firing. A top carriage was free to move

The left front view of the 60cm Karl howitzer, *Geraet* 040, in driving position with the crew platforms along the sides raised. The driver and assistant driver sat in the left front section with the gun itself pointing to the rear. This is Gun No. I, named "Adam," the first of seven to be built. *U.S. Army Ordnance Museum*

inside the hull, controlled by a hydro-pneumatic recoil system. The 60cm cannon was fitted into a ring cradle that had a separate recoil system connected to the breech ring. Thus the gun had a dual recoil system.[4]

Because of the huge caliber of 60cm (600mm), and relatively short barrel, 16 feet, 8 inches (5.08 meters) long, its range was limited to only about 4,921 yards (4,500 meters), depending on the propelling charge and angle of fire.[5] The gun was therefore mounted to fire to the rear from its special carriage. It was backed into position for firing so it could be quickly driven away under its own power in case of enemy counter-battery fire. The barrel could be elevated up to 75 degrees for firing and had a limited traverse. For major changes in aim, the entire vehicle had to be moved by turning on its tracks.

The special munition was specifically designed to penetrate and destroy the steel reinforced concrete forts of the French Maginot Line. The ammunition was referred to as a *schwere Betongranate 040* or concrete-piercing shell 040. This shell weighed 4,839 pounds (2,195 kilograms) and had an explosive charge weighing 617 pounds (280 kg). A lighter high-explosive shell 040 weighing 3,472 pounds (1,575 kg) with a longer range of up to 7,300 yards (6,675 meters) was also provided.[6] Shells could penetrate concrete 8.2 feet (2.5 meters) thick.

As mentioned, because of the heavy weight and substantial recoil, the chassis was designed so that it could be lowered with the power of the engine to rest on the ground for firing. When it was necessary to move on its tracks or to reposition, the engine was started and the chassis raised so it cleared the ground. The chassis could also be raised and lowered by hand using a crank handle, not an easy job.

Firing tests and experiments with various powder charges continued, as well as loading and driving trials and practice with the tracked chassis. They proved successful enough to allow

The left rear view of Karl howitzer No. I "Adam." The huge self-propelled gun, called a *Moerser* by the Germans, was designed to fire to the rear. The special concrete-piercing shell weighed 4,839 pounds (2,195 kg) and contained 617 pounds (280 kg) of high explosive. *U.S. Army Ordnance Museum*

six complete weapon systems to be ordered for operational use. There were still "bugs" to be worked out and it was understood that modifications and improvements would be made during production. A seventh gun was also ordered that would be used only for testing, firing table experiments, and training of crews.

Along with the gun, chassis, and ammunition, a special tracked ammunition carrier was designed called a *Munitionsschlepper*. This was also built on a modified Pz. Kpfw IV chassis. It featured a unique seesaw crane called a *Wippkran* that was powered by electricity and specially designed to move the heavy projectiles. An ingenious device for gripping the projectiles was attached to the end of the crane by cables. For traveling, the entire crane could be folded back across the box-like top of the vehicle. Eventually, three variations were built and used in action. In addition, a 35-ton crane on a special, wheeled trailer was provided for use in assembling and disassembling the gun from its chassis. As can be seen, very few items of equipment for this weapon could be "taken off the shelf."

The guns were self-propelled over short distances, but a means was required for moving them over long distances. For road travel, the gun assembly itself could be removed from its tracked chassis, which was carried on a specially designed 24-wheel trailer called a *Culemeyer–Strassenfahrzeug*. The gun assembly was carried in three separate loads: The gun tube and breech; the carriage with dual recoil system; and the loading tray for the ammunition and upper recoil and buffer housing. Each load was transported separately on special 16-wheel trailers differing in design from that used for the tracked chassis. In the field, all four loads were concealed by camouflaged canvas covers.

The Culemeyer-Strassenfahrzeug, the special heavy duty trailer provided for the tracked chassis, was designed so that the chassis could climb on and off the trailer under its own power. Consideration also had to be given to the weight that could be supported by bridges in the field, including military bridges built by the engineers. The chassis alone often had to be driven over some bridges under its own power.

The beginning of World War II in September 1939 began with the German invasion of Poland. Great Britain and France then declared war on Germany, which added new urgency to this weapon development project. In late 1939 design work commenced, in conjunction with engineers from the *Reichsbahn* (National Railway), on special railcars for transporting the guns. Here again, the great weight and size involved required ingenuity in design and manufacture. The special rail carriages produced allowed the complete gun, on its chassis, to be carried, supported by traversing pedestals, mounted on the two rail carriages. The gun was lifted on supporting arms on its chassis by powerful hydraulic cylinders, so it could be suspended between the rail carriages. The railcars and guns could pass under all existing railroad overpasses.

The guns were not ready for use during the German invasion of France in May and June 1940, but in any event were not needed because the Army Panzer units thrust through the Ardennes and bypassed the Maginot Line. The first tests of a complete, operational Geraet 040, including its support vehicles, began at a troop training area in July 1940, and test firing started in November. Many complex problems had been encountered in the development of this new weapon, and not all of the questions had been resolved to the complete satisfaction of the Army Ordnance Office and Rheinmetall-Borsig. Hitler had decided to invade the Soviet Union; the original date was set for May 1941. Production of the guns was ordered accelerated even though testing of some components, including the chassis, was still continuing. Between October 1940 and June 1941, six operational gun systems were completed by Rheinmetall and delivered to the Army for testing and acceptance. Training of a staff and crewmen was also underway. All of the tests and trials were completed successfully and at least two units formed to operate the guns in the field.

Because of the urgent need to complete the guns and have them ready for action, each of the seven weapon systems differed from the others in minor or major ways. Differences in the chassis and suspension can be seen with the number of road wheels varying from eight for guns I and II, to eleven for III through VII. Guns I, II, VI, and VII were powered by Daimler-Benz 12-cylinder MB 503A gasoline engines while III, IV and V were equipped with 12-cylinder MB 507C diesel engines.[7] If additional guns had been ordered, the most successful model would have been produced.

The gun crew for the Geraet 040 consisted of the gun captain, eighteen gunners, and two drivers. Extensive training was given to the drivers who had to learn to handle the operation and loading of the vehicle and to back it into a firing location that had previously been leveled and cleared of obstacles. The driver sat in a low compartment at the left front of the chassis and the assistant driver sat above and behind the driver.

The personnel, organization, and equipment of a 60cm Geraet 040 battery varied during World War II. Experience necessitated the addition of more vehicles for transporting supplies and equipment, especially if more than one gun was assigned.

Personnel assigned to the six main sections of a typical one-gun Karl-Geraet 040 battery late in the war included:

3 officers, 30 noncommissioned officers, and 122 enlisted men.

Vehicles assigned included:

One *Karl-Geraet 040*, on its tracked chassis.

Three *Munitionsschlepper*, tracked ammunition carriers.

Eight *Personenkraftwagen Gelaendegaengig (Pkw. gl.)*, light military cars with cross-country capability, for the commander, staff officers, etc.

Eighteen 2-, 3-, and 5-ton *Lastkraftwagen* (Lkw.), trucks for hauling equipment, tools, supplies, fuel, mess gear, rations, etc.

Four 12-ton *Zugkraftwagen.* (Zgkw.), large half-track prime movers for towing three 16-wheel Culemeyer trailers, the 35-ton crane, and the three 3.7cm Flak 43Z (Zwilling-twin AAA guns) assigned.

Two 18-ton *Zgkw.* were assigned for towing a 24-wheel Culemeyer trailer and probably a portable electric generator.

About this time the seven Geraet 040 were designated *Karl-Geraet* in honor of *Generalleutnant* (Lieutenant General) Karl Becker, former Chief of the Army Ordnance Office.

The following Karl-Geraet were produced, and each was given a nickname except number VII.[8]

Gun	Nickname	Engine	Metric H.P.	Speed	Range
I	Adam	MB 503A	580	10 km/h	42 km
II	Eva	MB 503A	580	10 km/h	42 km
III	Odin	MB 507C	580	6 km/h	60 km
IV	Thor	MB 507C	580	6 km/h	60 km
V	Loki	MB 507C	580	6 km/h	60 km
VI	Ziu	MB 503A	580	6 km/h	42 km
VII	—	MB 503A	580	Unknown	Unknown

Number VII, the *Versuchs-Geraet* (test gun), probably had the same performance as gun number VI.

After studying the test results and seeing the gun, Hitler decided that the range should be increased. The Heereswaffenamt responded to the wish of the Fuehrer by issuing a contract to Rheinmetall-Borsig for a modification of the Karl-Geraet to develop an interchangeable barrel and accessories with a reduced caliber of 54cm (21.2-inch). This would provide a range of about 11,500 yards (10,500 meters). This version was designated as the *Karl-Geraet 041*. The same chassis, support vehicles, and most of the accessories were used with both the 60cm and 54cm versions.

The new barrel was not completed until July 1942, and gun number VII was used as the test vehicle. Early tests of the 54cm barrel were unsatisfactory, and development problems with the ballistics and ammunition delayed production until 1944. The problems were finally solved and guns number I, IV, and V were converted to use the 54cm barrel. A new loading tray was also required. With the new, longer barrel, the vehicle actually increased in weight and length. As with the 60cm gun, range varied with the elevation of the barrel and propellant charges employed. The intended rate of fire for both guns was one round every ten minutes. It should be remembered that the Karl guns required their special crane and ammunition for operation.

Meanwhile, on June 22, 1941, Operation Barbarossa began and, as previously described,

A Karl gun of smaller caliber but longer range was introduced in 1942. The 54cm *Geraet* 041 used most of the components of the 60cm gun and, in fact, the 54cm barrel and breech were interchangeable with the 60cm gun on the same carriage. This photo shows the 54cm gun with the special ammunition carrier, built on the PzKpfw IV's chassis, that served both types of guns with slight modification to the crane. The crane on the ammunition carrier loaded the heavy shells onto the gun-loading tray. *U.S. Army Ordnance Museum*

two Karl guns were used to fire against the Soviet fortress of Brest-Litovsk. The Karl guns were only useful against heavy, fixed fortifications; smaller, more mobile artillery was more practical for the invasion of the Soviet Union. With no appropriate targets immediately available after Brest-Litovsk, the *2. Batterie, schwere Artillerie Abteilung (Motorisert) 833* (2d Battery, Heavy Artillery Detachment [Motorized] 833), as it was now redesignated, was returned to the *Truppenuebungsplatz* Bergen, the training area at Bergen in Germany. Within a few weeks the Karl guns were placed in storage and the highly trained unit was reorganized and reequipped with more mobile 21cm Moerser 18 guns for use in the fast-moving campaign in Russia.

The march of events during the first months of war on the Eastern Front led to the Crimea and Sevastopol in the fall of 1941. In March 1942, *s. Art. Abt. 833* was directed by OKH to form a Karl-Batterie of three guns and proceed immediately to the Crimea where it would be placed under command of *Harko 306*, the Eleventh Army artillery command. While the unit was forming up and moving by rail to the Crimea, firing positions for the three 60cm guns were selected and prepared by *Pioniere* (Engineers). Manual labor was accomplished by workers from the *Organisation Todt (OT)* construction organization, and by civilian workers hired and paid in bread. Because of the rocky and hilly terrain, and the need to build smooth dirt approach roads to the firing sites, this required considerable time and effort. Work was accomplished mainly at night by hundreds of men under tight security because the sites were close to the front line. Everything was camouflaged immediately to protect against Russian observation and subsequent air attack or artillery fire.

The Karl Battery with all its gear arrived in the area behind the Sevastopol front in mid-May. The unit was equipped with three 60cm guns, support vehicles, and 72 heavy and 50 light concrete-piercing shells. The crews and support vehicles were ready for action by May 25, and

A 60cm projectile is rammed off the loading tray and into the breech of the Karl gun. The shell was followed by the bagged propellant charge and the shell case that sealed the breech. *U.S. Army Ordnance Museum*

received orders from *Harko 306* for targets that had been selected in collaboration with the staff of the LIV Corps. The initial targets included Fort Maxim Gorki I and its Bastion, key to the Soviet defense of the northern front. The Karl guns lumbered into position the night of June 1–2, just hours before the assault on Sevastopol began. Every effort was made to conceal the preparations for the offensive all along the front, including maintaining normal radio transmissions.

On command, the Karl guns belched forth their huge shells, creating a great cloud of smoke and dust at the time of firing. Some crew members donned gas masks in the choking dust. As the sun came up and the temperature steadily climbed, they were soon coated with sweat and dust that added to the surreal scene of half-naked men struggling to load and fire the giant steel guns that were too hot to touch.

According to German reports, the shells from Karl guns that hit Fort Maxim Gorki I caused such severe damage that they materially aided in its capture.[9] The Karl battery fired eighteen heavy and fifty light shells at targets between June 2 and 13, with good effect. Interrogation of Russian prisoners disclosed that few adverse effects were experienced inside Fort Maxim Gorki I when bombed by the Luftwaffe or shelled by field artillery. However, the giant shells from the Karl guns shook even the lower levels and caused extensive damage to the exposed turrets, blockhouses, and other defenses. The numerous casualties spread fear and helped undermine the morale of the dazed defenders, bracing for the inevitable German ground assault that finally took the fort by storm.

The Karl guns ran out of ammunition around mid-June and had to wait until a new supply finally arrived by rail from Germany. Twenty-five heavy shells and fifty lightweight shells were fired on June 30 and July 1, respectively, as the troops of the Eleventh Army stormed the last fortifications and fully occupied the city of Sevastopol and environs. A total of 197 rounds were fired from the Karl guns during the siege. Photos in several references show Gun Nr. IV, "Thor," in action at Sevastopol.[10] The shock and devastation caused by the powerful 60cm shells certainly contributed to the final collapse of Soviet resistance in Sevastopol, the world's strongest fortress.

The following month the men of the *Karl-Batterie, s. Art. Abt. 833* packed up their guns and equipment, boarded a special train, and returned to Hillersleben, Germany, where they refurbished their gear and prepared for further assignment. Shortly thereafter, the commander was directed to make ready three 60cm guns and support vehicles for action on the Eastern Front. A new unit was formed for this deployment, designated *schwere Batterie 628 (Karl)*. It was transported by rail to the Leningrad area to participate in the siege of the city, but the counterattack by the Red Army caused the plan to be canceled. The unit was subsequently returned to Germany by rail to prevent capture by the advancing Soviet forces.

During 1943, various reorganizations occurred and training of crews continued, with some personnel sent to other artillery units at the front. In mid-year, the unit, now designated *schwere Artillerie Abteiling 628*, was reorganized again and formed into two batteries equipped with 21cm Moerser 18 heavy guns for use at the front. The big Karl guns and their vehicles were placed in storage, but not forgotten.

In early August 1944, the Soviet Army was advancing on the city of Warsaw in German-occupied Poland. The Polish resistance, called the Polish Home Army, began an uprising in the capital against the German occupation. The Russians callously decided to halt on the banks of the Vistula River and let the Germans slug it out with the Polish resistance, which the Soviets believed would also oppose occupation and communization by the Russians.

The OKH ordered that a battery of two 60cm Karl guns be formed immediately and sent to Warsaw without delay. *Heeres-Artillerie Batterie 638* was quickly organized from cadre and shipped with gun number I, "Adam," and number VI, "Ziu," by express train to Warsaw, where it entered action in August. A third gun was sent to Warsaw with *Batterie 428* in mid-September and replaced gun number VI, which was returned to Germany for repair. Guns number

A 60cm Karl gun ready for firing. The crew has withdrawn, the gun is aimed, and the gun captain needs only to give the order to fire. *U.S. Army Ordnance Museum*

The 60cm Karl gun in full recoil at the instant of firing. The huge shells caused heavy damage to even the most massive enemy fortifications. *U.S. Army Ordnance Museum*

I and VI are known to have been in almost continuous action at Warsaw during August and part of September 1944.

The SS was in charge of crushing the insurrection in Warsaw, and the bombardment of certain sections of the city helped break the resistance. The huge Karl shells striking the old, multistory brick buildings lining the streets resulted in massive destruction. Most shells punched through several floors to explode in the basement, causing whole blocks of buildings to collapse in great clouds of smoke and dust. Many streets were soon blocked with hundreds of tons of rubble. Countless civilians were killed and injured, as well as many of the heroic resisters.

Battery 428 with one gun and Battery 638 with gun number V, "Loki," were sent to Budapest, Hungary, by rail in late September. They were returned by rail to the Warsaw area sometime in late October. In mid-November, both Battery 428 and Battery 638 were returned to their base at Jueterbog in Germany with orders to rearm with the Geraet 041 54cm guns. However, only Karl Battery 638 was reequipped with the 54cm guns.

At Jueterbog, Karl-Batterie 428 was soon ready with 60cm guns II and VI, and prepared for a new assignment: support of the top secret offensive in the Ardennes, which became known in the West as the "Battle of the Bulge." Moving at night and in bad weather, this battery traveled west with all its gear by mid-December 1944. Karl Batterie 638 was also sent west armed with the 54cm Geraet 041, for the first combat use of this longer-range weapon. Both Karl units were placed under the direct control of the *Oberbefehlshaber West* (Commander in Chief, West).

The German offensive in the Ardennes began on December 16 with a heavy artillery barrage, but no record of the actual use of any of the Karl guns has been found. It is believed that the 60cm gun number VI, "Ziu," fired some rounds in December before being withdrawn for use on the Eastern Front. It was eventually captured intact by the Soviets and ended up after the war in a military museum in Kubinka, Russia.

Gun number II, "Eva," was damaged by bombs from USAAF fighter-bombers on its way to the assembly area behind the Ardennes front and was returned to Jueterbog. It was repaired, returned to the Western Front, and it fired several rounds at the Remagen bridge and bridgehead in March 1945, apparently with little success. It was captured on its railway cars by the advancing troops of the U.S. Army, probably in April.[11]

Karl Gun number I, "Adam," remained at Jueterbog and was used for spare parts to repair Gun number II, "Eva." Gun number III, "Odin," was severely damaged at Jueterbog during test firing of a 60cm 040 barrel in September 1944, and repairs were never completed.

Gun number IV, "Thor," veteran of the Sevastopol siege, now with the 54cm barrel, also sustained damage in the field and was returned by rail to Jueterbog in January for repair. It was probably destroyed by the Germans before the arrival of the Russians.

Repair and conversion of Gun number V, "Loki," to the 54cm configuration was completed by February, and in March it was sent with its crew to the front in the west where it was damaged on its railcars before capture by the U.S. Army.

Gun number VII remained at Jueterbog during most of the war for testing, training, and the preparation of firing tables for the 60cm and 54cm ammunition. It was probably destroyed by the Germans.

Immediately after the end of the war in Europe on May 8, 1945, U.S. Army Ordnance personnel collected all the parts of Karl Gun number II, "Eva," and Gun number V, "Loki," along with examples of both 54cm and 60cm ammunition and support vehicles. One complete Karl gun along with its ammunition carrier with the special crane on the Pz. Kpfw. IV chassis, and all equipment, was shipped to the U.S. Army Ordnance Center at Aberdeen Proving Ground, Maryland. After it was examined, it was scrapped before the U.S. Amy Ordnance Museum was officially established.

In the desperate days of April 1945, with the Wehrmacht disintegrating and Allied forces advancing on all fronts, Karl Batterie 638 was disbanded and remaining personnel and equipment transferred to Karl Batterie 428. Any further use of the Karl guns is unknown, and the home base at Jueterbog, 31 miles (50 km) south of Berlin, was captured by the triumphant troops of the Red Army on Hitler's birthday, April 20, 1945.

SUNDAY PUNCH:

"Dora," The World's Biggest Cannon

F EUER! A thunderous roar, followed by a huge cloud of smoke, heralded Dora's first shot in anger as its enormous shell whistled toward its target 15.5 miles (25 kilometers) distant. As the first rays of the morning sun illuminated the gray steel colossus, it resembled a giant, fire-breathing monster from Norse mythology, ready to rain destruction on its enemies. But this was not a myth, it was the 80cm "Dora," the biggest gun of all time, and its enemy in June 1942 was Sevastopol, the world's strongest fortress.

It was just over six years since Hitler had first proposed the construction of a giant cannon to officials of the Krupp works.[1] It would be a gun even larger and more powerful than any in history, just the sort of super weapon that could back up Hitler's plans for the domination of Europe. The origin of this gun is similar to that of the 60cm "Karl" self-propelled howitzer. It was designed and built at the specific request of Hitler for use in bombarding the French Maginot Line of heavy fortifications along the Franco-German border. A variety of large railway guns and other heavy artillery were included in the massive German rearmament program that commenced shortly after Hitler became Reichs Chancellor in January 1933.

This gun, however, was different from other heavy weapons being developed for Germany's new arsenal. Built by the famous cannon-making firm of Friedrich Krupp of Essen, it would be enormous; the design and construction of this complex gun, carriage, and ammunition would challenge the state of the art in metallurgy, ballistics, and mechanics, as well as other aspects of the operational use of artillery. This was, after all, the biggest gun ever built, and it had several unique features.[2] When first proposed, several experts from OKH and the Heereswaffenamt (Army Ordnance Office) recommended the production of railway guns of smaller and more practical size. The Fuehrer, however, personally directed Krupp to explore the feasibility of building this super gun. When this became known, no more disparaging suggestions were made, and the initial design work was immediately commenced by Krupp on its own initiative.

An official development contract was signed by the Heereswaffenamt with the Krupp firm in early 1937 for the design and development of an *80cm* (800mm or 31.5 inch) *Kanone (E)* (E-*Eisenbahngeschutz*—Railway Gun). The chief of construction was Dr. Erich Mueller, often called "*Kanonen-Mueller*," who was eventually honored by the Fuehrer with the *Kriegsverdienstkreuz* (War Merit Cross) for his accomplishments. The gun was originally called the "*Gustav Geraet*" (Gustav Equipment) in secret documents, and later "*Schwerer Gustav*" (Heavy or Fat Gustav) after the former head of the Krupp firm, Gustav Krupp von Bohlen und Halbach. When finally delivered in early 1942, it was given the cover name "Dora," and was sometimes referred to in documents as the "D–Geraet." The entire program, including training of the crews, was conducted in secret.

The gun weighed approximately 1,170 tons and was designed to have a range of about 25 miles (40 kilometers) at an elevation of 45 degrees. Original estimates suggested a barrel life of 100 rounds. The special projectiles had to be capable of penetrating at least five to six meters of the strongest type of steel-reinforced concrete fortification.[3]

Not since the famous 21cm "Paris Gun," that bombarded the French capital in 1918 from a range of 72 miles (132 km), had a weapon of this size been planned.[4] A large team of designers, engineers, and staff were employed, not only for the research and design of the gun, but the development of special cranes for the assembly and disassembly of the gun, the rail cars, and the special ammunition and equipment. Even the locomotives for use with the huge cannon had to be specially designed and built. Conventional electric engines were not powerful enough, and regular steam engines, of large size, burned coal and would be impractical for maneuvering the gun at the front while aiming, which required precise operation. Smoke and steam would also belch high into the air and would invite attack by the enemy before the gun even entered action.

A special diesel-electric locomotive of about 1,000 hp was designed, which would not only precisely maneuver the gun but provide the large amount of electric power needed to elevate the gun barrel and operate the other electric and hydraulic components and accessories— in effect, an auxiliary power plant. Two engines were ordered for each of the three guns planned, with the designation D 311, and the two engine sections for each were referred to as sections "A" and "B."

Three guns were ordered in 1939, and construction commenced immediately under a veil of secrecy. Detailed progress reports had to be submitted periodically to Hitler. In anticipation of the production contract, Krupp had already begun preparing and fabricating components of the gun and its accessories, and arranging subcontracts for certain electrical and other systems was under way.[5]

One of the special diesel-electric locomotives that maneuvered Dora at the front and produced electric power for elevating the barrel and other functions. It was hastily camouflaged after reaching the gun assembly area for Dora north of Sevastopol in May 1942. The crew gave it the nickname "Walli," which can be seen painted on the cab. *U.S. Army Ordnance Museum*

The beginning of World War II in September 1939 placed an even heavier work load on Krupp, and the giant railguns were far from completion when the German campaign in the west began on May 10, 1940. The German Army simply bypassed the vaunted Maginot Line by striking through the Ardennes region; with the fall of France there were no fortifications to attack with this mighty weapon. Still, work continued with the possible intention of using Schwere Gustav to fire across the English Channel at targets in southern England, already under bombardment by smaller railway guns. Planners at OKW also suggested using the gun to shell fortifications on Gibraltar in case an attack, with Spanish cooperation, would be made on this British bastion guarding the entrance to the Mediterranean.

In the smokey, cavernous shops of the Krupp Works, the construction of the oversize components continued: the huge steel carriage, the gun cradle, the breech block of finest steel, and the massive two-part barrel, about 95.14 feet (30 meters) long, with a caliber of 80cm. Large hydraulic and electrical systems were also designed and produced. Two giant ten-ton cranes were designed and specially built for use in the assembly of the gun and its parts in the field.

Special railway cars for trains were developed and built with the cooperation of the *Reichsbahn* (National Railway), for transporting the entire weapons system. This was a complex management job even for the experienced specialists at the Krupp Works, as well as ordnance and railway engineers. Lastly, crewmen with railway gun and heavy artillery experience were selected after the fall of France and trained on smaller guns to be ready for use in testing and deploying the super-gun upon its completion.

The design and manufacture of the special ammunition proceeded concurrently with the fabrication of the guns. Two types of shells were developed. A high-explosive projectile weighing 4.8 tons (9,600 pounds) or 4,354 kilograms, and a *"Panzergranate"* (armored shell), a concrete-penetrating projectile of chrome-nickel steel with an especially hard point. It had a soft, streamlined pointed cover for aerodynamic purposes and contained 551 pounds (250 kg) of high explosive with a base fuze. The shell not only had to pierce the fortification but also to explode inside. This shell weighed 7.1 tons (14,200 lbs) or 6,440.9 kg, making it probably the heaviest artillery shell ever built. Experiments showed the maximum range with the high-explosive shell to be 29.2 miles (47 km) and a range of about 23.6 miles (38 km) was attained with the huge concrete-piercing projectile. The range was extended somewhat through continuing experiments with projectiles and propellants.[6]

A study for the U.S. Army Ordnance Department prepared in 1945, in the files of the U.S. Army Ordnance Museum, states that the 80cm (31.5 inch) projectile for Dora weighed over seven tons. The pointed ballistic cap was threaded to the actual armor and concrete-piercing projectile, which had a large base fuze. This steel shell had a hollow, thick-walled body 11 feet, 6 inches long (3.51 meters), and 31.5 inches (80cm) in diameter. Four copper rotating bands were around the base of the shell. The shell had a smaller piercing cone on top with a neck for seating the ballistic cap or windshield at the front of the shell. The projectiles were transported in wooden crates in a horizontal position, on flat cars or in ammunition cars.

The propellant was contained in the metal shell case (*Hauptkartusche*) and two additional propellant charges (*Vorkartusche 1 und 2*). The one—piece shell case (*Hauptkartusche* or *Kartuschhuelse*) was made of steel, plated with brass, and was manufactured in 1942. It was marked with the secret manufacturer's code "bwn," indicating the firm of Friedrich Krupp AG, Essen.

The two separate bagged propellant charges were carried crated in wooden boxes and were marked with the manufacturer's code "dbg," indicating that they were made by Dynamit A.-G., vormals (formerly) Alfred Nobel & Co., Werk Dueneberg. The total weight of the three propellant charges was 2,500 pounds, and according to the U.S. Army report, the muz-

An 80cm Dora anti-concrete projectile with ballistic cap (left) and the shell case. The 6-foot, 1-inch man in the center is Col. F. B. Porter, FA, U.S. Army, who investigated the gun and ammunition captured in Bavaria in April 1945. *U.S. Army Ordnance Museum*

zle velocity of the gun was 2,500 feet per second with a maximum range of 51,000 yards or about 30 miles (48.2 km).

By early 1941 the first of the two complete guns to be built and assembled was complete enough for test at the Hillersleben range, as part of the proofing trials. Acceptance tests were then made on a curved track at Ruegenwalde. The biggest gun of all time fired its first shot as a complete system, with a military crew, on November 25, 1941. Dora's firing was an impressive event that could be heard for miles and left a huge cloud of smoke floating over the test range. Almost everything worked well, and the mighty detonation shook windows and caused nearby trees to sway from the force of the blast. Eight operational test firings were made until December 5. The muzzle velocity was recorded at between 592 and 708 meters a second. The longest range achieved was 22.9 miles or about 37.2 kilometers. The gun successfully demonstrated its ability to easily penetrate reinforced concrete 22.9 feet (7 meters) thick and steel armor plate 39.3 inches (1 meter) thick.[7]

The first of the special diesel-electric locomotives had arrived the previous fall; after a few more firing tests and a check-out of the many accessories, the crews practiced the disassembly and assembly of the complete system under operational conditions. Everything was now functioning properly, and in early 1942 the 80cm K (E), now called "Dora," was declared ready for operational use. The new name was chosen by the crew and used for security purposes.

The operational army unit that had been formed, *schwere Artillerie Abteilung (E) 672*, celebrated the official acceptance with a party at the Ruegenwalde range. The unit soon received secret orders from OKH for its first combat deployment. The gun and its seemingly countless accessories were immediately disassembled and all components loaded on the special railway cars. Four trains were formed and each included *Eisenbahnflak*, cars equipped with antiaircraft guns. On board was the unit commander, *Dipl.-Ing. Oberst-leutnant* (Certified Engineer, Lieutenant Colonel) Robert Boehm, and the gun captain, *Oberleutnant* (First Lieutenant) Knoll, whose title was *Geschuetzfuehrer*.[8]

The Dora trains rolled east in April 1942 just as the landscape in German-occupied Poland was awakening to the beauty of spring. The trains were pulled by large steam locomotives to avoid wear and tear on the vital diesel-electric locomotives. The Russian railroads had been changed to the west European gauge after the German invasion so that German rolling stock could be used. The artillerymen riding in the passenger cars gazed out the windows as the vast expanse of Russia unfolded in seemingly endless monotony. But all agreed that if they had to go to the *Ostfront* (Eastern Front), this was the way to travel. A field kitchen had been set up in a freight car on each train to prepare rations for the troops on board. Since this was an *Eilzug* (express train), few stops were made despite the heavy rail traffic. All equipment on board the cars was carefully covered with camouflaged canvas, and on the few occasions when the train pulled off on a siding, or stopped to take on water or coal, armed guards made sure no one approached the train.

The trains rumbled on past ruined villages and fallow fields to Dniepopetrowsk, Melitopol, and finally south into the Crimea. Their progress was temporarily delayed at Dzhankoi by heavy rail traffic and fighting in the east around the Kerch Peninsula. Finally, at the end of April, Dora and its many railcars of equipment, along with the passenger cars for the crew, arrived at Simferopol where it halted before steaming on in mid-May to the southwest towards its secret destination—the besieged city of Sevastopol.

Weeks before the arrival of Dora, about 1,500 laborers under the direction of German Army and railroad engineers, and about 1,000 men of the *Todt* Construction organization began preparations for the deployment of the gun and its gear. The site selected was north of

Sevastopol and its defensive perimeter. First, a railroad spur was built running from the main rail line between Simferopol and Sevastopol west to the village of Bachtschissarai. About 1.2 miles (2 km) south of the village, a large, level field about 2,186 yards (2000 meters) long was cleared and four parallel double tracks, connected with switches, were laid to provide an assembly area for Dora. The actual firing position was just south of the assembly area and was created by cutting through a small hill and building a curved section of double track.

Upon arrival, the two diesel-electric engines maneuvered the twenty-five railcars carrying the components of the gun into the assembly area. These included the left and right sections of the chassis, the two sections of the barrel, the gun mantle, the breechblock, and other components. The engines provided electric power as required. The two large cranes were assembled and positioned on the outer tracks where they were used in the assembly process, in accordance with a complex and carefully prepared plan. After Dora was assembled the cranes were used in handling the ammunition.

The two barrel sections were joined in the mantle and on the chassis. Eventually the accessories were installed, including the platforms and ladders for the crew and the elevators for the projectiles, powder bags, and shell cases. The gun was almost two stories high when fully assembled and moved on forty axles and eighty wheels. The difficult assembly was actually performed in only three days and nights by about 250 men, including engineers, artillerymen, and railway troops, plus technicians from the Krupp factory who provided technical assistance during the entire operation.

Hoeheresartilleriekommandeur 306 (Harko 306), the Eleventh Army artillery command section, was notified that Dora was ready for action. As explained in Chapter V, the German plan for the conquest of Sevastopol called for five days of intensive artillery and air bombardment before the ground assault began. Now, everything was in readiness as German offensive power challenged the Soviet defensive might in the world's strongest fortress.[9]

At *X-Uhr* (the German designation for H-hour), early on the morning of June 2, 1942, the night sky lit up along most of the front, followed by a great roar, as hundreds of guns opened their barrage on the Soviet defenses. This was certainly the greatest concentration of artillery and rockets since the beginning of Barbarossa, and it included the heaviest guns in the Wehrmacht arsenal. Even some captured and obsolescent artillery pieces were moved to the Sevastopol front for the attack, which was a logistical marvel in itself because of the huge amount of ammunition of different calibers required, transported on

During the assembly of Dora near Sevastopol in May 1942, the barrel cradle is emplaced on the upper carriage by the use of the two special mounting cranes. *U.S. Army Ordnance Museum*

only one railroad line. While the artillery bombardment and air attacks continued around the clock, Dora remained silent.

Finally, before dawn on June 5, the complete gun was slowly eased forward out of the assembly area by the two engines, into the cut that had been made in a small hill, and onto the curved section of double track facing south toward Sevastopol. The cut in the hill also provided protection and concealment for the gun. The long barrel could be raised electrically for aiming, but lateral or horizontal movement for adjusting the aim was made by inching the gun back and forth on the curved track. The ammunition in cars was brought forward and everyone waited impatiently for the order to load and commence firing.

Oberstleutnant (Lieutenant Colonel) Boehm set up an observation post 1.2 miles (2 km) south of the village of Bachtschiessarai and personally observed the targets previously selected. About 450 men were assigned to the actual gun crew, most employed in arming and moving the huge shells, powder bags, and steel cases in their small railcars. Personnel not required for firing withdrew to the tent camp established in an orchard behind the assembly area for a meal and a well-earned rest. All in all, about 5,000 men were required to place Dora in action, including laborers, guards and Flak crews.

Dora was camouflaged by large nets along each side, and smoke generators were positioned around the area. Because of its size and all of the railcars involved, Dora was brazenly vulnerable to air attack. A number of light antiaircraft guns were placed to provide defense in case of an air raid. However, thanks in part to the work of the Luftwaffe fighter patrols over the front, the gun itself was never attacked. Some barbed wire had been hastily laid and men of the Army *Feldgendarmerie* (Military Police), with guard dogs, were also brought in to patrol the area of the gun, its ammunition, and support vehicles and equipment.

The alert to fire was received in the dark hours before dawn on June 5, and the crew loaded and prepared the gun for firing. Tensions ran high among the men who had spent long months training, transporting, and erecting the gun for use in this important battle. The first targets selected by Harko 306, in cooperation with the LIV Army Corps and the Eleventh Army commander, were a barracks block and fortified Soviet artillery batteries along the coast, out of range of other German artillery. The barracks was probably selected to check the accuracy of the gun.

The loading and firing procedure was as follows:[10]

1. The seven-ton projectile was removed from the ammunition car and brought forward on the ammunition cart.
2. The ammo cart was loaded on the electrical elevator platform (lift).
3. The lift brought the projectile up to the loading stage (platform).
4. The projectile was moved from the cart to the loading table and moved by the hydraulic rammer into the barrel chamber.
5. The propellant (powder) bags and shell case for sealing the breech were brought up on the second lift and inserted into the chamber.
6. The breech was closed and the loading table withdrawn.
7. The barrel was raised to the firing position and the entire gun was inched along the tracks for lateral aim.
8. The gun was fired on command.
9. The barrel was then lowered to the horizontal position, the empty shell case was removed, the chamber cleaned, and the gun was ready for the process to be repeated.

The barrel, of course, had to be elevated to the absolutely correct angle and adjusted for horizontal aim by moving the gun along the twin-tracks with the diesel-electric engines. Other requirements for firing included determining the temperature of each charge as well as the air temperature, winds aloft, and overall weather conditions.

At 5:35 A.M. on June 5 the order to fire was received by the gun captain. The bright flash of fire and thunderous roar was unlike any gunshot the observers could remember. Everyone in the area had been warned to

Preparing Dora for action at Sevastopol in early June 1942. This photo shows a projectile on the loading tray (left) before it was chambered by use of the rammer. Note the shell case at right. *U.S. Army Ordnance Museum*

plug their ears at the time of firing. The recoil of the gun made even its massive carriage tremble, but all components functioned properly. A flight of Luftwaffe Fieseler Fi 156 *Storch* observation planes was assigned to cooperate with Dora and report the results of the firing by radio

while watching the fall of the shells. The first round apparently scored a direct hit (*Volltreffer*), shaking the very earth and causing a pillar of smoke to climb high into the sky. When this was reported to the crew by the gun captain, a cheer went up, but there was no time to celebrate. Eight more rounds were ordered fired at the Soviet coastal batteries and Fort Maxim Gorki I, which required rapid loading and re-aiming of the gun with the help of the locomotives. The shells reached the targets and did some damage, although most fell 300 meters (over 325 yards) short or beyond.

That afternoon six rounds were fired at Fort

Dora on the curved, double-rail spur near Sevastopol in June 1942. The ammunition cars are behind the gun. *U.S. Army Ordnance Museum*

Stalin, again with mixed results; however, one round was a direct hit. A crater 28 meters (91 feet) across was reported. Other craters observed during the siege were about 49 feet (15 meters) deep and some, with a narrow opening, were up to 104.9 feet (32 meters) deep, exploding far underground. Colonel General Erich von Manstein, Marshal Ion Antonescu, Alfried Krupp, and Dr. Erich Mueller, witnessed the firing of Dora from a safe distance.

Firing commenced the next morning with seven rounds fired at Fort Molotov, again with mixed results. A new and perhaps the most important target came under fire that afternoon. A major Soviet underground ammunition storage facility had been identified through aerial reconnaissance and interrogation of prisoners and deserters. Called the *Weisse Klippe* or *Munitionsberg* (White Cliff or Ammunition Mountain) by the Germans, it was thought by the Russians to be immune to attack because it consisted of a large cavern situated under a hill facing Severnaya Bay. Heavy steel doors protected the entrance in the hillside and it was, in fact, invulnerable to air attack and bombardment by conventional artillery. This was a job for Dora!

Nine rounds of concrete-penetrating shells were fired with great success, with six direct hits on the target. Firing continued on June 7, with more hits scored by the huge shells. Rounds 33, 34, and 35 were also direct hits, and at least one punched through about 98 feet (30 meters) of earth and rock and exploded inside the ammunition storage chamber.[11] The result was a tremendous blast, with secondary explosions adding to the destruction of the large stocks of artillery ammunition. A huge column of smoke soared high into the sky, announcing the success of this attack. The loss of ammunition at this critical time in the siege certainly weakened the Red Army's ability to defend Sevastopol. Strangely, when Hitler learned of this, he sent an angry message to the Eleventh Army commander directing that Dora was to be used only against concrete fortresses. This is just another minor example of the supreme war lord trying to micromanage the war, often with insufficient information at his disposal.

Fort Sibirien was bombarded by Dora with five rounds on June 11, with three direct hits that caused massive damage, rendering it vulnerable to ground attack by infantry and combat engineers. Dora roared again on June 17, with the shelling of Fort Maxim Gorki II, with its heavy gun turrets and coastal battery. The five rounds softened up this modern fort for the coming ground attack.

Dora had performed well in the hands of its well-trained and dedicated crew, with only minor mechanical problems. The forty-eight rounds fired during the siege demolished several important targets. The detonation of the giant shells on and near the Soviet fortifications also caused severe casualties, and the resulting panic had a damaging effect on the morale of the defenders, even more terrible than that caused by the shells from the 60cm Karl howitzers or the bombs from Stuka dive-bombers.

Five high-explosive shells were reportedly also fired on June 25, with one against the city of Sevastopol itself. This was a test of this type of ammunition, and four shells landed in the bay. The last round caused a huge column of smoke to rise over the city. These were in addition to the forty-eight concrete-penetrating shells fired during the siege.[12]

With the fall of Sevastopol, Dora was disassembled, loaded on its railcars, and on orders from Hitler moved to Army Group North for the bombardment of the city of Leningrad. It was assembled on a hastily laid railspur in a woods but not fired because a Soviet offensive required it to be disassembled and returned to Germany. Back at Ruegenwalde, Dora was serviced and a new barrel installed while the original sections were returned to Krupp for relining.[13]

Dora was parked under camouflage at the Ruegenwalde firing range in early 1943, and eventually it was joined by Schwerer Gustav 2, the other 80cm railway gun to be completed. They were occasionally fired for testing and experiments with new concrete-penetrating projectiles with longer range, and a few demonstration rounds were fired to impress important foreign guests. Altogether, a total of about 300 rounds were expended by Dora, including the forty-eight Panzergranate fired during the siege of Sevastopol.

There was great excitement at Ruegenwalde on March 19, 1943. An official visit to inspect Dora and its crew was made by Hitler and a number of high-ranking German and foreign dignitaries. The group included Field Marshal Wilhelm Keitel, Chief of OKW, the German High Command; Professor Albert Speer, Chief of Armament and War Production; Alfried Krupp; Dr. Erich Mueller of Krupp; Colonel General Heinz Guderian, then Inspector of Panzer Forces; General Emil Leeb, Chief of the Army Ordnance Office; and many other "bigwigs." A Spanish military commission was also invited to attend the impressive demonstration because Hitler was still trying to get Spain to join or participate more actively in the war on the Axis side. Three rounds were fired, observed by the distinguished visitors from the safety of a bunker.

Dora, the biggest gun of all time, ready for a firing demonstration for Hitler and other German and foreign dignitaries at the Ruegenwalde test firing range on March 19, 1943. *U.S. Army Ordnance Museum*

Although Dora was ready for action, the changing tides of war made its further use impractical. OKW planners considered using Dora and Schwerer Gustav 2, the other 80cm gun to be completed, for shelling London and important targets in southeast England. (The third gun, Langer Gustav, 52cm, was wrecked during construction at the Krupp factory by an Allied air raid). For the bombardment of England, it was proposed to use rocket-assisted shells to provide the longer range needed to reach distant targets. For use against England, a large curved concrete-covered tunnel with a double railway track would have been dug in a hill near Cape Gris Nez on the English Channel. This would have been a mammoth construction project and would have been worthwhile only if the new rocket-shells were also ready for use. By 1943, it was realized that the construction project would be difficult because the bulk of the Luftwaffe was tied down in Russia and in the air defense of the Reich, and the RAF and USAAF airpower was growing stronger along the Channel. The tunnel project was abandoned before it was built. Most of Dora's crew members were eventually reassigned to other heavy artillery batteries and only a small cadre was retained at Ruegenwalde to fire and maintain the two giant "White Elephants."

By 1945, the Allies were advancing on Germany from both the east and the west, and British and American airpower ruled the skies over the Reich. The two complete 80cm K (E) guns, Dora and Schwerer Gustav 2, were still on camouflaged railcars, one near Chemnitz in

Dora's demise. The 80cm forward-barrel section (*Seelenrohr*), with the wreckage of an ammunition railcar in the foreground. This gun was destroyed by the Germans in April 1945 and parts from fourteen railcars were along some fifty miles of railway track near Grafenwoehr, Auerbach, and Weiden in Bavaria, northeast of Nuremberg. *U.S. Army Ordnance Museum*

eastern Germany where it was overrun by troops of the Red Army when the U.S. Army withdrew, and the other near Grafenwoehr in southern Germany. The special trains, parked and camouflaged on sidings, may have been damaged by air attacks, but the breeches, other key parts, and the ammunition cars were blown apart and rendered unusable by the Germans before they were abandoned. U.S. Army ordnance personnel inspected the remains of both guns and photographed the wreckage.[14] Only examples of the ammunition survive today. A projectile and shell case are in the collection of the Imperial War Museum in England, and another may be in a museum in Russia. The wreckage near Grafenwoehr, Bavaria, received special attention from U.S. technical experts. The remains were not scrapped until 1950. A projectile and its accompanying shell case were transported to Aberdeen Proving Ground, Maryland, after the war, and they are on exhibit today outside the U. S. Army Ordnance Museum. These last Dora relics are located a few hundred yards from a much smaller, but still impressive railway gun, the *28cm K 5 (E) "Leopold,"* known to American veterans of the Italian campaign as "Anzio Annie." Leopold was the standard German Army railway gun, and twenty-five were completed during World War II.

After the war, there was a shortage of locomotives for the German railways. Three of the big diesel-electric locomotives built for the Dora-type guns survived. One was used for spare parts and two were rebuilt and used by the West German *Bundesbahn* until 1972.

In retrospect, Dora was a remarkable achievement in ordnance development. However, it is obvious that the great expense involved and

The muzzle of the barrel from the 80cm railway gun found scattered along the rail tracks near Grafenwoehr, Bavaria, by Col. F.B. Porter and the men of the U.S. Army 417th Field Artillery, in April 1945. *U.S. Army Ordnance Museum*

the use of so many valuable resources, including raw materials, manpower, and design and production facilities, did not justify the building of the guns. Still, Dora and Schwerer Gustav 2 were available from 1942 had the fortunes of war created appropriate targets for the world's biggest guns and the armies of the Third Reich.

Only the 280mm M65 "Atomic Cannon," developed for the U.S. Army in the 1950s, could claim to be a more powerful and destructive gun than Dora. Dora was grandiose in size and power but finally came to naught, like Hitler's maniacal dreams of conquest.

NOTES

Introduction

1. Field Marshal Erich von Manstein, *Lost Victories* (Chicago: Henry Regnery, 1958), 175.
2. Alan Clark, *Barbarossa: The Russian-German Conflict, 1941–1945* (New York: Wm. Morrow, 1965), 43.
3. H. R. Trevor-Roper, *Blitzkrieg to Defeat: Hitler's War Directives, 1939–1945* (New York: Holt, Rinehart and Winston, 1964), 49.
4. U.S. Department of the Army, *The German Campaign in Russia—Planning and Operations, 1940–1942*, Dept. of the Army Pam. No. 261a (Washington, D.C., 1955), 38–41.
5. Ibid. See also John Toland, *Adolf Hitler* (New York: Doubleday & Co., 1976), 648–649.
6. Von Manstein, *Lost Victories*, 176–177.
7. Ibid., 177.
8. U.S. Dept. of the Army Pam. No. 261a, 42.
9. Toland, *Hitler*, 659. See also General Heinz Guderian, *Panzer Leader* (New York: E.P. Hutton, 1952), 142–143.
10. Adolf Hitler, *Hitler's Secret Conversations, 1941–1944* (New York: Farrar, Straus and Young, 1953), 26.

CHAPTER I. Storm Across the Steppe

1. U.S. Army, Dept. of Military Arts and Engineering, *The War in Eastern Europe, June 1941 to May 1945* (West Point, New York: 1949), 15.
2. Hanson W. Baldwin, *The Crucial Years, 1939–1941* (New York: Harper and Row, 1976), 336.
3. Susan B. Glasser, "Pope Highlights Suffering in Ukraine." *Washington Post*, June 26, 2001, A14.
4. Ibid.
5. Heinrich *Graf* von Einsiedel, *The Onslaught: The German Drive to Stalingrad* (New York: Norton, 1984), 56.
6. Louis L. Snyder, *Encyclopedia of the Third Reich* (New York: McGraw-Hill, 1976), 191–192. See also Thomas Parrish and S. L. A. Marshal, *The Simon and Schuster Encyclopedia of World War II* (New York: Simon and Schuster, 1978), 329–330.
7. Baldwin, *Crucial Years*, 330.
8. U.S. War Department, Military Intelligence Division, *Order of Battle and Handbook of Rumanian Armed Forces* (Washington, D.C.: GPO, January 1944), 2.
9. Norman Polmar and Thomas B. Allen, *World War II: An Encyclopedia of the War Years, 1941–1945*, (New York: Random House, 1991), 703.
10. Kurt Passow, *Taschenbuch der Heere* (Muenchen-Berlin: J. F. Lehmanns, 1939), 310.
11. Trevor J. Constable and Col. Raymond F. Toliver, *Horrido!: Fighter Aces of the Luftwaffe* (New York: Macmillan, 1968), 118. See also Don McCombs and Fred L. Worth, *World War II Strange and Fascinating Facts* (New York: Greenwich House, 1983), 92.
12. Von Manstein, *Lost Victories*, 206.

13. Ibid., 207. By the Prussian tradition, von Manstein meant respect, confidence in the fairness and efficiency of officers, NCOs, and men, and obedience to orders.

14. U.S. Army, *The War in Eastern Europe*, 20–21.

15. U.S. Dept. of the Army Pam. No. 261a, 38.

16. Paul Carell, *Hitler Moves East, 1941–1943* (Boston: Little, Brown, 1963), 64. Note that after the war, both Field Marshal von Manstein and Colonel General Herman Hoth stated that the Soviet forces were organized in depth for defensive operations, but the Red Army could have regrouped for offensive operations within a very short time.

17. C. G. Sweeting, *Hitler's Personal Pilot: The Life and Times of Hans Baur* (Washington, D.C.: Brassey's, 2000), 170.

18. U.S. Army, *The War in Eastern Europe*, 38.

19. Ibid., 39.

20. Abteilung lc, 11. Armee, *Bessarabien, Ukraine-Krim: Der Siegeszug Deutscher und Rumaenischer Truppen* (Berlin: Verlag Erich Zander, 1943), 15.

CHAPTER II. Luftwaffe: The "Air Weapon" in Action

1. Constable and Toliver, *Horrido!*, 125.

2. Hanfried Schliephake, *The Birth of the Luftwaffe* (Chicago: Henry Regnery, 1971). See also Herbert Molloy Mason, Jr., *The Rise of the Luftwaffe, 1918–1940* (New York: Dial Press, 1973), and Major Hermann Adler, *Ein Buch von der neuen Luftwaffe* (Stuttgart: Franckh'sche Verlagshandlung, 1938).

3. Charles Messenger, *The Blitzkrieg Story* (New York: Charles Scribner's Sons, 1976).

4. William Green, *Warplanes of the Third Reich* (Garden City, New York: Doubleday, 1970). See also U.S. Army Air Forces, Office of the Asst. Chief of Air Staff, Intelligence, *German Aircraft and Armament* (Washington, D.C.: Brassey's, 2000, reprint of October 1944 Intelligence Summary No. 44–32)

5. Len Deighton, *Blitzkrieg* (New York: Alfred A. Knopf, 1980). See also Alistair Horne, *To Lose a Battle, France 1940* (Boston: Little, Brown, 1969), and Heinrich Hoffmann, *Mit Hitler im Westen* (Berlin: Zeitgeschichte Verlag, 1940).

6. Roger Parkinson, *Summer 1940, The Battle of Britain* (New York: McKay, 1977), and Winston S. Churchill, *Their Finest Hour* (Boston: Houghton Mifflin, 1949). See also Gavin Lyall, ed., *The War in the Air, The Royal Air Force in World War II* (New York: Wm. Morrow & Co., 1969).

7. Adolf Galland, *The First and the Last: The Rise and Fall of the German Fighter Forces, 1938–1945* (New York: Henry Holt, 1954), 43.

8. U.S. Dept. of the Army, *The German Campaign in the Balkans, Spring 1941*, Dept. of the Army Pam. No. 20–260 (Washington, D.C.: GPO, 1953). See also Alan Clark, *The Fall of Crete* (New York: Wm. Morrow, 1962), and Gen. der Flieger Kurt Student, *Kreta, Sieg der Kuehnsten* (Graz: Steirische Verlagsanstalt, 1942).

9. Friedrich Heiss, *Der Sieg in Suedosten* (Berlin: Volk und Reich Verlag, 1943), 168.

10. Dr. Von Hardesty, *Red Phoenix: The Rise of Soviet Air Power, 1941–1945* (Washington, D.C.: Smithsonian Institution Press, 1982), 250.

11. *German Aircraft and Armament*, 107.

12. Generalfeldmarschall a.D. Albert Kesselring, *Kesselring: A Soldier's Record* (New York: Wm. Morrow, 1954), 93.

13. Williamson Murray, *Strategy for Defeat: The Luftwaffe 1933–1945* (Maxwell AFB, Ala.: Air University Press, 1983), 80.

14. Constable and Toliver, *Horrido!*, 13.

15. Ibid., 14.

16. Ibid., 123.

17. Ibid., 213.

18. Cajus Bekker, *The Luftwaffe War Diaries* (Garden City, New York: Doubleday, 1968), 224. See also Air Ministry, *Notes on the German Air Force*, Air Pub. 1928 (London, April 1943), 24–25.

19. Bekker, *War Diaries*, 224.

20. Margaret Bourke-White, *Shooting the Russian War* (New York: Simon Schuster, 1942), 189.

21. Dr. Ing. Wolf Ruemmler, *Ein Fliegerkorps im Einsatz Ost* (Muenchen: F. Bruckmann Verlag, 1943), 65.

22. Air Ministry, *Notes*, 25.

23. Hans Ulrich Rudel, *Stuka Pilot* (Dublin: Euphorion Books, 1953), 32–34.

24. Ibid., 223. See also Generalleutnant a.D. Hermann Plocher, *The German Air Force Versus Russia, 1941.* (Maxwell AFB, AL.: USAF Historical Division, 1965), 151–152.

25. Plocher, *German Air Force*, 49.

26. Constable and Toliver, *Horrido!*, 118. See also Hermann Plocher, *German Air Force*, 77–78.

27. Plocher, *German Air Force*,53.

28. Constable and Toliver, *Horrido!*, 218.

29. Plocher, *German Air Force*, 73.

CHAPTER III. Breakthrough at Perekop Isthmus

1. Von Manstein, *Lost Victories*, 203.

2. The Kuebelwagen, le Pkw (Kfz 1), literally "Bucket Car," was developed for the Wehrmacht from the Volkswagen passenger car. It was the closest German equivalent of the American military Jeep. See John Milsom, *German Military Transport of World War Two* (New York: Hippocrene Books, 1975), 24–25, 71–74.

3. The Tatars of the Crimea were an ethnic group descended from the original Mongol invaders but usually referred to as "Turkic Peoples." See Basil Dmytryshyn, *A History of Russia* (Englewood Cliffs, N.J.: Prentice Hall, 1977) 116–123.

4. Von Manstein, *Lost Victories*, 214.

5. Ibid., 216. See also Plocher, *German Air Force*, 211–212.

6. Plocher, *German Air Force*, 212.

7. Ibid., 212.

8. Ibid., 212.

9. US. Department of the Army, Historical Study, *Small Unit Actions During the German Campaign in Russia*, Dept. of the Army Pam. No. 20–269 (Washington, D.C.: GPO, 1953), 61–62.

10. Von Manstein, *Lost Victories*, 220.

CHAPTER IV. Crimean Combat

1. *Bessarabien, Ukraine-Krim*, 18, and U.S. Army Pam. 20–261a, 81.

2. Plocher, *German Air Force*, 213.

3. Von Manstein, *Lost Victories*, 221.

4. *Bessarabien, Ukraine-Krim*, 19.

5. Ibid., 19.

6. M. M. Minasyan, (ed.), *The Great Patriotic War of the Soviet Union, 1941–1945* (Moscow: Progress Publishers, 1970), 106.

7. *Bessarabien, Ukraine-Krim*, 20.

8. Ibid., 21.

9. U.S. War Department, Military Intelligence Division, *Handbook on German Military Forces*, TM-E 30–451 (Washington, D.C.: 1 September 1943), 214–215. See also the edition from 15 March 1945.

10. U.S. War Department, Military Intelligence Division, *Order of Battle of the German Army* (Washington, D.C., 1 March 1945), 17.

11. Von Manstein, *Lost Victories*, 233.

12. Ibid., 234.

13. Ibid., 238. See also *Bessarabien, Ukraine-Krim*, 22–23, which gives a figure of 294 tanks, 1,500 machine guns, 283 Pak and 131 Flak.

14. *Bessarabien, Ukraine-Krim*, 23.

CHAPTER V. The Siege of Sevastopol

1. C. G. Sweeting, *Hitler's Squadron* (Washington, D.C.: Brassey's Inc., 2001), 70–71.

2. Sweeting, *Hitler's Personal Pilot*, 158–165.

3. Von Manstein, *Lost Victories*, 238.

4. Ibid., 243.

5. Minasyan, *Patriotic War*, 119.

6. *Order of Battle of the German Army, 1 March 1945*, 620, 632, 645.

7. Earl F. Ziemke and Magna B. Bauer, *Moscow to Stalingrad: Decision in the East* (New York: Military Heritage Press, 1988), 312. See also Terry Gander and Peter Chamberlain, *Weapons of the Third Reich* (Garden City, New York: Doubleday & Co., 1979), 363.

8. Werner Baumbach, *The Life and Death of the Luftwaffe* (New York: Ballantine Books, 1960), 140.

9. Letter to Dr. John Schmitt, Ammunition Consultant, from Herbert Jaeger, Gesellschaft fuer Artilleriekunde e.V. an der Artillerieschule, Idar Oberstein, Germany, dated 3 July 2001.

10. Von Manstein, *Lost Victories*, 246–247.

11. Carell, *Hitler Moves East*, 467.

12. Ibid., 467.

13. U.S. War Department, *German Military Dictionary*, Technical Manual TM 30–506 (Washington, D.C.: 20 May 1944), 123.

14. Information from the Archives of U.S. Army Ordnance Museum, Aberdeen Proving Ground, Md., October 17, 2001. See also Gerhard Taube, *Die Schwersten Steilfeuer-Geschuetze*, 1914-1945 (Stuttgart: Motorbuch Verlag, 1981), 32–91, and F. M. von Senger und Etterlin, et al., Die *deutschen Geschuetze, 1939–1945* (Muenchen: J. F. Lehmanns Verlag, 1960), 138 and 147.

15. F. M. von Senger und Etterlin, *Geschuetz*, 137.

16. Information from the Archives of U.S. Army Ordnance Museum. See also F.M. von Senger und Etterlin, 161–164, and Ian V. Hogg, *German Artillery of World War Two* (New York: Hippocrene Books, 1975), 138–140.

17. Baumbach, *Life and Death*, 140–141.

18. Plocher, *German Air Force*, 189.

19. Ibid., 191.

20. Ibid., 193.

21. U.S. Department of the Army, *Small Unit Actions During the German Campaign in Russia*, Dept. of the Army Pam. No. 20–269 (Washington, D.C.: GPO, 1953), 144–145.

22. Von Manstein, *Lost Victories*, 250.

23. Ibid., 255.

24. Ibid., 255.

25. Ziemke and Bauer, *Moscow to Stalingrad*, 321.

26. Ibid., 321.

27. Plocher, *German Air Force*, 202.

28. Ibid., 199.

29. Von Manstein, *Lost Victories*, 258.

30. Ibid., 259.

31. David Littlejohn and Col. C. M. Dodkins, *Orders, Decorations, Medals and Badges of the Third Reich* (Mountain View, Ca.: R. James Bender, 1968), 142–145. See also Dr. Heinrich Doehle, *Die Auszeichnungen des Grossdeutschen Reichs* (Berlin: Berliner Buch und Zeitschriften Verlag, 1943), 81–84.

32. *Bessarabien, Ukraine-Krim*, 25–26, 226.

33. Von Manstein, *Lost Victories*, 261–262.

Epilogue

1. Major General F. W. von Mellenthin, *Panzer Battles* (London: Cassell & Co., 1955), 173.
2. Major General F. W. von Mellenthin, *German Generals of World War II as I Saw Them* (Norman, Ok.: University of Oklahoma Press, 1977), 19. For information on von Manstein's career, see *Lost Victories*. The most comprehensive short biography of his life is included in the book by Correlli Barnett, *Hitler's Generals* (New York: Grove Weidenfeld, 1989).
3. Samuel W. Mitcham, Jr., *Hitler's Field Marshals and Their Battles* (Chelsea, Mi: Scarborough House, 1988), 243.
4. Von Manstein, *Lost Victories*, 175.
5. Von Mellenthin, *German Generals*, 32.
6. B. H. Liddell Hart, *The Other Side of the Hill* (London: Cassell & Co., 1948), 72–73.
7. Von Mellenthin, *German Generals*, 36.
8. Richard Brett-Smith, *Hitler's Generals* (San Rafael, Ca.: Presidio Press, 1977), 229.
9. Ibid., 229.
10. Mitcham, *Hitler's Field Marshals* 253.
11. Hart, *Other Side*, 73.

APPENDIX B. Ranks, Uniforms, Insignia, Medals

Illustrations reproduced from Oberstleutnant W. Reibert, *Der Dienstunterricht im Heere* (Berlin: E. S. Mittler & Sohn, 1943).

APPENDIX C. Weapons of Barbarossa

1. C. G. Sweeting, *German Proof Marks and Arms Codes, 1860–1960* (Colorado Springs, Col., 1960).
2. Oberkommando des Heeres, Heereswaffenamt Wa Z 2, *Liste der Fertigungskennzeichen fuer Waffen, Munition und Geraet* (Berlin; OKH, Oktober 1941) (Geheim-Secret)
3. Ludwig E. Olson, *Mauser Bolt Rifles* (Montezuma, Iowa: F. Brownell, 2nd ed., 1976). See also H.Dv. 257, *Schusswaffen 98* (Berlin: E. S. Mittler & Sohn, 1942), and D 136, *Karabiner 98k-Zf 41* (Berlin: 1942).
4. Edward C. Ezell, *Small Arms of the World* (Harrisburg, Pa.: Stackpole Books, 12th ed. of W. H. B. Smith's classic work, 1983), 506–517. See also George Markham, *Guns of the Reich* (London: Arms and Armour Press, 1989), 105–116, and Daniel D. Musgrave & Thomas B. Nelson, *The World's Assault Rifles* (Alexandria, Va.: T.B.N. Enterprises, 1967), and OKH, Heereswaffenamt, *K 43 mit Gewehr Zielfernrohr 4-fach* (Berlin: 1944).
5. Ezell, *Small Arms*, 488–500, Markham, *Guns*, 52–70, John Walter, *Luger* (New York: Sterling Pub., 1991), Fred A. Datig, *The Luger Pistol, 1893–1945* (Hollywood, Ca., Fadco Pub. Co., 4th Revised ed., 1958), and W. H. B, Smith, *Walther Pistols and Rifles* (Harrisburg, Pa., Stackpole Co., 2nd ed., 1962), 89–121.
6. Ezell, *Small Arms*, 524–535, Markham, *Guns*, 122–144, Daniel D. Musgrave, *German Machineguns* (Alexandria, Va.: Ironside International Pub., Rev. ed., 1992), Dolf F. Goldsmith, *The Devil's Paintbrush, Sir Hiram Maxim's Gun* (Toronto: Collector Grade Publications Inc., 1989).
7. Ezell, *Small Arms*, 519–523, Markham, *Guns*, 80–92, Thomas B. Nelson and Hans B. Lockhoven, *The World's Submachine Guns* (Cologne, Germany; International Small Arms Pub., Vol. I, 1964), 224–280.
8. Terry Gander and Peter Chamberlain, *Weapons of the Third Reich* (Garden City, N.J.: Doubleday & Co., 1979), 100–106. See also A. J. R. Cormack, *German Small Arms of World War II* (New York: Exeter Books, 1979), 112–117, and U.S. War Department, TM-E 30–451, *Handbook on German Military Forces* (Washington, D.C.: G.P.O., 15 March 1945), VII-9–VII-l2.

9. Gander and Chamberlain, *Weapons of Third Reich*, 348–352, TM-E 30–451, VII-95–VII-103, and U.S. Dept. of the Army and Air Force, TM 9–1985–2, *German Explosive Ordnance* (Washington, D.C.: G.P.O., 16 March 1953), 319–346.

10. Gander and Chamberlain, *Weapons of Third Reich*, 345–347, TM-E 30–451, VIII-117–VIII-121.

11. Gander and Chamberlain, *Weapons of Third Reich*, 298–309, TM-E 30–451, VII-13–VII-18.

12. TM-E-30–451, VII-19–VII-56, and Ian V. Hogg, *German Artillery of World War Two* (London: Arms and Armour Press, 1975), 7–12.

13. Albert Mueller, *Germany's War Machine* (London: J. M. Dent & Sons, 1936), 35–45. See also John Milsom, *German Military Transport of World War Two* (London: Arms and Armour Press, 1975).

14. Ian V. Hogg, *The Illustrated Encyclopedia of Ammunition* (Secaucus, N.J.: Chartwell Books, 1985), 234–235. Good reference for all types of ammunition.

15. Hogg, *German Artillery of World War II*, 18–28, see also Gander and Chamberlain, *Weapons of Third Reich*, 282–288.

16. Hogg, *German Artillery of World War II*, 37–80, see also Gander and Chamberlain, *Weapons of Third Reich*, 170–193, and Basil T. Fedoroff, Picatinny Arsenal Technical Report No. 2510, *Dictionary of Explosives, Ammunition and Weapons* (Dover, N.J.: Picatinny Arsenal, 1958)

17. Hogg, *German Artillery of World War II*, 61–112. See also Gander and Chamberlain, *Weapons of Third Reich*, 194–230, TM-E 30–451, VII-25–VII-30; J. Engelmann, *Das Buch der Artillerie, 1939–1945* (Friedberg, Germany: Podzun-Pallas-Verlag, 1983), and U.S. Army, Office of Chief of Ordnance, *Catalogue of Enemy Ordnance Materiel* (Washington, D.C.: 1 May 1945), 320–323.

18. Hogg, *German Artillery of World War II*, 82–112, and Gander and Chamberlain, *Weapons of Third Reich*, 194–230. See also Ian V. Hogg, *The Illustrated Encyclopedia of Artillery* (Secaucus, N.J.: Chartwell Books, 1987), 148–157, and SHAEF, G-4, *Recognition Handbook of German Technical Equipment* (HQ SHAEF, June 1945).

19. F. M. von Senger und Etterlin, *Die deutschen Geschuetze, 1939–1945* (Muenchen; J. F. Lehmanns Verlag, 1960), 151–170. See also Eugen Beinhauer, *Artillerie in Osten* (Berlin: Wilhelm Limpert Verlag, 1944), 170–199, and Gander and Chamberlain, *Weapons of Third Reich*, 231–251.

20. Gander and Chamberlain, *Weapons of Third Reich*, 289–297, and von Senger und Etterlin, *Geschuetz*, 29–37.

21. Fritz Pachtner, *Waffen* (Leipzig: Wilhelm Goldmann Verlag, 1942), 188.

22. Gander and Chamberlain, *Weapons of Third Reich*, 127–169, and von Senger und Etterlin, *Geschuetz*, 173–213.

23. U.S. War Department, TM E9–369A, *German 88-MM Antiaircraft Gun Materiel* (Washington, D.C.: G.P.O., 29 June 1943)

24. Gander and Chamberlain, *Weapons of Third Reich*, 107–126, and von Senger und Etterlin, Geschuetz, 57–74.

25. Gen. Heinz Guderian, *Panzer Leader* (New York: E. P. Dutton, 1952), and Maj. Gen. F. W. von Mellenthin, *Panzer Battles: A Study of the Employment of Armor in the Second World War* (Norman, OK., Univ. of Oklahoma Press, 1956).

26. Duncan Crow, ed., *Armored Fighting Vehicles of Germany* (New York: Aero Pub. Co., 1978). See also U.S. War Dept., FM 30–40, *Recognition Pictorial Manual on Armored Vehicles* (Washington, D.C.: G.P.O., 1943), 71–94, and TM-E 30–451, editions of 1 September 1943 and 15 March 1945.

27. B. H. Liddell Hart, *The Red Army* (New York: Harcourt, Brace & Co., 1956), 134–139.

28. John Milsom, *Russian Tanks, 1900–1970* (New York: Galahad Books, 1970), 119.

29. E. J. Hoffschmidt, *German Aircraft Guns and Cannons* (Old Greenwich, CT,: WE Inc., 1969). See also Louis Bruchiss, *Aircraft Armament* (New York: Aeroephere, Inc., 1945).

30. TM 9-1985-2, 1–260, and U.S. War Dept., *Enemy Bombs and Fuses* (Washington, D.C.: G.P.O., November 12, 1942). See also Bruchiss, 18–25.

31. U.S. Department of the Army Pamphlet No. 30–2, *The Soviet Army*, (Washington, D.C.: GPO, July 1949), iii.

32. Ibid., 8.

33. Moisin is also often spelled Mosin in some references.

34. Ezell, *Small Arms of the World: 11ᵗʰ* edition, 36.

35. Ibid., 476.

36. A. W. F. Taylerson, *Revolving Arms*, (New York: Walker and Co., 1967), 91–92.

37. Thomas B. Nelson and Hans B. Lockhoven, *The World's Submachine Guns*, (Cologne, Germany: International Small Arms Publishers, 1963), 591–593.

38. Ibid., 600.

39. DA Pam. No. 30–2, 11.

40. Ibid., 22.

41. J. N. Westwood, *The Illustrated History of the Russo-Japanese War*, (Chicago: Henry Regnery, 1973).

42. Hart, *The Red Army*, 142.

43. DA Pam. No. 30–2, 14.

44. U.S. Army Europe, *Identification Handbook, Soviet and Satellite Ordnance Equipment* (APO 403, U.S. Army, 1960), 114.

45. Hart, *The Red Army*, 19.

46. U.S. Department of the Army Field Manual 30–40, *Handbook on Soviet Ground Forces*, (Washington, D.C.: G.P.O., June 1975) 6–37.

47. DA Pam. No. 30–2, 43.

48. Ibid., 34.

49. Ibid., 34. See also U.S. Department of the Army Technical Manual 5–223, *Foreign Mine Warfare Equipment* (Washington, D.C.: G.P.O., Nov. 8, 1957), 28–30.

50. George Forty, *United States Tanks of World War II in Action*, (Poole, U.K.: Blanford Press, 1983), 13.

51. Milsom, *Russian Tanks*, 104–111.

52. Ibid., 119.

53. Von Hardesty, *Red Phoenix: The Rise of Soviet Air Power, 1941–1945*, (Washington, D.C.: Smithsonian Institution Press, 1982), 36.

54. Bill Gunston, *Aircraft of the Soviet Union*, (London: Osprey Publishing Co., 1983), 21.

55. Ibid., 21.

56. U.S. Department of the Air Force Technical Order 11A-1-35, *USSR Bombs and Fuzes* (Washington, D.C.: G.P.O., October 12, 1954), 1.

57. Ibid., 26–27.

58. DA Pam. No. 30–2, 21.

APPENDIX D. The "Karl" *Geraet* Super Howitzer

1. Information and photographs pertaining to the Karl guns were obtained from several sources, including the archives of the U.S. Army Ordnance Museum, Aberdeen Proving Ground, Maryland. Much research on German weapons has been accomplished by Karl Pawlas of Germany, publisher of *Waffen Review* magazine. Many books on weapons and artillery refer to this gun, but an excellent source, in English, on the Karl guns is the monograph by Thomas L. Jentz, *Bertha's Big Brother, Karl-Geraet (60cm and 54cm)*, published by Panzer Tracts, Boyds, Md., in 2001. Extensive details on the weapon are contained in F. M. von Senger und Etterlin, *Die deutschen Geschuetze, 1939–1945*, 138–142 and 147–158. See also J. Engelmann, *Das Buch der Artillerie, 1939–1945* (Friedberg: Podzun-Pallas-Verlag, 1983), and Kenneth Allen, *Big Guns* (Hove: E. Sussex, 1976), 62–69.

2. U.S. War Department, TM 30–506, 123.

3. Charles Messinger, *The Blitzkrieg Story* (New York: Charles Scribner's Sons, 1976).

4. Ian V. Hogg, *The Illustrated Encyclopedia of Artillery* (Secaucus, N.J: Chartwell Books, 1988), 182–183. See also von Senger und Etterlin, 147–148.

5. ETO Ordnance Technical Intelligence Report No. 95, *German Heavy Self-Propelled Mortar* (ETOUSA, APO 887, 24 December 1944), 2.

6. *Waffen Review*, Nr. 3, Dezember 1971, 350–354.

7. ETO Ordnance Technical Intelligence Report No. 95, 2.

8. Hogg, *Encyclopedia of Artillery*, 182.

9. Svein Wiiger Olsen, "Battery Maxim Gorki I," *After the Battle* magazine, issue 112, n.d., p. 50. See also Francois de Lanney, "Les Forces Germano-Roumaine s a la Conquete de la Crimee," *Tactiques* (Paris: n.d.) pp. 29–30. Another interesting reference is Eugen Beinhauer, *Artillerie in Osten* (Berlin: Wilhelm Limpert Verlag, 2. Auflage, 1944).

10. Oberkommarido der Wehrmacht (OKW), *Die Wehrmacht* (Berlin: Verlag "Die Wehrmacht," 1942), 240–241. See also Gerhard Taube, *Die Schwersten Steilfeuer—Geschuetze, 1914–1945* (Stuttgart: Motorbuch Verlag, 1981), 85.

11. Compiled mainly from documents in the archives of the U.S. Army Ordnance Museum, Aberdeen Proving Ground, Maryland.

Appendix E. Sunday Punch: "Dora," The World's Biggest Cannon

1. William Manchester, *The Arms of Krupp, 1587–1968* (Boston: Little, Brown, 1964), 416–418. See also Peter Batty, *The House of Krupp* (New York: Stein and Day, 1966), 179–182.

2. The archives in the U.S. Army Ordnance Museum at Aberdeen Proving Ground, Maryland, is a good source of information and photographs of Dora, just as it is for the Karl howitzer and numerous other items of ordnance. Most of the books already cited that deal with the Karl gun also have information and photos of Dora. The most comprehensive published work on Dora is the book by Gerhard Taube, *Eisenbahngeschuetz Dora: Das groesste Geschuetz aller Zeiten* (Stuttgart: Motorbuch Verlag, 1981). Information and photos of the Karl and Dora guns, and the siege of Sevastopol, will also be found in certain issues of *Die Wehrmacht*, the German armed forces magazine, especially the issues from July 15 and September 9, 1942.

3. Ian V. Hogg, *German Artillery of World War Two*, 139–140. See also F. M. von Senger und Etterlin, 161–164, 169–170.

4. Henry W. Miller, *The Paris Gun* (New York: Jonathan Cape & Harrison Smith, 1930).

5. Hogg, *German Artillery of World War Two*, 138.

6. Taube, *Steilfeuer-Geschuetze*, 30.

7. William Manchester states on pages 416 and 417 in his book that Hitler, Albert Spear, and Alfried Krupp observed the firing of Dora at Ruegenwalde in the spring of 1941, and this is repeated by Peter Batty in his book on page 181. However, this has not been confirmed from other authoritative sources such as the book by Gerhard Taube.

8. Taube, *Steilfeuer-Geschuetze*, 42.

9. Von Manstein, *Lost Victories*, 24.

10. Taube, *Steilfeuer-Geschuetze*, 74.

11. Von Manstein, *Lost Victories*, 245. See also Taube, *Steilfeuer-Geschuetze*, 82–84.

12. Gerhard Taube, *Steilfeuer-Geschuetze*, 93–94.

13. One source indicates that Dora may have returned briefly to Ruegenwalde for overhaul before moving to Army Group North. (Secret letter cited by Gerhard Taube dated July 2, 1942, from OKH ordering the movement of the *Dora-Geraet* to the *Heimatkriegsgebiet* [Germany] and then to *Heeresgruppe Nord* [Army Group North]).

14. Col. F. B. Porter, FA, "World's Biggest Guns," *Army Ordnance Journal*, 1945, 545–547, and "Big Bertha—World War II," *Army Ordnance Journal*, November–December 1946, 254–256.

Glossary

References:

Oberst Dr. Fritz Eberhardt, *Militaerisches Woerterbuch* (Stuttgart: Alfred Kroener Verlag, 1940).

U.S. War Department, Military Intelligence Service, Special Series No. 12, *German Military Abbreviations* (Washington, D.C.: April 12, 1943).

U.S. War Department, Technical Manual TM 30-506, *German Military Dictionary* (Washington, D.C.: May 20, 1944).

British General Staff, The War Office, *Vocabulary of German Military Terms and Abbreviations* (London: HMSO, October 1939).

British Air Ministry, *Manual of German Air Force Terminology* (London: HMSO, n.d., Ca. 1944–45).

GLOSSARY

SOME ABBREVIATIONS, acronyms, and terms not in the book have been included in this glossary to make it a more comprehensive and useful reference for future reading.[1]

A	Amt	office, official position
a/A	alter Art	old type. e.g., 7.7cm FK a/A
AA, AAA		Antiaircraft Artillery, AA fire (U.S. & British terminology)
AAF		(U.S. Army Air Forces, 1941–47), also USAAF
Abt.	Abteilung	detachment, section, branch
Abw.	Abwehr	defense
Abz.	Abzeichen	insignia, badge, marking
ac	Waffenfabrik Walther, Zella-Mehlis, Thueringen	Code for manufacturer found on weapons, e.g. P.38
Achse	Achsenmaechte	Axis. Alliance between Germany and Italy (1936) and Japan (1940)
a.D.	ausser Dienst	retired. e.g., Oberst a.D.
AG, A.G.	Aktiengesellschaft	Joint Stock Company
Allg.SS	Allgemeine SS	General SS organization
AP		armor-piercing (U.S. & British)
Ar	Arado Flugzeugwerke Gmbh, Potsdam-Babelsberg	Aircraft manufacturer name abbreviation, e.g. Ar 96
Ar	Mauser-Werke AG, Berlin-Borsigwalde	Code for manufacturer found on weapons, e.g. Kar. 98k
Art., Artl.	Artillerie	artillery
asb	Deutsche Waffen-und Munitions fabriken AG, Berlin-Borsigwalde	Code for manufacturer found on weapons, see also DWM
AGr., Aufk. Gr.	Aufklaerungsgruppe	Reconnaissance Group, Lw
Ausb.	Ausbildung	training
	Axis	Alliance between Germany and Italy (1936) and Japan (1940)

	Balkenkreuz	square cross insignia on German aircraft, tanks, vehicles, etc.
(b)	belgisch	Belgian. German mark indicating weapon or equipment of Belgian origin, e.g. Pistole P.35(b)
	Barbarossa	German code name for invasion of Soviet Union on June 22, 1941
Batt.	Batterie	Battery (artillery)
	Beton	concrete
	Bau	construction
BB, Br.B.	Brandbombe	incendiary bomb
Beob.	Beobachter	observer, e.g. Lw, art, etc.
Bf, BFW	Bayerische Flugzeugwerke AG	Bavarian Aircraft Works AG (Messerschmitt)
BK	Bordkanone	aircraft cannon
	Blitzkrieg	lightning war
BMW	Bayerische Motorenwerke, Muenchen	Bavarian Motor Works, Munich
Bramo or BRAMO	Brandenburgische Motoren Werke Berlin-Spandau	Company and type of aircraft engine, e.g. BMW-Bramo 323R-2
	Brotbeutel	bread bag, musette bag
byf	Mauser-Werke AG, Oberndorf am Neckar	Code for manufacturer found on weapons, e.g. MG 151
ce	J. P. Sauer & Sohn, Suhl	Code for manufacturer found on weapons, e.g. P. Mod. 38(H)
CinC		Commander in Chief (U.S. & Brit.)
cm	Zentimeter	centimeter
Co.		Company
CO, C.O.		Commanding Officer
cpo	Rheinmetall-Borsig AG, Berlin-Marienfelde	Code for manufacturer found on weapons, e.g. MG 15 & MG 17
D	Dienst	service
DB	Daimler-Benz AG, Stuttgart	Engine and vehicle manufacturer
Dipl.	Diplom	Diploma, as in Dipl. Ingenier
DLH	Deutsche Lufthansa AG	German National Airline
Do	Dornier Werke GmbH, Friedrichshafen	Aircraft manufacturer, e.g. Do 17
Dora	80cm Kanone (E)	German 80cm railway gun
DR	Deutsche Reichsbahn Dreibein Dritten Reich	German National Railway tripod, e.g. Dreibein 34 Third Reich. Germany, 1933–1945
D.R.P.	Deutsches Reichs Patent	German national patent
DRK	Deutsches Rotes Kreuz	German Red Cross organization

DWM	Deutsche Waffen und - Munitions fabriken AG, Berlin-Borsigwalde	Arms manufacturer, marking on weapons, see also asb
E, (E)	Eisenbahn	railway, railroad
(e)	english	English. German mark indicating weapon or equipment of English origin. e.g. s.MG 230(e)
	Ehrenzeichen	decoration, medal
Ei.Hgr.	Eihandgranate	egg-shaped hand grenade
	eiserne Portion	iron ration
EK	Eisernes Kreuz	Iron Cross medal (see also RK)
EL	Eichenlaub zum Ritterkreuz des EK	Oakleaves to Knight's Cross
Ele	Einheitslafette	Dual-purpose gun mount or carriage
E.M, EM	Uffz & Mannschaften	enlisted man, U.S. forces
	Erd	ground
Ers.	Ersatz	substitute or replacement
Ers. Abt.	Ersatzabteilung	replacement unit
F	Fern-	long-range, long-distance
F, Fl., Flg.	Flieger	flyer, airman, pilot, aviator, private in Lw.
F	Flugzeug	airplane, aircraft
(f)	franzoesisch	French. German mark indicating weapon or equipment of French origin. e.g. MG 106(f)
F, Fld.	Feld	field
F, Fest.	Festung	fortress
F	Feuer	fire
FA, F.A.	Feldartillerie	field artillery
FAGr.	Fernaufklaerungsgruppe	long-range reconnaissance group, Lw.
FBB	Fuehrerbegleitbatallion	Leader's Escort Battalion (Hitler)
Fd, F.	Feind	enemy
F.d.F.	Fliegerstaffel des Fuehrers	Aviation Squadron of the Leader (Hitler)
Fdw., Fw.	Feldwebel	technical sergeant (sgt. in general)
FF, FlFhr.	Flugzeugfuehrer	airplane pilot
FFS	Flugzeugfuehrerschule	flying school
FH, F.H.	Feldhaubitze	field howitzer
FHQu.	Fuehrerhauptquartier	Hitler's supreme headquarters
Fi	Gerhard Fieseler Werke GmbH, Kassel	aircraft manufacturer, e.g., Fi 156
FJ, Fschj.	Fallschirmjaeger	paratrooper
FK, F.K.	Feldkanone	field gun
Flz, Fz	Flugzeug	airplane
Fla.	Flammenwerfer	flamethrower

Flak.	Flugabwehrkanone(n)	antiaircraft gun(s) or fire
Fldgen.	Feldgendarmerie	military police
Fl.Hst.	Fliegerhorst	military air base
F1K	Fliegerkorps	air corps, Lw unit
Flugh.	Flughafen	airport, airfield
Flugkapt.	Flugkapitaen	flight captain (senior civilian pilot)
FP	Feldpost	military postal service
	Freie Jagd	fighter sweep without ground control
	Freiherr	baron
	Frontflugspange	Front Flight (combat) Badge, Lw
F.St.	Funkstelle	radio station
Ft.	Fuss (als Masseinheit)	foot (feet) (unit of measure)
Fu, F, Fhr.	Fuehrer	leader, commander, driver of vehicle or aircraft
	Fuehrerbunker	Hitler's HQ bunker
FuG	Funkgeraet	radio set, radar, or electronic equipment
Fw	Focke—Wulf Flugzeugbau AG, Bremen	aircraft manufacturer, e.g., Fw 200
G	Geschwader	Lw wing, 3 (sometimes 4) Gruppen & Stab, e.g. JG, KG, ZG, etc.
g, Ge,Gel.	gelaendegaengig	capable of cross-country travel
GAF		German Air Force (U. S & GB, WW II)
Gamma	42cm Gamma Moerser	420mm Gamma howitzer
Ge,Geb.	Gebirgs-	mountain-
Geb.L.	Geballte Ladung	concentrated explosive charge
Gen.	General	general
Gen.d.Flg.	General der Flieger	general of aviation, Lw
Gen.d.JF.	General der Jagdflieger	general of fighters (position, not a rank) (Adolf Galland), Lw
Gen.Lt.	Generalleutnant	lieutenant general (equivalent to U.S. major general)
Gen.Maj.	Generalmajor	major general (U.S. brigadier gen.)
Gen.d.Inf., Art., Pz, usw.	General der Infanterie, Artillerie, Panzer, etc.	general of infantry, etc. (equivalent to U.S. Lieutenant general)
Gen.Oberst	Generaloberst	col. general (U.S. four-star gen.)
Ger.	Geraet	equipment, apparatus, ordnance
Gesch., G.	Geschuetz, Geschoss	gun, artillery piece, shell, bullet
Gestapo	Geheime Staatspolizei	Secret State Police
Gew., G.	Gewehr	rifle, gun, e.g. Gew. 98
GewGr, G.G.	Gewehrgranate	rifle grenade
GFM	Generalfeldmarschall	general field marshal (usually referred to simply as field marshal)

Gfr., Gefr.	Gefreiter	corporal (corresponds roughly to U.S. Army acting corporal)
ghKdos.,	geheime Kommandosache	secret document or matter
GmbH, G.m.b.H.	Gesellschaft mit besch- raenkter Haftung	limited liability company
	Graben	trench, ditch, grave
Gr.	Gruppe	Lw group, 3 Staffeln & Stab, also army unit
Gr., G.	Granate	shell, artillery projectile
GrW.	Granatwerfer	trench mortar
H	Haubitze	howitzer
H	haupt	head, main, chief
H	Heimat	home, zone of interior
H	Heer	army
Harko	Hoeresartilleriekommandeur	GHQ artillery
H.Dv.	Heeresdruckvorschrift(en)	army regulation(s)
He	Ernst Heinkel Flugzeugwerke GmbH, Rostock	aircraft manufacturer, e.g. He 111
H.E., HE		high explosive
HG	Heeresgruppe	army group, 2 or more armies
Hgr, HdGr.	Handgranate Hakenkreuz, Hakenkreuzfahne	hand grenade swastika, swastika flag
Hpqt., HQu.	Hauptquartier	headquarters
Hptm., Hpt.	Hauptmann	captain (army and air force)
HQ		headquarters (U.S. & G.B.)
Hs	Henschel Flugzeugwerke AG, Berlin-Schoensfeld und Johannisthal	aircraft manufacturer, e.g. Hs 123
H.Wa.A, HWA	Heereswaffenamt	Army Ordnance Office
I, Inf.	Infanterie	infantry
(i)	italanisch	Italian. German mark indicating weapon or equipment of Italian origin, e.g. MG 259(i)
i.G.	im Generalstab	on the general staff
IG	Infanteriegeschuetz	infantry support gun or howitzer
Insp.	Inspektor, inspektion	inspector, inspection
J.	(see "I")	Used especially in typewritten documents for capital I; e.g. J.R. for I.R.
J	Jaeger	fighter, hunter, rifleman in light infantry
Jabo	Jagdbomber	fighter bomber
	Jagdflieger	fighter pilot
JG	Jagdgeschwader	fighter wing
JGr.	Jagdgruppe	fighter group

Ju	Junkers Flugzeug und Motoren-werke AG, Dessau	aircraft and engine manufacturer, e.g. Ju 88
Jumo	Junkers Motorenbau	Junkers engine factory, e.g. Jumo 211
K	Kanone	cannon
K	Kampf	battle, struggle, fight
K	Kette	Lw element of 3 aircraft
K	Kraftrad	motorcycle
K	Kreuz	cross (as in Ritterkreuz)
K	Krieg	war
Kb, Kar.	Karabiner	carbine
k	kurz	short
K(E)	Kanone (Eisenbahn)	railway gun
Karl	60cm Karl Moerser (Geraet 040)	600mm Karl howitzer
Kdo.	Kommando	detachment, special unit
KFz	Kampfflugzeug	war plane, bomber
Ffz	Kraftfahrzeug	motor vehicle
KG	Kampfgeschwader	bomber wing, Lw
K.G., KG	Kommandit-Gesellschaft	limited partnership company
Kg	Kilogram	kilogram, metric unit of measure, 1 Kg = 2.205 lb
Kgef.	Kriegsgefangener	prisoner of war (POW)
KGr.	Kampfgruppe	bomber group, Lw
KGz.b.V.	Kampfgeschwader zur besonderne Verwendung	bomber wing for special duties, later transport wing, Lw
KM	Kriegsmarine	(German) Navy, 1935–1945
Km	Kilometer	Kilometer, 1 Km = 0.621 mile
Km/h, Km/Std.	Kilometer pro Stunde	Kilometers per hour
Kom.	Kommodore	commander (Lw title, not a rank)
Kp.	Kompanie	company (military unit)
Kp	Alfried Krupp GmbH, Essen	Krupp industrial complex, famous for cannon and heavy steel equipment
	Kriegsflagge	national war flag
KrGl.	Kriegsgliederung	order of battle (OB)
k.v, kv.	Kriegsverwendungsfaehig	fit for active service
KVK	Kriegsverdienstkreuz	War Merit Cross (decoration)
KW	Kampfwagen	tank
KW	Kuebelwagen	military Volkswagen-lit: bucket car, German equivalent of Jeep
KwK, KWK	Kampfwagenkanone	tank gun

L	Lafette	gun mount, carriage
L	Lauf	barrel
l	lang	long
l	leicht	light
LAH, LSSAH	Leibstandarte SS "Adolf Hitler"	Fuehrer's personal bodyguard regiment, later W-SS Pz Div.
	Landser	German "G.I." (slang), soldier
	Lebensraum	living space
	Lehr	instruction, training
leGrW	leichter Granatwerfer	light trench mortar
l.F.H.,leFH	leichte Feldhaubitze	light field howitzer
Lfl, LF	Luftflotte	air fleet, Lw
LG	Luftgau	air force district
Lkw.	Lastkraftwagen	truck
l.MG, LMG, LeMG	leichtes Maschinengewehr	light machine gun, e.g. lMG 34
Lotfe	Lotfernrohr	telescopic bomb sight
LPist.	Leuchtpistole	signal or flare pistol
L.S.M.	Leuchtspurmunition	tracer ammunition
Lt., Lnt.	Leutnant	lieutenant (U.S. 2nd Lt.)
Lw, LW	Luftwaffe	air force (German, 1935–1945)
m	Magazine	magazine, dump, store
m	Meter	meter, 1m = 3.281 ft.
m	mit	with
Maj.	Major	Major
Masch.	Maschine	machine, engine
Me	Messerschmitt Flugzeugwerke AG, Augsburg	Aircraft manufacturer, e.g., Me 410
MG, M.G.	Maschinengewehr	machine gun, e.g. MG 81
Min.	Minen-	mine
MK, M.K.	Maschinenkanone	machine (automatic) cannon, e.g. MK 108
m.K	mit Kern	with core (usually armor-piercing)
mm	millimeter	millimeter, 1mm=0.039 inch
Mot.	motorisert	motorized, mechanized, mobile
MP, M.P., MPi.	Machinenpistole	machine pistol, submachine gun, e.g. MP 40
mph		miles per hour
Mrs.	Moerser	mortar, short large-caliber howitzer
MV	(German-Muendungsgesch-windigkeit)	muzzle velocity

N.	Nacht-	night-
N	Nord	north
n.A.	neuer Art	new type, e.g. LMG-08/15n.A.
NAGr.	Nahaufklaerungsgruppe	short-range recon group, Lw
NASM		National Air and Space Museum, Smithsonian Institution, Washington, D.C.
Nazi	Nationalsozialist	Acronym formed from the first syllable of National and the second syllable of Sozialist. A member of the NSDAP
Nb	Nebel	fog, mist, artificial smoke
NbW	Nebelwerfer	smoke shell projector, rocket launcher
NCO		noncommissioned officer (U.S.)
	Niemandsland	no man's land
NKVD	(Russian) Narodnyy Komissariat Vnutrennikh Del.	Peoples Commissariat of Internal Affairs-Soviet Security Police 1938–1946
Nr.	Nummer	number
NSDAP	Nationalsozialistische Deutsche Arbeiterpartei	National Socialist German Worker's Party (Nazi Party)
O, Ob.	Oberst	colonel
(ö)	oesterreichisch	Austrian. German mark indicating weapon or equipment of Austrian origin, e.g. P. 12(ö)
O.	Osten, Ost	east
Ob.	Oberbefehlshaber	commander in chief
obr.	(Russian) obrazets	pattern, model (year)
Obergruf.	Obergruppenfuehrer	SA and SS rank equivalent to a general
Oblt.	Oberleutnant	first lieutenant
Oberstlt.	Oberstleutnant	lieutenant colonel
Ofw.	Oberfeldwebel	master sergeant
Ogfr.	Obergefreiter	corporal
OKH	Oberkommando des Heeres	High Command of Army
OKL	Oberkommando der Luftwaffe	High Command of Air Force
OKM	Oberkommando der Kriegsmarine	High Command of Navy
OKW	Oberkommando der Wehrmacht	High Command of Armed Forces
Org.	Organisation	organization
ORPO	Ordnungspolizei	Order Police
Ost	Ost (Ostfront)	east (Eastern Front)
OT	Organisation Todt	Todt organization was semi-military engineering and construction org. named for leader, Dr. Fritz Todt

P, Pz.	Panzer	armor, tank, armored unit
P	Patrone	cartridge, round of ammunition
P	Pioniere	combat engineer
(p)	polnisch	Polish. German mark indicating weapon or equipment of Polish origin, e.g. MG 30(p)
PAK, PaK	Panzerabwehrkanone	antitank gun
Patrh.	Patronenhuelse	cartridge case
PC	Panzerbombe, Cylindrisch or Panzerdurschschlagbombe, Cylindrisch	cylindrical armor-piercing bomb, Lw
PD	Panzerdickenwandbombe	armor-piercing thick-walled bomb, Lw
Pkw.	Personenkraftwagen	passenger automobile, motor car
PGren.	Panzergrenadier	armored infantry(man)
Pol.	Polizei	police
POW		prisoner of war (U.S. & British term)
PS	Pferdestaerke	horsepower. 1 PS = 0.9861 hp
PzB.	Panzerbuechse	antitank rifle
Pzbr.	Panzerbrechend	armor-piercing
Pz.Kpfw. or PzKw	Panzerkampfwagen	tank, armored vehicle
Q, Qu.	Quartier	Quarters, billets
R	Reich	state, empire, national
R.	Richtkreis	aiming circle (gunnery)
R	Rotte	A pair of planes, flying in loose formation, Lw
R	Ruestsatz	field conversion kit, Lw
(r)	russisch	Russian. German mark indicating weapon or equipment of Russian origin, e.g. MG 216(r)
RAD	Reichsarbeitsdienst	National Labor Service
RAF		Royal Air Force (Great Britain)
RB	Reichsbahn	National Railroad
R.d.L.u.-Ob.d.L.	Reichsminister der Luftfahrt und Oberbefehlshaber der Luftwaffe	Reichs Minister of Aviation and Commander in Chief of the Air Force (Goering)
Rdf.	Rheindorf	name of German arsenal (esp. ammo.)
Res.	Reserve	reserve
Revi.	Reflexvisier	reflex sight for aircraft gun
RFSS	Reichsfuehrer-SS	National Leader of SS (Himmler)
RFSS	Reichsfuehrung-SS	High Command of SS & Waffen-SS
RhB	Rheinmetall-Borsig	arms manufacturer
Rk.	Richtkanonier	gunner (artillery)

RK	Ritterbreuz des Eisernen Kreuzes	Knight's Cross of the Iron Cross
RLM	Reichsluftfahrtministerium	German Air Ministry (headed by Goering)
	Ritter	knight
RM	Reichsmark	Reichsmark=U.S. $0.40
RM	Reichsmarschall	Reichs Marshal (Goering)
RM	Reichsminister	Reichs Minister
RP	Reichspost	German national postal service
RSD or SD	Reichssicherheitsdienst	National Security Service of SS
RSHA	Reichssicherheitshauptamt	SS Main Security Office
RW	Reichswehr	German Army and Navy, 1920–1935
Rue.	Ruestung	armament, equipment
RZM	Reichszeugmeisterei	NSDAP Quartermaster Bureau
S	Seitengewehr	bayonet
S	sonder	special
S, St.	Staffel	squadron (Lw), section
S	Sprengstoff	explosive
S, St.	Sturm	storm, assault
St.	Sturmtruppen	storm troops, SA and SS battalion-size unit
S	S-Vorserie	pre-production models
s	schwer	heavy, hard, difficult
SB	Sprengbombe, Cylindrisch	cylindrical H.E. fragmentation bomb, Lw
SC	Splitterbombe, Cylindrisch	cylindrical H.E. fragmentation antipersonnel bomb, Lw
	Schwarm	four fighters in formation, Lw
schw.Art.	schwere Artillerie	heavy (actually medium) artillery
	Schwerpunkt	main effort, center of gravity
SD	Spreng Dickenwandbombe	thick-walled H.E. semi-armor-piercing bomb, Lw
Sd	sonder	special
Sd.Kfz.	Sonderkraftfahrzeug	spec. motor vehicle, e.g. SdKfz.6
sFH	schwere Feldhaubitze	heavy field howitzer
SG	Schlachtgeschwader	close support or ground attack wing, Lw
SGr.	Schlachtgruppe	close support or ground attack group, Lw
Sgt.	(in German: Unteroffizier)	sergeant (U.S. and Great Britain)
sGrW	schweres Granatwerfer	heavy trench mortar
ShePzWg.	Schuetzenpanzerwagen	armored personnel carrier
SlGew.	Selbstladegewehr	self-loading or automatic rifle, e.g. Gew. 43
sMG	schweres Maschinengewehr	heavy machine gun, e.g. 13mm MG 131
	Sieg	victory
	Soldbuch	pay and I.D. book, carried by each soldier
	Sperrkreis	restricted area

Sperrf.	Sperrfeuer	barrage
	Spiess	first sergeant, top sergeant (slang)
SP	Splitterbombe	fragmentation antipersonnel bomb, Lw
Sp	Schwerpunkt	point of main effort
Sp	Spreng-	explosive-, demolition-
Sq., SQ.		squadron, U.S., British
SS	Schutzstaffel	Protective Unit (Elite Guard of NSDAP, formed in 1925.) See Waffen-SS.
SSHA	SS-Hauptamt	SS main office (Berlin)
SS-Ofu.	SS-Oberfuehrer	SS senior colonel
St.	Stab	staff
St.	Staffel	squadron, Lw, section, unit
	Stahlhelm	steel helmet, for Wehrmacht, the M35
Sthg.	Stielhandgranate	stick hand grenade, e.g. M24
Stalag	Stammlager	POW camp, for E.M., run by Lw
Stavka	(Russian) Stavka Verkhovnogo Glavnokomandovaniya	HQ Soviet Supreme Command, WW II (Moscow)
St.G, Stu.G.	Sturmgeschuetz	assault gun, self-propelled
St.G.	Sturzkampfgeschwader	dive-bomber wing, Lw
Stl., St.	Stelle, Stellung	office, position
	Stoerfang	Sturgeon haul or catch, code for German assault on Sevastopol, June 1942
	Storch	stork-Fi 156
St.A.	Sturmabzeichen	assault badge (decoration)
St.H.	Sturmhaubitze	assault howitzer, self-propelled
Stuka	Sturzkampfflugzeug	dive-bomber, e.g. Ju 87
	Sued	south
	Tagesbefehl	Order of the Day
T	Teil	part, component, piece
t	tief	deep, low
t	Tonne	ton; metric ton = 2,205 lbs.
Ta, Tk.	Tank	tank
Ta	Tarnung	camouflage
T., Tr.	Treffer	hit (gunnery)
(t)	tschechisch	Czechoslovakian. German mark for weapons and equipment of Czech origin, e.g., MG 37(t)
TG	Transportgeschwader	Transport wing, Lw
TGr.	Transportgruppe	Transport group, Lw
	Trappenjagd	Bustard Hunt, code name for German offensive on Kerch front, May 1942
TN	Technische Nothilfe	Technical Emergency Corps

Tragt.	Tragtier	pack animal
Trbst.	Treibstoff	fuel
Tr.P.	Treffpunkt	point of impact
T.Ueb.Pl.	Truppenuebungsplatz	training area, drill ground
U	Umruest-Bausatz	Factory Conversion Kit. A set or modification, e.g. Fw 200C-4/Ul
u	und	and
Uffz.	Unteroffizier	noncommissioned officer (NCO)
	unter	under, subordinate
USAAF		U.S. Army Air Forces (1941–47)
umg.	umgeaeandert	changed, modified, altered
U.d.S.S,R.	Union der sozialistischen Sowjet-Republic	Union of Soviet Socialist Republics; U.S.S.R.
U.Z., UZ	Uhrzuender	clockwork time fuze
V	Verband	formation, unit
V, VD	Verdienst	merit. e.g., Verdienstkreuz
V	Verein	association, society, union
V	Verfuegung	disposition, order, decree
V	Versuchs-	experimental-
VT	Volltreffer	direct hit (gunnery)
VVS	Voyenno—vozdushnyye sily	Soviet Air Force
VW	Volkswagen	People's Car, VW Company
V-Waffe	Vergeltungswaffe	vengeance or retaliation weapon
W, Wa	Waffe(n)	weapon(s), arm(s), branch of service; e.g., Inf., Art., etc.
W	Wagen	vehicle, wagon
W, WM, Wm.	Wehrmacht	Armed Forces. German, 1935–1945, Army, Navy, Air Force, and from 1941 also Waffen-SS
W	Werfer	launcher (rocket, etc.)
WaA	Waffenamt, Heeres	Ordnance Office, Army. (There was also a Waffen-SS Waffenamt)
WB	Waffenbehaelter	weapons container, Lw
	Werwolf	Hitler's HQ at Vinnitsa, Ukraine (1942–43)
WG	Wurfgeraet	heavy rocket launcher
Wgr.	Wurfgranate	mortar shell
WH	Wehrmacht-Heer	Armed Forces-Army (on army vehicle license plates)
	Wehrmachtbuehne	armed forces entertainment group
	Wehrpass	soldier's official service record
	Wilhelmstrasse	famous street in Berlin, location of Reichs Chancellery and important government HQs.

WK	Wehrkreis	military district
WL	Wehrmacht-Luftwaffe	Armed Forces-Air Force
WM	Wehrmacht-Marine	Armed Forces-Navy
W.Nr.	Werk-Nummer	works number. Manufacturer's serial number
	Wolfsschanze	Wolf's Redoubt. Hitler's HQ in East Prussia (1941–44)
WPrue(f)	Waffenpruefung (Waffenpruefungstelle)	weapons proving and testing, weapons test center
W-SS	Waffen-SS	Armed SS. Full military combat units of the SS
WW – I	(in German: Weltkrieg)	World War I (1914–1918), for U.S. (1917–1918)
WW-II	(in German: Zweite Weltkrieg)	World War II (1939–1945), for U.S. (1941–1945)
X-Uhr	X-Uhr	German equivalent of H-hour
Z	Zeit	time, period
Z	Ziel	target, objective, goal
Z, Zdr.	Zuender	fuze, detonator, igniter
Z, Zw.	Zwilling	twin, double
Zb.	Zweibein	bipod, e.g. Zb. fuer lMG 34
	Zentralverlag der NSDAP	Nazi publishing house since 1922, formerly Franz Eher Vlg.
z.b.V, or zbV	zur besonderen Verwendung	for special use. (shown after unit designation, e.g. KG 200 z.b.V.)
Zf.	Zielfernrohr	telescopic sight
ZG	Zerstoerergeschwader	Destroyer Wing, Lw
ZGr.	Zerstoerergruppe	Destroyer Group, Lw
Zgkw.	Zugkraftwagen	half-track prime mover, e.g. Sd.Kfz. 7
Zg, Z	Zug	train, pull, platoon, section
Zt.Z	Zeitzuender	time fuze, e.g. for artillery shell
Z.Z., ZZ	Zugzuender	pull igniter, e.g. Z.Z. 35

INDEX

Page references to illustrations are in italics.

ABOUT THE AUTHOR

C. G. Sweeting, a U.S. Air Force veteran, is a military and aviation historian and a former curator at the Smithsonian's National Air and Space Museum, the Air Defence Command Museum in Colorado Springs, and the Air Force Space Museum at Cape Canaveral. Considered an authority on German military history, he assembled one of the world's largest and most comprehensive collections of German military uniforms, small arms, equipment, and memorabilia of the 1870–1945 period. This unique collection was acquired by the Imperial War Museum in London in 1978, and much of it is on exhibit today in the main museum in Lambeth. He is the author of numerous books, including *Hitler's Personal Pilot: The Life and Times of Hans Baur; Hitler's Squadron: The Fuehrer's Personal Aircraft and Transport Unit, 1933–45; Combat Flying Clothing: Army Air Forces Clothing During World War II;* and *Combat Flying Equipment: U.S. Army Aviators Personal Equipment, 1917–1945.* He lives in Clinton, Maryland.